AI iQ for a
Human-Focused Future

AI iQ for a Human-Focused Future: Strategy, Talent, and Culture offers a pioneering approach to integrating artificial intelligence (AI) and generative AI (GenAI) in business, emphasizing a business strategy first mindset over a technology-centric one.

This book challenges the usual hype surrounding AI, advocating for a more realistic perspective. It delves into the evolution of AI, from traditional data science and machine learning to GenAI, all through the lens of strategic business application. Unlike other texts, this book moves away from case studies, favoring practical, real-world advice from extensive field experience. This book presents strategies for creating an environment that not only accepts but thrives on AI, focusing on strategic leadership, talent development, and inclusivity. It highlights crucial roles, such as the Chief AI Officer, and emphasizes the importance of diversity in AI teams.

Uniquely, each chapter concludes with key takeaways, offering actionable steps, and implementation tips. This practical approach transforms theoretical concepts into actionable business strategies, providing leaders with the tools to apply AI initiatives effectively in their organizations.

This book is more than an informative resource; it's a practical toolkit for any business leader aiming to navigate the evolving landscape of AI and GenAI, ensuring their organization is prepared for sustainable growth and success in an AI-driven future.

As a renowned expert in the field, Seth Dobrin shines a light on the importance of artificial intelligence within organizations. AI is no longer futuristic; it is a present-day technological reality offering vast potential for businesses across multiple sectors. Seth's strategic and practical insights will assist leaders in evaluating their existing business strategies and, to hopefully embrace the full potential of AI capabilities whilst recognizing the challenges it presents from a legal, privacy and ethical perspective, in order to shape and develop an AI governance framework that creates et

– Jenna Franklin, *Partner in Data, Privacy and AI at Stephenson Harwood, LLP*

Dive into a journey where AI meets heart and strategy in business. This book isn't just a guide; it's an intimate Masterclass with a wise friend who's walked the path of integrating AI in business and in everyday life. Seth Dobrin teaches us to use AI not just as a tool but as a partner in achieving greater organizational strategy and impact. This book provides a comprehensive understanding of the opportunities and benefits of AI and Gen AI and gently challenges the hype, guiding us through its evolution with insightful takeaways and action steps we can use immediately. It's a beacon for leaders seeking to blend AI with humanity, focusing on nurturing talent, streamlining processes, and building inclusive culture within their organization. Let this book inspire you to lead with both innovation and soul in the AI era.

– Lisa Mae Brunson, *Founder and CEO, Wonder Women Tech*

Have you been named as Chief AI Officer? Are you a C-Suite leader whose organization is trying to figure out how to think about AI and how to derive business value from AI? Are you immersed in the AI ecosystem of your organization but not sure how all of the pieces fit together?

If you want to raise your "AI iQ" Seth Dobrin's book provides a practical approach to help you guide your organization's AI transformation journey. Together your leadership team and key stakeholders need to determine how AI can and will reshape your business, and what will it take to make your organization "AI-ready". The book is like having a master class series with Seth, who brings his years of expertise as a recognized AI leader.

Each chapter takes you further into the dimensions of AI that will drive your organization's decisions regarding AI transformation, innovation and responsibility. I agree with his use of on-going readiness assessments to shape the roadmap and measure progress along the way. The AI landscape continues to rapidly evolve—the "key points and actions" at the end of each chapter give you a starter kit to move forward and to adjust as conditions change.

– Nancy Ellis Morgan, *CEO, Ellis Morgan Enterprises and Former Intelligence Community Chief Data Officer*

Unlike other publications, this book shifts the narrative from a technology-centric perspective to a strategy-first mindset, aligning AI implementation with overarching business goals rooted in human-focused values. It challenges the prevailing hype around AI, offering a refreshingly realistic perspective on its evolution, from traditional data science to the transformative power of generative AI (GenAI).

What sets this book apart is its emphasis on practicality and real-world advice derived from extensive field experience, moving beyond mere case studies. The strategies outlined for fostering an AI-embracing environment are invaluable, focusing on strategic leadership, talent development, and practical steps for implementation. The book not only identifies the critical role of the Chief AI Officer but also underscores the significance of diversity within AI teams.

In a world inundated with AI literature, "AI iQ for a Human-Focused Future" stands out as a beacon of wisdom, guiding leaders towards a future where AI seamlessly integrates with human values, transforming businesses for the better.

– **Neil Taylor,** *Mastercard*

AI iQ for a Human-Focused Future: Strategy, Talent, and Culture provides a compelling argument for the need to address the issue of AI governance. Powerful and transformational technologies, throughout history, have been always followed by new business models that have changed the way we manage people, systems, and processes. And when the hype and the dust of the generative AI settle down, business leaders will be faced with the question of "How can I implement this technology in a responsible and in an engaging way?" Seth's book addresses exactly this question with the clarity and insights that engage the reader.

– **Dr. Sid Ahmed Benraouane,** *author, professor, and Government advisor; Member Expert of the US/ISO Group tasked with the draft of the ISO/IEC 42001:2023 Artificial Management System*

Chapman & Hall/CRC Artificial Intelligence and Robotics Series

Series Editor: Roman Yampolskiy

AI by Design: A Plan for Living with Artificial Intelligence
Catriona Campbell

The Global Politics of Artificial Intelligence
Edited by Maurizio Tinnirello

Unity in Embedded System Design and Robotics: A Step-by-Step Guide
Ata Jahangir Moshayedi, Amin Kolahdooz, Liao Liefa

Meaningful Futures with Robots: Designing a New Coexistence
Edited by Judith Dörrenbächer, Marc Hassenzahl, Robin Neuhaus,
Ronda Ringfort-Felner

*Topological Dynamics in Metamodel Discovery with
Artificial Intelligence: From Biomedical to Cosmological Technologies*
Ariel Fernández

A Robotic Framework for the Mobile Manipulator: Theory and Application
Nguyen Van Toan and Phan Bui Khoi

AI in and for Africa: A Humanist Perspective
Susan Brokensha, Eduan Kotzé, Burgert A. Senekal

*Artificial Intelligence on Dark Matter and Dark Energy: Reverse Engineering
of the Big Bang*
Ariel Fernández

Explainable Agency in Artificial Intelligence: Research and Practice
Silvia Tulli and David W. Aha

An Introduction to Universal Artificial Intelligence
Marcus Hutter, Elliot Catt, and David Quarel

Transcending Imagination: Artificial Intelligence and the Future of Creativity
Alexander Manu

Responsible Use of AI in Military Systems
Jan Maarten Schraagen

AI iQ for a Human-Focused Future: Strategy, Talent, and Culture
Seth Dobrin

AI: Unpredictable, Unexplainable, Uncontrollable
Roman V. Yampolskiy

For more information about this series please visit: https://www.routledge.com/
Chapman–HallCRC-Artificial-Intelligence-and-Robotics-Series/book-series/
ARTILRO

AI iQ for a
Human-Focused Future
Strategy, Talent, and Culture

Seth Dobrin, PhD

CRC Press
Taylor & Francis Group
Boca Raton London New York

CRC Press is an imprint of the
Taylor & Francis Group, an **informa** business
A CHAPMAN & HALL BOOK

Designed cover image: Tabitha Rudd.
Title of Artwork: *Resisting Technological Colonialism*
©2024

First edition published 2025
by CRC Press
2385 NW Executive Center Drive, Suite 320, Boca Raton FL 33431

and by CRC Press
4 Park Square, Milton Park, Abingdon, Oxon, OX14 4RN

CRC Press is an imprint of Taylor & Francis Group, LLC

© 2025 Seth Dobrin

ISBN: 978-1-032-78204-1 (hbk)
ISBN: 978-1-032-78203-4 (pbk)
ISBN: 978-1-003-48672-5 (ebk)

DOI: 10.1201/9781003486725

Typeset in Minion
by KnowledgeWorks Global Ltd.

Access the Support Material: https://ai-iq.online and https://www.routledge.com/ 9781032782034

*To my wife and partner, Tabitha,
whose never-ending support has
gotten me where I am.*

Contents

Foreword

In the complicated world of artificial intelligence, where the line between hype and reality often blurs, this book emerges as a beacon for those eager to navigate the complexities of AI integration. It meticulously unpacks the essential elements required to embark on the AI journey, addressing the excitement surrounding its potential while grounding expectations in the practicalities of implementation. Seth's enthusiasm and expertise for the subject make this a great read.

Beyond the allure of AI's capabilities, this book delves into the critical aspects of governance and responsibility, urging a balanced approach to innovation. It outlines how organizations and individuals can prepare for AI adoption, emphasizing the importance of ethical considerations, data integrity, and the need for continuous learning and adaptation. This forward-thinking guide not only equips readers with the knowledge to make informed decisions about AI but also inspires confidence and optimism about the future it holds. The author's commitment to demystifying AI, while advocating for responsible use, makes this book an invaluable resource for anyone looking to understand and leverage artificial intelligence.

Sol Rashidi
Former CDO/CAO/CDAO of Fortune 100s
February 2024

Preface

In an era where technological advancement is not just rapid but revolutionary, the role of AI in shaping business futures cannot be overstated. *AI iQ for a Human-Focused Future: Talent, Culture, and Strategy* is born out of a compelling need to address a critical gap in contemporary business practice – the alignment of AI with human values, strategic acumen, and organizational culture. As a seasoned author and strategist, I aim to guide you, the leaders of large complex organizations, through the complexities of AI, focusing on its integration with talent, culture, and strategic business imperatives.

THE GENESIS OF THIS BOOK

My journey, culminating in the creation of Qantm AI, revealed a striking insight: many organizations need a structured methodology to extract real, tangible value from AI, starting with a solid business strategy. This book distills more than 15 years of real-world experience, aiming to fill this gap with a human-focused and value-based approach to AI.

UNRAVELING AI'S EVOLUTION AND IMPACT

This book begins with Chapter 1, "The Foundation," a critical examination of AI's evolution since 2006 and the significant pivot marked by GenAI's advent. It challenges conventional wisdom, provocatively discussing traditional AI methods' overuse and potential pitfalls. This sets the stage for a deeper exploration into AI's impact on business, urging leaders to rethink their strategies and adopt a comprehensive AI perspective for sustainable success.

BRIDGING AI AND BUSINESS STRATEGY

In Chapter 2 "The Uncomfortable Truth About AI" and "Connection to Tangible Value" focuses on AI's strategic integration within businesses. It goes beyond the hyped narratives, providing a pragmatic view of

AI's impact and potential in enhancing business strategies. Chapters 2–3 advocate for a "strategy-first" versus technology-first approach, ensuring AI investments align with and drive core business objectives.

FOSTERING AN AI-READY CULTURE AND STRUCTURE

Understanding that technology alone doesn't drive change, Chapters 4 and 5, "AI-Ready Culture" and "Organizational Structure" delve into the human aspects of AI integration. They provide actionable insights for building an AI-conducive environment, emphasizing the need for innovation, ethical AI development, and a comprehensive talent strategy.

COMPREHENSIVE READINESS FOR AI'S FUTURE

This book also tackles the foundational aspects of AI readiness – infrastructure, data, compliance, ethics, social and environmental responsibility, and the role of the Chief AI Officer. Chapters 6–12 offer a holistic view of the prerequisites for a successful AI journey, addressing the technical, ethical, societal, and leadership dimensions necessary for future-proofing organizations in the AI era.

A STRATEGIC BLUEPRINT FOR AI INTEGRATION

Chapter 13 synthesizes these insights, offering a strategic blueprint for effectively navigating the dynamic AI landscape. It emphasizes agility, ethical considerations, and strategic alignment, projecting AI's transformative potential across various business sectors.

A STRATEGIC IMPERATIVE FOR LEADERS

This Preface and the book's chapters are crafted to resonate with your strategic mindset, offering not just insights but a call to action. The aim is to empower you with the knowledge and tools necessary for strategic and human-focused integration of AI in your organizations, ensuring a future that is not only technologically advanced but also aligned with core human values and business strategies.

About the Author

Dr. Seth Dobrin is a renowned AI and Data Science Leader known for his transformative work. At Monsanto, he revolutionized agriculture by integrating AI to enhance farming through precision agriculture. As IBM's first Global Chief AI Officer, he led the IBM Data Science Elite Team, driving ethical AI development and diversity across multiple projects. His leadership was instrumental in IBM's AI and data transformation.

He continued his journey by founding Qantm AI, championing a human-focused approach centered on ethical AI in business. His work at Qantm AI guides Fortune 500 companies and Private Equity firms in developing responsible AI strategies. A strong advocate for diversity and against technological colonialism, he supports organizations like Women Leaders in Data and AI (WLDA) and Wonder Women Tech (WWT). His multidisciplinary expertise, combining molecular and cellular biology with industry experience, sets AI leadership benchmarks, shaping its future to be responsible, ethical, and inclusive.

Introduction

In the dynamic landscape of modern business, the emergence of artificial intelligence (AI) and generative AI (GenAI) is a beacon of innovation and a challenge to conventional strategies. *AI iQ for a Human-Focused Future: Strategy, Talent, and Culture* is crafted as a vital resource for business leaders, equipping them with the insights and tools necessary for navigating this transformative era.

My journey, which began in 2006, has been rich with experiences in leading data and AI transformations at global Fortune 500 companies and advising numerous others. This book culminates these experiences, offering a unique blend of technical expertise and business acumen. It serves as a bridge, translating the intricate world of AI into actionable strategies for business growth and sustainability.

The essence of this book lies in its pragmatic approach to AI and GenAI. Moving beyond the often overhyped narratives, it focuses on strategically integrating these technologies within the business sphere. Covering a spectrum of topics from readiness assessment to capacity building, governance, and execution, this book provides a comprehensive guide to AI implementation in organizations.

Each chapter delves into different aspects of AI in the business context, thoroughly exploring its adoption, critical evaluation, strategic alignment with business goals, and the cultivation of an AI-ready culture. This book challenges conventional narratives, advocating for a balanced and strategic approach to AI adoption and implementation, and emphasizes the importance of ethical considerations and sustainable strategies.

A distinctive feature of this book is its direct approach to controversial topics, encouraging leaders to assess AI's role and impact in their

DOI: 10.1201/9781003486725-1

organizations critically. It confronts misconceptions about AI, promoting a nuanced understanding of its capabilities and limitations.

Furthermore, this book includes a detailed methodology for AI readiness assessments, a critical tool for organizations embarking on their AI journey. These assessments evaluate an organization's preparedness across various dimensions: culture, skills, data, infrastructure, systems, and compliance. The methodology provides a structured approach to identify strengths, uncover gaps, and develop targeted strategies for AI integration. Regular and comprehensive assessments are emphasized as essential practices, ensuring organizations remain aligned with evolving AI technologies and business objectives.

AI iQ for a Human-Focused Future: Strategy, Talent, and Culture is more than a guide; it is a strategic partner for business leaders serious about leveraging AI and GenAI in their organizations. It offers a vision and practical grounding necessary to navigate the complexities of AI, driving transformative change and sustainable growth.

This book is structured and meticulously designed to offer a comprehensive and profound understanding of AI, emphasizing its ethical application and the transformative potential of GenAI. Each chapter within this book serves as a gateway into different facets of AI, ranging from its foundational principles to the intricacies of seamlessly integrating it into organizational strategies and daily operations.

- **In-Depth Exploration:** This book is structured to provide a thorough and well-rounded exploration of both traditional AI and the emerging field of Generative AI. It takes you on a journey that begins with fundamental concepts, gradually progressing to more advanced applications. This progressive approach ensures you develop a surface-level grasp and a profound and holistic understanding of AI in all dimensions.

- **Real-World Relevance:** Unlike books that dwell solely on theoretical concepts, the content within each chapter is deeply rooted in real-world applications. This emphasis on real-world relevance is a distinctive feature, ensuring that the knowledge you acquire is theoretical, highly practical, and actionable. You'll gain insights that are immediately applicable to address current business challenges and real-life scenarios, making you a more effective and adaptable professional in the rapidly evolving landscape of AI.

- **Ethical and Strategic Focus:** A prominent and recurring theme throughout this book is the ethical use of AI. As AI technologies continue to advance, ethical considerations become increasingly crucial. The book equips you with the knowledge and tools to navigate the complex ethical landscape of AI. You'll learn to identify and address ethical dilemmas, ensuring that your AI strategies and implementations are practical, responsible, and ethically sound.

- **Insights into Organizational Transformation:** Beyond presenting theoretical concepts, this book sheds light on how AI can be a powerful catalyst for profound organizational transformation. It elucidates how AI can influence and reshape various aspects of an organization, from decision-making processes and operational efficiency to business models and corporate culture. By understanding the transformative potential of AI, you'll be well-prepared to harness it as a driving force for positive change within your organization. This perspective enables you to envision AI not merely as a tool but as a transformative agent that can revolutionize your organization's approach to problem-solving and innovation.

In summary, this meticulously structured book is a valuable resource that empowers you with a deep and practical understanding of AI, specifically focusing on ethics and transformative potential. It guides you through a journey from fundamental concepts to real-world applications, ensuring you can effectively acquire knowledge and apply AI concepts in your professional endeavors. As you progress through its chapters, you'll gain insights that are relevant to the present and indispensable in shaping your organization's future in the AI-driven landscape. This book is more than a passive source of information; it is a dynamic tool that equips you with the expertise to navigate the evolving AI landscape, make informed decisions, and drive positive change within your organization, ultimately contributing to your success in AI's exciting and transformative world.

At the end of each chapter, you will find a "Key Points and Actions" section, a valuable resource for translating theoretical knowledge into practical steps. These sections are designed to provide you with actionable steps for implementation, offering clear guidance on applying the concepts discussed in your professional context. These actionable steps bridge theory and practice, allowing you to turn abstract ideas into concrete actions.

Moreover, the "Key Points and Actions" sections offer strategies for real-world applications. They provide a roadmap for applying the critical points in various scenarios, helping you navigate the complexities of the ever-evolving field of AI. These strategies ensure that you can effectively apply AI concepts regardless of the specific context you encounter in your work.

Additionally, these sections serve as a tool for review and reflection. After completing a chapter, revisiting the "Key Points and Actions" helps consolidate your understanding and plan how to integrate these insights into your work. This reflection process is essential for long-term retention and practical application, enabling you to make informed decisions and adjustments in your AI implementation journey.

Furthermore, these sections can also be utilized as a framework for discussion and collaboration within your team or organization. They provide a structured way to effectively engage others in conversations about implementing AI strategies. Collaborative efforts and communication are crucial when integrating AI into an organization, and these sections facilitate discussions, idea sharing, and collaboration on AI-related projects.

As you progress through this book, consider each chapter a building block in your AI knowledge. The "Key Points and Actions" sections help you construct a solid foundation for applying AI in your business practices. They equip you not only with knowledge but also with the tools for action. By actively engaging with these sections, you will be well-prepared to leverage AI effectively in your professional context, turning your AI knowledge into actionable results that drive innovation and improvement within your organization.

Besides the rich content within each chapter, this book is further enhanced by three carefully curated appendices maintained on an external website and not contained in this book as they need to be updated regularly for relevance. These appendices are not mere afterthoughts but integral components that add significant value to your understanding and application of AI in business. Let's explore how each appendix contributes to this book's overall value. These appendices are found at the website for this book: https://ai-iq.online.

Appendix 1 is a comprehensive resource that covers AI standards and frameworks on a global scale. It includes a list of international standards and best practices related to AI, such as International Standards Organization (ISO/IEC Standards and IEEE Guidelines. Understanding these standards is crucial to ensure your AI initiatives are globally compliant and adhere to best practices. Moreover, this appendix includes ethical guidelines and frameworks from reputable organizations like the OECD and UNESCO, which are invaluable for navigating the ethical landscape of AI. It ensures that your AI strategies are not only practical but also responsible and ethical. This appendix serves as a key resource for those involved in policymaking or governance. It offers a foundation for developing or refining AI policies within your organization, aligning with international norms and ethical considerations.

Appendix 2 provides insights into global AI strategies and initiatives undertaken by various countries, including the UAE, EU, and China. Understanding these strategies offers valuable insights into how different nations approach AI, which can inform your strategic planning and market analysis. It also helps benchmark your AI initiatives against global trends and standards, primarily if your business operates internationally or plans to expand. The governmental initiatives outlined here can inspire your organization's AI strategy. They offer examples of comprehensive approaches to AI adoption and integration that can be adapted to your specific organizational context.

AI is a field filled with complex terminology and jargon. Appendix 3 provides clear and concise definitions of essential AI and GenAI terms, ensuring you have a solid grasp of the language used in the field. This appendix lays the foundation for a deeper understanding of the concepts discussed throughout this book by demystifying this terminology. It is an essential tool for AI novices and seasoned professionals looking to refresh their knowledge. Additionally, it is a valuable resource for training and education within your organization. You can use it to bring team members up to speed on AI terminology, facilitating more effective communication and collaboration on AI projects.

Each of these appendices is thoughtfully designed to complement and enhance this book's primary content, providing a comprehensive toolkit for navigating the AI landscape. Whether you are a business leader, a policymaker, or an AI enthusiast, these appendices offer additional layers of depth and practicality. They make "AI iQ for a Human Focused future" a genuinely invaluable resource in your AI journey, equipping you with the knowledge, standards, and insights necessary to succeed in the dynamic world of AI-driven business transformation.

The stage is set for a profound exploration of AI and GenAI in the modern business landscape. This book, authored by an experienced professional who has led AI transformations at Fortune 500 companies globally, is a valuable resource for business leaders. It offers insights and tools to navigate the transformative era of AI, focusing on a pragmatic and strategic approach.

This book's essence lies in its practicality, moving beyond the hype to provide a comprehensive guide to AI implementation in organizations. It covers topics ranging from readiness assessment to ethical considerations, challenging conventional narratives, and advocating for balanced AI adoption. The preface introduces a methodology for AI readiness assessments, emphasizing their importance in identifying strengths, uncovering gaps, and developing targeted strategies for AI integration.

CHAPTER 1

The Foundation

INTRODUCTION

Since 2011, the business world has focused on big data, data science, and machine learning. That all changed in November 2022 when OpenAI released ChatGPT, a consumer-accessible interface for their generative artificial intelligence (AI) models. The public release of ChatGPT initiated a new era of AI – the GenAI Era – relegating data science and machine learning to being old school and boring, much like the on-premises data center and the mainframe were old school and boring when the cloud computing was the new shiny object.

We must understand these technologies' differences as we leverage the new and the old. We need to examine the mistakes and the success of the old school. We must adopt and modify the successful transformation from the old-school AI to the new-school AI. Much like applying any technology, we must ask the right questions.

OLD SCHOOL AI: DATA SCIENCE AND MACHINE LEARNING

Like anything else, the most straightforward approach is generally the best approach. Successfully implemented data science and machine learning uses this as a core tenant. Approach these as one of many tools in a toolbox: If basic rules work for a use case, that's the right solution. If statistical modeling works, use that. If a simple regression works, that's the right solution. Data science and machine learning were the two prized pieces of the decade buzzword bingo. Because of this, they became overused terms, leading to overselling, under-delivering, and diluting the value of these compelling tools.

DOI: 10.1201/9781003486725-2

But what is the difference between data science and machine learning? They are two sides of the same coin. Data science is the practice of building machine learning models. Data scientists also work with data engineers to develop data pipelines that feed machine learning models; they often make statistical models and simulations. Data scientists come with a wide array of skill sets and experiences. Machine learning is part of a spectrum of tools that combines math and computer science to solve business problems at scale. Most machine learning models are the same as some very old statistical models. The main difference is the ability of the models to learn over time. On the other hand, deep learning is a type of machine learning that usually uses newer mathematical models. When you hear the term "black box" in this field, it is a deep learning model.

> These problems (bias) do not stem from math or computer science, as neither are inherently biased. The models learn from the provided data. This data is the permanent record of humans' past decisions – the good, the bad, and the ugly.

There are, however, inherent problems with machine learning that result in a biased outcome. These problems do not stem from math or computer science, as neither are inherently biased. The problem comes from the learning component of machine learning. The models learn from the provided data. This data is the permanent record of humans' past decisions – the good, the bad, and the ugly. So, math teaches the model to mimic the choices humans have made in the past. The fact that many past decisions are biased is problematic because these mathematical models aim to predict what will happen based on past choices by picking up on patterns in the data. And they are very good at doing this, so much so that they often pick up on data elements related to a past biased decision that a human may not pick up on.

Today, the problem of bias is handled directly in the model development life cycle, and models are adjusted to minimize the bias toward protected classes. Adjusting model parameters and hyperparameters to account for bias often comes at a cost for model performance. It sometimes needs to solve the problem of applying these models. Some regulations require the examination of disparate impact – measuring the outcomes for one population versus another in the actual decision-making in the entire implementation. Disparate impact is a much more effective measurement of bias in the models as you can over-correct the model for a specific bias, and it does not impact the actual decision. Alternatively, you can have a very unbiased model. However, it creates a differential impact on one population over another in the implementation context.

NEW SCHOOL AI: GenAI

In November 2022, GenAI took off when OpenAI released ChatGPT. This conversational interface allows anyone who can type or speak to interact with the model. ChatGPT was initially a front end for GPT-3 (Generative Pre-trained Transformer version 3). The GPT models have been around and accessible to the AI and software development communities since 2017, more than five years before the release of ChatGPT. The advent of the technology goes back even further than that. GenAI is not a new technology. ChatGPT is merely a way for the public to use GenAI.

Like statistics, machine learning, and deep learning, GenAI is part of a hierarchy as well. The base of the hierarchy is deep learning. The first layer under that is a concept known as foundation models. These deep learning models are pre-trained on an extensive data set (in the case of ChatGPT, a considerable portion of the internet). Foundation models train on a specific domain. Then, one can apply the model to their proprietary data to get the power of the extensive data without having the data, the skill, or the resources it took to build the foundation model. GenAI is a foundation model pre-trained on vast data sets to generate new data. GenAI comes in multiple flavors: language, speech, text, image, video, 3D images, and scientific-focused models (genetics, chemistry, pharmaceuticals, etc.).

To sum this up. ChatGPT is a large language model, a kind of GenAI, and various foundation models, deep learning, and machine learning models, all based on statistics.

Some examples of the different GenAI models you may be familiar with are as follows:

- **Large Language Models (LLM):** Bard, ChatGPT, and Claude

- **Text to Image:** DALL-E, Stable Diffusion, and Midjourney

- **Text to Video:** Stable Diffusion Video

As of the writing of this book, OpenAI has made ChatGPT a pseudo multimodal interface bringing together GPT and DALL-E, while Google has built a multimodal model from the ground up in Gemini.

A QUICK LOOK BACK

Data science and machine learning started to enter the mainstream of the business world as a concept and a desire around 2011. However, few companies that were not digital natives captured value at scale from these tools. For over a decade, self-declared AI implementation has hovered below 25%. From 2011 until 2016, it hovered below 10%. The most recent surveys have shown that only 25%–30% of organizations have adopted more than one AI model. As of today, only a small subset of organizations genuinely realize the value of data science and machine learning.

GenAI is all the rage. It is the topic de jour of nearly every industry conference. It is the desire of every board of directors. It is the expectation of customers and employees alike. To understand how to implement GenAI in organizations successfully, we must examine what prevents the success of the data science and machine learning opportunities for more than two-thirds of organizations. What did successful organizations do differently?

Successful organizations myopically focus on connecting AI strategy to business strategy, organizational capacity, and technological capacity. And across these three, they measured Key Performance Indicators ((KPIs) that mattered to the business – cost savings and new revenues.

On the other side are the remaining two-thirds of the business world. In this group, there needs to be a tighter connection between AI and business strategies. More organizational capacity building and widespread adoption of modern technologies are required. Data science was a scam for this group – they invested millions and received little to no return.

> If you don't change your approach, generative AI will be a scam, just like data science and machine learning were.

There is a reliable way to align all the dots in an organization to enable the successful implementation of AI and, by extension, GenAI in the enterprise. The rest of this book will describe how I have used this approach at two companies and helped many companies, large and small, do the same. The method starts in the boardroom and ends in the mail room.

FINAL THOUGHTS

As we conclude this chapter, we reflect on a transformative journey in the realm of AI, from its roots in big data, data science, and machine learning to the advent of the GenAI Era, heralded by innovative platforms like OpenAI's ChatGPT. This chapter marks a significant shift in the AI landscape, transitioning from traditional data analysis to the creative capabilities of generative models, reshaping our understanding and application of AI technologies.

In this chapter, we explored the evolution of AI, understanding the nuances and differences between the old-school practices of data science and machine learning and the new-school wave of GenAI. The emphasis was on recognizing the value and limitations, understanding that the key to leveraging their potential lies in harmonizing their strengths, aligned with strategic business objectives. We delved into the successes and mistakes of the past, learning from them to adopt and modify these approaches for the future of AI.

However, as we transition to Chapter 2, "The Uncomfortable Truth About AI" the narrative takes a more critical turn. Chapter 2 challenges us to reevaluate our understanding and expectations of AI. Moving away from the foundational concepts and optimistic advancements discussed in this chapter, Chapter 2 confronts the harsher realities of AI's application in the business world. It questions the prevailing hopeful narratives and delves into a provocative exploration of AI's effectiveness and value, labeling its current form and application in many organizations as a "scam."

Chapter 2 is set to critically examine the discrepancies between AI's promise and its actual performance in businesses, underlining the gap between its potential and realized value. It aims to dissect AI's prevalent misunderstandings and misapplications, emphasizing the need for a strategic, realistic approach to its adoption and implementation. Chapter 2 promises to navigate the complex ecosystem of AI, addressing common pitfalls, ethical considerations, and the paramount importance of aligning AI initiatives with tangible business objectives and human-centric considerations.

The transition from this chapter to Chapter 2 represents a shift from a foundational understanding of AI's evolution and potential to critically examining its real-world impact and value. This progression reflects the multifaceted nature of AI as a field that is not only technologically advanced but also deeply intertwined with business strategy, ethics, and human impact.

KEY TAKEAWAYS AND ACTIONS

UNDERSTANDING OLD SCHOOL AI: DATA SCIENCE AND MACHINE LEARNING

- **Actionable Steps:** Utilize data science and machine learning as practical tools, applying them where they fit best.
- **Implementation:** Focus on simplicity and appropriateness in solutions, using basic rules, statistical modeling, or regression as needed.

DISTINGUISHING BETWEEN DATA SCIENCE AND MACHINE LEARNING

- **Actionable Steps:** Recognize and differentiate the roles of data science and machine learning in AI strategy.
- **Implementation:** Understand that data science involves building machine learning models and developing data pipelines, while machine learning is about applying mathematical and computer science principles to solve business problems at scale.

ADDRESSING BIAS IN MACHINE LEARNING

- **Actionable Steps:** Tackle inherent biases arising from biased data in machine learning models before deployment – before and after training.
- **Implementation:** Integrate bias-handling mechanisms directly into the model development lifecycle, adjust parameters to minimize bias, and measure ongoing disparate impacts.

EMBRACING GenAI: THE NEW SCHOOL AI

- **Actionable Steps:** Leverage the capabilities of GenAI models for innovative solutions.
- **Implementation:** Utilize GenAI across various applications like language, speech, text, image, and video to create new data and insights.

INTEGRATING OLD AND NEW AI APPROACHES

- **Actionable Steps:** Harmonize traditional data science methods with advanced GenAI techniques.
- **Implementation:** Combine old-school AI's reliability and tested approaches with new-school AI's innovative and creative capabilities for balanced solutions.

CRITICAL EVALUATION OF AI IMPLEMENTATION

- **Actionable Steps:** Critically assess the value and application of AI in business.

- **Implementation:** Evaluate AI initiatives for their real-world effectiveness, ensuring they align with business goals and offer a substantial return on investment.

STRATEGIC ALIGNMENT OF AI WITH BUSINESS GOALS

- **Actionable Steps:** Align AI strategies with overarching business objectives.
- **Implementation:** Ensure that AI initiatives are integrated into the business strategy, enhancing operations and contributing to growth.

REALIZING THE VALUE OF AI IN BUSINESS

- **Actionable Steps:** Transition AI from a conceptual tool to a strategic business driver.
- **Implementation:** Measure the impact of AI initiatives against business objectives, making necessary adjustments for continued alignment and improvement.

CHAPTER 2

The Uncomfortable Truth About AI

INTRODUCTION

In 2017, I embarked on an international journey spanning 6 continents and more than 40 countries, and I am still going. This was not leisurely travel but an expedition to uncover a truth about artificial intelligence (AI) that was as uncomfortable as it was undeniable. As the leader of AI at IBM and currently leading my advisory firm – Qantm AI, I found myself standing before diverse audiences. Not to sing the praises of AI but to make a startling declaration – AI, in its present form and application, is a scam.

Using "scam" here may raise more than a few eyebrows, especially considering my position. Why do I make such a claim? The answer is simple and originates from a complicated truth: AI was and continues to be a scam for most organizations. This assertion is not a critique of the technology itself – AI has shown promise in various fields – but rather an analysis of its deployment and utilization in the business world. The problem isn't the technology but the misunderstanding and misuse of it.

> *The net result is that many organizations spend millions or tens of millions of dollars on AI programs, realizing little to no value from them – this is the heart of the scam.*

During my journey, my talks often began with a series of questions, which I asked the audience to respond to by raising their hands. The

 DOI: 10.1201/9781003486725-3

instruction is to keep their hands raised as long as their answer remained affirmative:

1. Are you piloting AI anywhere in your organization?

2. Do you have AI in production in at least one business unit?

3. Do you have AI in production in multiple business units?

4. Do you have an AI system deployed across the entire company?

5. Can you measure how your AI programs directly support and accelerate your organization's objectives?

The progression usually moves from 80% to 90% for the first question, 30% to 40% for the second question, and 10% to 20% for the third question. By the time we reach the fourth question, less than 5% of hands remain raised. You usually drop to 2% to 3% for the fifth question, keeping their hands up. This anecdotal evidence is not meant to discourage business leaders but rather illuminate the harsh reality of AI adoption in most organizations. The idea is to create self-awareness of the truth about AI implementation in the business world. This book helps you raise your AI iQ to keep your hand up the next time these questions are asked.

According to analysts from top consulting firms such as McKinsey, BGC, and others, less than 30% of organizations have an AI system deployed across the entire organization.

If the goal of AI is to add value to an organization, it is backfiring now.

This is not to say that successful AI implementation is a myth. Some organizations can keep their hands raised through all the questions. These organizations are the ones that have successfully derived value from AI. Their AI strategy is derived from their business strategy, not vice versa. They have clearly articulated how AI initiatives support their organizational objectives. They view AI governance as an enabler, not a hurdle. They embrace diversity and ensure that their talent reflects the populations they serve. They have the proper architectures for deployment, and, most importantly, they start with the humans. They understand that AI is not just about technology; it's about people. Unsuccessful companies, at best, do some of these but most likely do none of these.

You might ask, "What are the differences?" It all starts with asking the right question. The question is, "What are the key decisions I need to make or tactics that need to be executed to reach our organizational objectives and commitments, and how can technology help me reach them?" The answer will undoubtedly involve data, AI, and generative AI (GenAI). But by starting with the business problem, your AI strategy is part of your business strategy and not separate in and of itself.

AI AND ITS MISUNDERSTANDINGS

AI stands at a crossroads, surrounded by myths and misconceptions. It's often hailed as a revolutionary force, a catalyst for change in businesses' operations. Yet, beneath these grandiose claims lies a more nuanced reality. AI has become a magnet for investments in many organizations, often driven more by its allure than a deep understanding of its potential and limitations. This trend has led to numerous initiatives where AI is aggressively pursued without a strategic compass, leading to investments resulting in more costly experimentation than actual value creation.

AI is not a magic wand that miraculously transforms business operations. Instead, it's a tool that thrives in an ecosystem with the correct data, infrastructure, skill sets, and cultural alignment. AI initiatives risk becoming little more than high-tech follies without these essential components. This widespread misunderstanding about AI doesn't render the technology useless. Instead, it underscores the necessity for a strategy-first approach to its adoption and implementation. This involves shifting from viewing AI as a standalone marvel to understanding it as part of a broader operational tapestry woven intricately with the threads of business strategy, human talent, and organizational culture.

To harness AI's true potential, organizations must look beyond the hype. They must cultivate a transparent, pragmatic understanding of AI's capabilities and limitations and strategically integrate this technology into their operations. This approach isn't about putting AI in an overly optimistic light or promoting it as a panacea. Instead, it's about adopting a balanced, realistic perspective, acknowledging AI's potential while being acutely aware of the groundwork required for successful implementation.

The forthcoming sections will explore the ecosystem supporting effective AI integration. This journey will navigate the crucial elements necessary for AI's success – data quality robust infrastructure, requisite skills, and conducive organizational culture. The narrative will confront common pitfalls and dispel prevalent myths about AI, offering insights into sidestepping these traps. It will guide leaders in aligning AI initiatives with their business objectives and provide metrics to gauge their efficacy.

Ultimately, AI's essence isn't encapsulated in its status as a modern buzzword or a subject of technological wonder. Its value lies in its ability to add tangible, measurable benefits to business operations. The objective of this discourse is not merely to demystify AI but to equip leaders with the insights and tools they require to make informed AI-related decisions and implement this technology in a manner that translates into tangible, palpable business value.

GenAI: A BIGGER SCAM?

The emergence of GenAI in the landscape of AI marks a significant evolution, presenting possibilities that many in the business world view with a mixture of awe and skepticism. GenAI, with its capability to produce novel content ranging from text to images and beyond, indeed carries an air of transformative potential. Yet, there's a pervasive misconception that GenAI is a universal solution, a silver bullet in content creation. This view is as misleading as it is potentially detrimental.

GenAI, much like its predecessors in the broader AI family, is not an all-conquering tool but a sophisticated instrument that requires precise handling. The efficacy of GenAI hinges not just on the technology itself but on a constellation of supporting elements: accurate and relevant data, contextual understanding, and careful oversight. Absent these, the outputs of GenAI can be, at best, underwhelming, and at worst, they can steer endeavors toward unanticipated, sometimes catastrophic, outcomes. GenAI, in its current form and application, introduces complexities and challenges that pose a greater risk compared to traditional AI approaches.

The potential of GenAI is undeniable, yet realizing this potential demands a strategic, nuanced approach. This approach must encompass not only the technology but also the people who wield it, the processes it is intended to enhance, and the business objectives it aims to fulfill. GenAI, like traditional AI, is not about supplanting human ingenuity but augmenting it, marrying human creativity, intuition, and judgment with the machine's speed, accuracy, and scalability. It's about leveraging these tools for their strengths – analyzing vast data sets, detecting patterns, and generating outputs – while allowing humans to excel in context, oversight, and strategic direction.

Furthermore, understanding GenAI requires recognizing its place within a broader ecosystem, including data, infrastructure, processes, and people. Leaders in the business realm must grasp this interconnectedness, ensuring that each component is aligned and contributing effectively toward a shared goal. Therefore, while GenAI – and AI at large – may not be the panacea some have proclaimed, it is far from a mere industry gimmick. These tools can unlock substantial value when approached with the right strategy, accurate data, effective oversight, and alignment with business goals and processes.

The true promise of GenAI is not merely in its technological prowess but in how it is integrated into the fabric of business operations. It calls for a strategic approach considering the entire ecosystem, balancing AI's strengths with human insight and expertise. With this balanced approach, business leaders can harness the power of GenAI, transforming its promise into a tangible, impactful reality.

THE REAL VALUE OF AI

AI has transitioned from a futuristic concept into a present-day technological reality, offering vast potential for businesses across various sectors. Properly utilized, AI can be a powerhouse for driving business value, automating mundane tasks to free up human talent for more strategic endeavors. It can delve into extensive data sets, extracting insights beyond human capability. In customer engagement, AI's ability to personalize experiences can significantly enhance satisfaction and loyalty, creating a more efficient, competitive business landscape.

Yet, unlocking AI's full potential is not as straightforward as it might seem. The journey to harnessing these benefits extends far beyond merely deploying AI technologies. It necessitates a robust connection to business strategy, a steadfast focus on specific business outcomes, and a commitment to continual learning and adaptation. AI should not be viewed as a universal remedy but as a strategic tool that, when applied effectively, can yield considerable returns. A crucial element in this process is a well-defined strategy that outlines the organization's AI objectives, the role of AI in achieving these goals, and the necessary resources and capabilities. This strategy must also consider potential risks and ethical concerns associated with AI, proposing practical measures to manage these aspects.

The pursuit of AI in the business world should be driven by a desire to achieve business goals, whether enhancing customer service, optimizing operational efficiency, or fostering innovation. The success of AI initiatives should be measured not by the technology's sophistication alone but by its impact on business objectives. In AI's dynamic, ever-evolving realm, leaders must embrace ongoing learning and adaptation to remain competitive.

This commitment requires cultivating a culture of continuous learning, encouraging employees to upgrade their skills, and staying informed about the latest AI advancements. Leaders should also be prepared to iterate and adapt AI strategies based on feedback and outcomes.

Investing in both people and processes is equally crucial. Effective AI implementation demands not just technological investments but also significant investments in human resources – their skills, knowledge, and ability to work with AI systems. It necessitates establishing processes that support efficient data management, ethical AI deployment, and agile management of AI projects. Understanding AI's capabilities and limitations is fundamental. Despite its potential, AI is not a panacea for all business challenges, nor can it replace all human functions. It should be seen as an augmentative tool that, when used judiciously, can significantly enhance business efficiency.

While AI presents an incredible opportunity for businesses to revolutionize their operations and offerings, realizing its full potential is complex. It requires a strategic approach encompassing business goal alignment, continuous learning, human and process capital investment, and a realistic appraisal of AI's capabilities. With these elements in place, businesses can unlock the actual value of AI, transforming its potential into tangible, measurable business outcomes.

AI AS A STRATEGIC IMPERATIVE

In today's business landscape, AI transcends being just a technological advancement; it has emerged as a strategic imperative. This profound tool harbors the capacity to revolutionize every aspect of business, encompassing customer service, operations, decision-making, and product development. However, the realization of this transformation is not automatic. It mandates a strategic approach where AI initiatives are not only in sync with the overarching business goals but also tailored to the unique needs and capabilities of the organization.

For organizations to harness the transformative power of AI effectively, they must develop a strategy that seamlessly integrates with their broader business objectives. This strategy should articulate the organization's aspirations with AI, delineate the role of AI in achieving these goals, and identify the requisite resources and capabilities. It should define the value AI is expected to create and establish key quantitative performance indicators for measuring its success. A meticulously formulated AI strategy acts as a navigational chart, guiding organizations through the intricacies of AI implementation and steering them clear of potential pitfalls.

Organizational leaders need to grasp the fundamental aspects of AI – its capabilities, limitations, potential risks, and ethical considerations – without the necessity of becoming data scientists. They should focus on understanding how AI can augment and align with their business strategy.

Clarity on the objectives of integrating AI is crucial. Whether the aim is to enhance customer service, optimize operations, bolster decision-making, or stimulate innovation, these goals will shape the AI strategy. They will influence the selection of AI technologies, determine data needs, and guide the implementation process. Navigating the AI landscape demands a commitment to continuous learning and agility. The domain of AI is dynamic, characterized by constant evolution, with new advancements and applications continually emerging. Staying informed about these developments and being agile enough to adapt AI strategies as needed is imperative for businesses.

Effective AI implementation is not a static project but an ongoing journey. It involves a process of exploration, experimentation, learning, and constant adaptation. Integrating AI into the business fabric means aligning it with business strategies and continually fine-tuning it to optimize its value. For companies today, implementing AI is more than a competitive edge; it is a strategic necessity that can redefine the business paradigm. By adopting a strategic approach to AI, an understanding of the technology, and a commitment to continual learning and adaptation, businesses can unlock AI's full potential and solidify their position in an AI-driven future.

THE HUMAN ELEMENT IN AI

In pursuing the vast potential of AI, it's a common oversight to primarily focus on the technology – the algorithms, the data, the computational capacity. However, the pivotal element in effective AI implementation transcends the technological realm and firmly resides in the human aspect. AI's true essence lies not just in the technology itself but in the people who develop, deploy, interact with, and are affected by it.

A comprehensive understanding of the human factor in AI involves a deep appreciation of human behavior, needs, and expectations. This perspective requires viewing AI through the lenses of sociotechnical – psychology, sociology, and anthropology, applying human sciences to machine intelligence. It's about acknowledging that AI, at its core, is a tool utilized by humans, and its success or failure hinges as much on the user as on the technology. Integrating this human aspect compels businesses to adopt a holistic approach to AI implementation. Organizations must consider the technical aspects and their implications on their employees, customers, and broader stakeholder groups. This involves preparing the workforce for the AI transition, equipping them with the necessary skills and knowledge, and addressing any fears or misconceptions they may harbor. For customers, AI-driven products and services must align with their needs, expectations, and values to enhance rather than detract from their experience.

Understanding the human element in AI also demands a steadfast commitment to ethical considerations. Like many potent tools, AI is dual-use – capable of being used for beneficial or detrimental purposes. Navigating AI ethics' complex and often controversial terrain requires a thoughtful approach. This includes grappling with issues such as bias, privacy, job displacement, and responsible decision-making within AI, always keeping in mind the sociotechnical context of its application. Employing AI should uphold human rights, promote fairness, and contribute to societal welfare rather than prioritizing efficiency or profit.

The human aspect of AI is far from a secondary concern; it is integral and should be woven into the fabric of AI strategy, from its conception to its full-scale implementation. Embracing AI necessitates a paradigm shift – from perceiving it as a solely technological venture to understanding it as a sociotechnical system that intricately intertwines technology with humanity. The accurate measure of AI's success transcends its operational efficiency or problem-solving capabilities; it is defined by how well it serves and enhances human lives, respects our values, and aligns with societal norms.

As we continue to advance in AI, we must focus on the humans at its core – those who build and use AI and those impacted by it. Ensuring that as we endow our machines with greater intelligence, we must not lose sight of our humanity is crucial. AI must be a tool that works for us, augmenting our capabilities and enriching our lives. After all, the future of AI is not solely about the advancement of machines; it is predominantly about people and how this technology can be harnessed to improve the human condition.

THE POTENTIAL OF AI AND GenAI

The escalating excitement around AI and GenAI, marked by predictions of significant economic value creation, is reshaping the business landscape. Consulting firm McKinsey projects that AI could contribute an additional $13.3 trillion to global GDP by 2030 (https://www.mck-insey.com/capabilities/mckinsey-digital/our-insights/the-economic-potential-of-generative-ai-the-next-productivity-frontier), with GenAI potentially adding another $4.4 trillion annually (https://www.mckinsey.com/mgi/overview/in-the-news/ai-could-increase-corporate-profits-by-4-trillion-a-year-according-to-new-research) This staggering economic potential, driven mainly by enhanced productivity and innovative applications across industries, highlights GenAI's capacity to double the overall impact of AI potentially.

However, amidst this economic optimism, there lies a nuanced reality. The focus on aggregate financial gains often shadows the complex challenges and disparities that may arise from these technological advancements. While net positive, the benefits of AI and GenAI are unlikely to be uniformly distributed. This uneven distribution underscores the need for proactive policies to ensure technological advancements contribute to broad-based prosperity.

In-depth insights from the McKinsey Global Survey on AI in 2023 illustrate that GenAI rapidly moves from a specialized technological focus to a mainstream business priority. With about a third of respondents already utilizing GenAI in various business functions, the technology is no longer confined to experimental labs. Still, it is being integrated into day-to-day business operations. Significantly, this integration is not just a tech-centric endeavor but is increasingly becoming a board and C-suite-level focus, with a substantial proportion of executives actively employing these tools in their professional tasks (https://www.mckinsey.com/capabilities/quantumblack/our-insights/the-state-of-ai-in-2023-generative-ais-breakout-year).

The transformative potential of GenAI is particularly pronounced in industries centered around knowledge work, such as technology, banking, pharmaceuticals, and education. These sectors are poised for substantial changes, anticipating workforce reductions in certain areas and extensive up-skilling to align with the new talent requirements. In contrast, sectors like manufacturing, which rely more on physical labor than knowledge-based activities, might experience less direct impact from GenAI advancements.

McKinsey's research reveals that organizations with a deeply ingrained culture of innovation are better positioned to leverage GenAI effectively. These companies excel in their strategic vision, ensuring that new ideas are pursued and rapidly scaled to achieve market relevance. Their innovative operating models, characterized by robust investments in R&D and digital tools, facilitate seamless integration of GenAI into their business processes, creating significant value. These organizations stand out for their ability to ask strategic questions, swiftly identify and rectify inaccuracies, build proprietary data, quickly adapt organizational learning, and develop efficient workflows that maximize the speed and capabilities of GenAI.

While the economic and operational promises of AI and GenAI are substantial, harnessing these benefits requires more than technological implementation. It demands strategic organizational adaptation, where companies with innovative and agile cultures are likely to excel. Navigating the integration of these technologies into business operations, these organizations can stay ahead in a rapidly evolving digital landscape, turning the potential of AI and GenAI into a tangible reality.

WINNERS AND LOSERS

The potential of AI and GenAI in transforming various industries and occupations is vast and nuanced. While offering significant economic value and advancements, these technologies also pose risks and challenges that must be addressed strategically.

The economic potential of AI and GenAI is staggering. Consulting firm McKinsey estimates that AI could add $13.3 trillion and GenAI an additional $4.4 trillion annually to global GDP. This growth primarily stems from increased productivity and new applications across diverse sectors. However, the aggregate focus often overshadows the individual and societal perils these technologies bring. While the overall impact is positive, the benefits are not uniformly distributed. This uneven distribution necessitates proactive policies to ensure technology drives broad prosperity.

The transformative nature of AI and GenAI will inevitably create winners and losers. Enhanced productivity and reduced costs could elevate profits and wages for some, but others may face job losses or pay cuts as tasks become automated. Particularly, GenAI threatens roles in content creation, customer service, data analysis, and managerial tasks. The disruption's pace will likely be faster than any previous technological change, requiring rapid adaptation.

Moreover, pre-existing disparities play a significant role in determining who benefits from these advancements. Entities with the resources to adopt new technologies swiftly will likely surge ahead, widening the gap with those who need to catch up, especially in developing countries and less affluent communities within advanced economies. These groups often need more access to the education and training needed to excel in an AI-centric world. Focusing policies on skill development, educational access, and robust social safety nets is crucial to counter these growing disparities.

While the economic and productivity potentials of AI and GenAI are undeniable, their impact is far from uniform. Addressing the challenges and risks associated with these technologies is as important as harnessing their potential. This approach ensures that the benefits of AI and GenAI are widespread and contribute to the overall betterment of society rather than exacerbating existing inequalities.

ECONOMIC AND POLITICAL POWER

AI's economic and political implications, particularly in the context of Big Tech's dominance, are subjects of significant concern and debate. The rise of GenAI, a powerful and versatile technology, has the potential to further consolidate power among leading AI firms like Google, Microsoft, and OpenAI. While this concentration of expertise and resources can drive innovation rapidly, it raises critical issues around monopolization, privacy, and freedom of expression.

The economic dominance of these tech giants not only impacts market competition but also poses risks to individual privacy and the autonomy of content creation and dissemination. A few significant players' control over AI technologies can lead to potential biases in AI algorithms and outputs and a lack of diversity in the perspectives these technologies represent and reinforce. Furthermore, countries and organizations' heavy reliance on proprietary AI systems can jeopardize national security and technological sovereignty. It becomes essential for governments to strike a balance between the interests of these influential tech firms and the broader public good. Smart regulations around data rights, interoperability, and anti-trust laws are critical steps in this direction.

A notable incident highlighting these issues occurred on 16 November 2023, when the Board of OpenAI dismissed Sam Altman (https://www.nytimes.com/2023/11/17/technology/openai-sam-altman-ousted.html), only for him to be reinstated due to pressure from Microsoft, which held a significant interest in the company (https://www.nytimes.com/2023/11/22/technology/openai-sam-altman-returns.html). This event raises questions about the independence of OpenAI and its alignment with Microsoft's business interests, particularly given Microsoft's considerable investment in and influence over OpenAI's operations and decision-making.

In addition to market concerns, AI technologies, especially generative models, enable the creation and spread of hyper-personalized misinformation and propaganda. The ease with which these technologies can fabricate convincing but false content poses significant risks to public discourse and democratic processes. It can sway public opinion, simulate voices or images for fraudulent activities, and undermine trust in media and information sources.

To mitigate these social harms, it's crucial to develop robust AI auditing mechanisms that ensure transparency and accountability in AI development and deployment. Additionally, digital literacy programs are necessary to educate the public about the capabilities and limitations of AI, enabling individuals to assess AI-generated content critically. Governments and regulatory bodies should also impose transparency requirements on AI developers and deployers to ensure that the public understands the nature and origin of AI-generated content.

The economic and political power dynamics surrounding AI and GenAI demand careful consideration and action. Balancing innovation with ethical considerations, market fairness, national security, and preserving democratic values is essential for harnessing the benefits of AI while mitigating its risks.

POLICY PRIORITIES

AI and GenAI are becoming ubiquitous, and the importance of astute policy priorities cannot be overstated. These priorities represent not just reactionary measures but embody a forward-thinking governance model, comprehensively addressing AI's multifaceted societal impact. The European Union has pioneered in this regard, as evidenced by the EU AI Act Cheat Sheet (https://iapp.org/resources/article/eu-ai-act-cheat-sheet/). It articulates a comprehensive AI regulation approach to balance advancing technology and protecting fundamental rights. This Act classifies AI systems according to their risk level and sets stringent requirements for those categorized as high-risk. These requirements include conducting impact assessments on fundamental rights, establishing robust risk management practices, implementing strict data governance measures, and conducting conformity assessments based on internationally recognized standards such as ISO/ECC to protect individual and societal interests.

Central to the policy focus is the investment in AI and technology education. This approach is pivotal in developing a workforce proficient in these rapidly evolving technologies. Equally critical is establishing a robust digital infrastructure, serving as the backbone for AI's development and deployment. Furthermore, enhancing social safety nets, expanding healthcare access, and launching retraining programs are essential steps in preparing the workforce to adapt to AI-induced changes in the job market.

Robust regulations around bias testing, transparency, accountability, and privacy are paramount in building public trust in AI technologies. The EU AI Act, for instance, prohibits AI systems designed to manipulate behavior or exploit the vulnerabilities of specific groups. It also places stringent controls on applications like biometric identification and predictive policing, reflecting a deep commitment to individual rights and societal welfare.

In terms of enforcement, the Act is extraterritorial. It proposes substantial fines as high as 7% of global turnover, indicating a severe commitment to compliance and aligning with the broader need for international coordination on critical issues like harmful content, human rights, and AI arms control. By establishing clear standards and penalties, the EU aims to ensure that AI development is safe and in line with the public interest.

Partnerships between government, academia, and industry are essential in fostering responsible AI innovation and sustaining public trust in technology. The Act encourages AI ethics training within tech firms and advocates for establishing oversight boards, promoting an approach that allows the industry to address emerging issues while adhering to regulatory standards proactively.

The Act strongly emphasizes a human-focused approach to AI. This approach prioritizes human oversight and minimizes risks to fundamental rights, maintaining a delicate balance between the benefits of AI and the protection of individual and societal values.

In response to the evolving landscape of AI, the United States has also taken significant strides in shaping its AI governance. The Executive Order on AI (https://www.whitehouse.gov/briefing-room/statements-releases/2023/10/30/fact-sheet-president-biden-issues-executive-order-on-safe-secure-and-trustworthy-artificial-intelligence/) and the Blueprint for an AI Bill of Rights (https://www.whitehouse.gov/ostp/ai-bill-of-rights/) are landmark documents reflecting a commitment to AI's safe, secure, and ethical development. They underscore a multifaceted approach that balances technological advancement with protecting fundamental rights and democratic values.

The Executive Order on AI prioritizes responsible AI governance, advocating a coordinated, government-wide strategy. It acknowledges AI's potential to enrich society while cautioning against its misuse, which could exacerbate societal harms like fraud, discrimination, and national security threats. The Order outlines guiding principles for AI development, focusing on safety and security, innovation and competition, workforce support, equity and civil rights, consumer protection, privacy and civil liberties, government's use of AI, and global leadership.

The Blueprint for an AI Bill of Rights complements the Executive Order by providing a governance framework that upholds human rights and ethical standards. It details principles to ensure AI systems are transparent and equitable and do not infringe on individual freedoms and privacy.

The policy frameworks from the EU and US governments provide a comprehensive approach to AI governance. They emphasize the importance of balancing innovation with ethical considerations and societal impacts. The focus on education, infrastructure, equity, privacy, and global cooperation sets a standard for responsible AI development. By embracing these principles, policymakers can guide AI development toward a future that maximizes societal benefits while addressing advanced technologies' inherent risks and challenges.

FINAL THOUGHTS

Chapter 2 of our exploration into AI culminates in a significant realization. This chapter dismantles the facade of AI as a universal solution, revealing instead a landscape where its implementation often falls short of the transformative potential it promises. This revelation underscores the critical disconnect between AI's capabilities and deployment. The journey through this chapter is sobering, where the harsh realities of its implementation temper the initial enthusiasm for AI's revolutionary potential.

Throughout this exploration, we confronted the overzealous adoption of AI, driven more by its allure as a buzzword than by a strategic understanding of its true potential and limitations. We delved into the need for a strategic, nuanced approach, especially concerning GenAI, emphasizing its role not as a panacea but as a sophisticated tool requiring precision and understanding. This chapter emphasized aligning AI with tangible business strategies and addressing the human element in its deployment.

As we transition from the revelations of this chapter to the insights of Chapter 3, "Connection to Tangible Value," our narrative shifts from the critique of AI's misapplication to a focus on how AI can be strategically integrated to realize tangible business value. This upcoming chapter promises to traverse the intricate connection between AI strategy and business success, moving beyond a simplistic view of AI as a technological tool to a deeper understanding of its role as a strategic asset.

Chapter 3 will explore the relationship between AI and business strategies. AI is not merely an isolated technological entity but a critical factor in achieving specific business objectives. Chapter 3 aims to illuminate the pathway for organizations to align their AI investments with their strategic goals, optimizing the return on investment and leveraging AI's capabilities to enhance business performance and drive significant value.

The journey through Chapter 3 is set to be transformative, shedding light on the practicalities of implementing AI within the fabric of business operations and emphasizing the need for a cultural shift within organizations to embrace the potential of AI fully. We will explore how a strategic approach to AI, commitment to ethical practices, and continuous adaptation can transform AI from a misunderstood technology into a cornerstone of business innovation and success.

KEY TAKEAWAYS AND ACTIONS

AI AS A SCAM
- **Actionable Steps:** Recognize the gap between AI's potential and business impact.
- **Implementation:** Reassess existing AI strategies to focus on tangible outcomes and actual value generation.

AI IMPLEMENTATION REALITY CHECK
- **Actionable Steps:** Conduct honest evaluations of AI projects in organizations.
- **Implementation:** Use a series of questions to assess AI's impact on business objectives and identify underperforming areas.

SUCCESSFUL AI IMPLEMENTATION
- **Actionable Steps:** Integrate AI strategies with business strategies and focus on human-centric approaches.
- **Implementation:** Embrace diversity, start with human needs, and ensure AI governance facilitates rather than hinders progress.

AI MISUNDERSTANDINGS

- **Actionable Steps:** Shift the narrative from AI as a standalone solution to a tool integrated into business operations.
- **Implementation:** Foster a practical understanding of AI, focusing on its capabilities, limitations, and strategic integration.

GenAI CHALLENGES

- **Actionable Steps:** Approach GenAI with a balanced, strategic perspective.
- **Implementation:** Ensure the correct data, context, and oversight for GenAI to avoid misaligned outcomes.

REAL VALUE OF AI

- **Actionable Steps:** Link AI initiatives to specific business outcomes and invest in people and processes.
- **Implementation:** Develop AI strategies tied to business value, focusing on enhancing customer service, operational efficiency, and innovation.

AI AS A STRATEGIC IMPERATIVE

- **Actionable Steps:** Align AI initiatives with overarching business goals while accommodating organizational needs.
- **Implementation:** Develop an AI strategy connected to the business strategy and adapt it per evolving AI advancements and market conditions.

HUMAN ELEMENT IN AI

- **Actionable Steps:** Emphasize the importance of the human aspect in AI implementation.
- **Implementation:** Focus on understanding human behavior, needs, and ethics in AI deployment.

POTENTIAL OF AI AND GenAI

- **Actionable Steps:** Harness AI's economic potential while addressing societal challenges.
- **Implementation:** Develop proactive policies for broad prosperity and adapt to the transformative impact of AI across sectors.

WINNERS AND LOSERS IN AI ERA

- **Actionable Steps:** Address the disparities and risks associated with AI advancements.
- **Implementation:** Formulate policies around skill development, educational access, and social safety nets.

ECONOMIC AND POLITICAL POWER OF AI

- **Actionable Steps:** Balance innovation with ethical considerations and market fairness.
- **Implementation:** Develop robust AI auditing mechanisms and digital literacy programs.

POLICY PRIORITIES FOR AI

- **Actionable Steps:** Implement comprehensive policy frameworks for responsible AI governance.
- **Implementation:** Embrace principles ensuring AI systems are transparent, equitable, and do not infringe on individual freedoms and privacy.

CHAPTER 3

Connection to Tangible Value

INTRODUCTION

Integrating artificial intelligence (AI) into business strategies marks a pivotal shift in organizational dynamics, moving beyond the mere adoption of technology to a strategic realignment of corporate goals and technological capabilities. This chapter delves into this profound transformation, exploring the intricate connection between AI strategy and tangible business value. It transcends the conventional focus on AI's technological aspects to emphasize its role as a strategic asset, capable of reshaping business models and driving significant value.

This chapter's core is the concept of a deeper understanding of AI strategy, not just as a technological tool but as an integral component of the overarching business strategy. This understanding necessitates departing the prevalent "technology-first" mindset, advocating for a "strategy-first" approach. In this paradigm, AI is not an isolated entity but a critical factor in achieving specific business objectives, ensuring that investments in AI technology are in harmony with the organization's strategic goals. This alignment is pivotal, optimizing the return on investment, enhancing revenue, and improving profit margins.

This chapter further explores the dynamic interplay between business strategy and AI strategy, emphasizing the need for agility and adaptability. This interplay is characterized by a mutual influence where business strategy informs AI initiatives, and AI insights, in turn, shape business

DOI: 10.1201/9781003486725-4

strategy. Real-world examples in this chapter illustrate how AI can unveil new opportunities, prompting strategic pivots and reshaping business goals. This synergy demands a continuous review and modification, aligning AI strategies with changing market conditions and technological advancements.

The cultural shift within the organization is central to the successful integration of AI into business strategy. This shift involves preparing and equipping employees at all levels to embrace AI as a collaborative tool in achieving business objectives. This chapter underscores the importance of leadership in driving this cultural transformation, advocating for an organization that values innovation, agility, and data-driven decision-making. Furthermore, the quality of data available plays a crucial role, as AI systems are only as effective as the data they process. Thus, ensuring data accuracy, relevance, and accessibility is paramount, necessitating significant investment in data management and analytics capabilities.

Ethical considerations and regulation compliance are also critical aspects of an AI strategy. In an era where AI's impact is pervasive, addressing issues surrounding data privacy, ethical use of AI, and compliance with evolving regulations becomes increasingly significant. This chapter navigates these challenges, advocating for responsible and sustainable AI initiatives.

This chapter presents a comprehensive examination of the role of AI in business strategy, emphasizing its strategic alignment with business goals, the necessary cultural shift, and the commitment to ethical and sustainable technology use. Understanding and leveraging this interplay between AI and business strategy is advantageous and essential for senior leaders in an increasingly digital world.

A DEEPER UNDERSTANDING OF AI STRATEGY

In business, integrating AI strategy is not merely adopting new technologies but a profound shift in how organizations align their technological capabilities with overarching business objectives. The essence of a well-crafted AI strategy lies in identifying how AI can bolster specific business goals and developing a plan to actualize this integration. This perspective steers the discourse away from the simplistic query of "How do we use AI?" to a more nuanced consideration of "What are our business objectives, and how can technology facilitate their achievement?" In this context, data, AI, and generative AI (GenAI) emerge as tools and integral components of a strategic vision.

This approach marks a decisive departure from the prevalent "technology-first" mindset, where organizations hastily invest in new technologies without clearly understanding their role in advancing business goals. Such a misaligned approach often leads to squandered resources and overlooked opportunities. In contrast, a "strategy-first" philosophy ensures that investments in AI are not just technologically sound but are also in harmony with the organization's strategic objectives. This alignment is crucial for optimizing the return on investment, enhancing revenue, and improving profit margins.

In practice, the implementation of a strategy-first AI approach demands a thorough understanding of both the capabilities of AI and the specific needs and goals of the business. This requires a detailed analysis of the market, customer behavior, operational efficiencies, and potential growth areas. AI can then be tailored to address these areas, offering insights and solutions that might not be apparent through traditional methods. For instance, AI can analyze vast customer data to identify emerging trends, preferences, and behaviors, enabling businesses to anticipate market shifts and respond proactively.

Moreover, integrating AI into business strategy necessitates a cultural shift within the organization. Employees at all levels must be prepared and equipped to work alongside AI technologies. This preparation involves technical training and an adjustment mindset to embrace AI as a partner in achieving business objectives. Leaders play a crucial role in this cultural transformation, setting the tone for an organization that values innovation, agility, and data-driven decision-making.

The successful integration of AI also hinges on the quality of data available. AI systems are only as effective as the data they process. Thus, ensuring data accuracy, relevance, and accessibility is paramount. This entails a significant investment in data management and analytics capabilities, laying the groundwork for AI systems to function optimally.

Developing and implementing an AI strategy within a business context is more than deploying technology. A strategic alignment of AI capabilities with business goals, a cultural shift toward embracing AI, and a commitment to responsible and sustainable use of technology is critical. This holistic approach ensures that AI becomes a driving force in achieving business objectives, transforming operational efficiencies and the entire business landscape. Understanding and leveraging this interplay between AI and business strategy is advantageous and necessary for senior leaders in an increasingly digital world.

THE INTERPLAY OF BUSINESS STRATEGY AND AI STRATEGY

In the contemporary organizational landscape, the integration of business and AI strategies is emerging as a vital element for organizational success. This fusion signifies a dynamic interplay where business strategy informs AI initiatives, and AI insights, in turn, influence business strategy. For C-Suite leaders, grasping this synergy is not merely beneficial – it's crucial.

This relationship's heart is how business strategy sets the goals and objectives an organization aims to achieve. AI strategy serves as a means to support these objectives with data-driven insights and intelligent automation. Yet, this relationship is not one-way. AI often unveils new opportunities or threats, significantly reshaping business strategy.

Consider the example of a corporation employing AI to analyze customer behaviors, leading to the discovery of a significant demand for a product or service not currently offered. This insight isn't just data; it's a potential strategic pivot, elevating AI from a supportive role to a driver of strategic transformation.

This nexus between business and AI strategy demands agility as market conditions, technological advancements, and organizational capabilities are in constant flux. Therefore, business and AI strategies must be aligned and adaptable, requiring continuous review and modification in response to internal and external changes.

Real-world examples further illustrate this point. A global retail giant, for instance, used AI to optimize its supply chain, discovering inefficiencies and proposing predictive stocking models. This insight shifted the company's business strategy toward just-in-time inventory, enhancing efficiency and profitability. Similarly, a financial services firm employed AI for customer data analysis, uncovering an untapped market segment and leading to a diversification of product offerings. These cases demonstrate AI's transformative impact on business strategy.

Beyond just technology, effective AI implementation requires its integration into the organizational fabric, ensuring it complements and enhances business strategy. This involves a comprehensive approach, considering corporate culture, infrastructure readiness, and data quality.

Success in AI strategy is closely linked to an organization's AI readiness, which encompasses technological infrastructure, data readiness, cultural readiness, and compliance readiness. Each aspect ensures AI initiatives are effective and aligned with business objectives. Cultivating an AI-ready culture means promoting a mindset open to data-driven decision-making and continuous learning, with leadership playing a pivotal role.

The technical foundation of AI strategy lies in infrastructure and data readiness. This includes the hardware and software, as well as the quality and accessibility of data. Organizations must invest in data management and analytics capabilities to ensure their data is accurate, relevant, and available for AI applications.

Compliance readiness is essential today, where data privacy and ethical AI use are paramount. Organizations must navigate the complexities of regulations and ethical guidelines to ensure their AI initiatives are responsible and sustainable.

The synergy between business and AI strategies is fundamental to modern organizations. Leveraging AI as a strategic asset can reshape business models and uncover new opportunities, making mastering this interplay not just a competitive edge but a necessity in the digital age.

AI STRATEGY AND ORGANIZATIONAL CULTURE

The success of an AI strategy within any organization is deeply rooted in its culture, particularly one that endorses innovation, experimentation, and learning. Such a culture is likelier to foster a successful AI strategy than one that resists change and discourages risk-taking. The adoption of AI often heralds significant change, typically met with resistance, especially from employees accustomed to the status quo. This resistance is most pronounced among middle management, whose roles and responsibilities often intertwine with the current business structure. To navigate this "clay layer" of resistance, organizations must adopt a comprehensive approach to change management, encompassing both top-down and bottom-up strategies.

Effective change management in the realm of AI requires a multifaceted approach. It starts with training and support to help employees adapt to new ways of working, easing the transition into the AI-augmented workplace. Another critical aspect is communicating the benefits of AI clearly and effectively, ensuring that all employees, regardless of their position, understand how AI can enhance their work and contribute to the organization's overall success. Moreover, involving employees in the decision-making process related to AI initiatives is vital. This involvement mitigates resistance and empowers employees, making them active participants in the organization's transformation journey.

However, involving employees in decision-making is necessary but not sufficient. Organizations must also empower their staff with the autonomy and authority to take risks. Implementing AI is not a straightforward process; it requires trial and error, and an organizational culture that punishes failure or discourages risk-taking is less likely to realize the full potential of AI. Instead, companies should encourage experimentation, celebrate successes, and approach failures as valuable learning experiences.

The concept of "AI iQ" is pivotal in this context. AI iQ is more than just a term; it represents an organization's comprehensive understanding and capability in AI, encompassing knowledge, strategy, and clarity of execution at all levels. Over the years, it has become clear that certain focus areas are crucial in developing a robust AI iQ. These include creating a culture of innovation, ensuring complete data management, investing in AI training and literacy, and aligning AI initiatives with business goals. Ethical considerations and compliance readiness also form an integral part of AI iQ.

For an AI strategy to succeed, it must be embedded in an organizational culture that supports change, empowers risk-taking, and views failures as opportunities for learning. The concept of AI iQ serves as a guiding framework in this journey, encapsulating the necessary knowledge, strategy, and execution clarity for successful AI implementation. For leaders, nurturing these values and focusing on these critical areas is beneficial and essential to leverage AI's full potential in their organizations.

BUILDING AI iQ: DEFINING AN AI STRATEGY

Building an organization's robust AI iQ begins with crafting a clear and potent AI strategy. This strategy is a pivotal indicator of a successful AI program. It is typically initiated at the board and senior management levels to bolster or expedite existing and future business strategies.

Developing an AI strategy should adopt a repeatable and practical approach, entailing the mapping of organizational decisions essential for achieving business goals and pinpointing areas where AI can contribute substantial value. This necessitates engagement across various administrative tiers: the Board and C-Suite, Senior Management, and individual lines of business.

The process commences with the engagement and commitment of the Board and Senior Management Team. At the highest echelons of the organization, they should spearhead the strategic direction for AI adoption, ensuring alignment with the company's mission, vision, and objectives. Their primary responsibility is comprehending how AI can generate business value and advocating for its importance across the organization. The Senior Management Team and executives should be deeply involved in the AI strategy development process, participating in workshops and planning sessions. They are responsible for setting high-level priorities and delegating execution specifics to lower management levels. Securing this leadership buy-in is fundamental for the success of AI initiatives.

Following establishing the strategic framework by the Senior Management Team, the focus shifts to the line-of-business leaders. They play a pivotal role in bridging the overarching strategy with tactical implementation. These leaders should conduct targeted sessions to convert the AI strategic priorities set by Senior Management into actionable objectives for their departments. Given their oversight of daily operations, line-of-business leaders are uniquely positioned to identify specific opportunities where AI could enhance decision-making, productivity, efficiency, and overall performance. They should also identify existing challenges and pain points where AI solutions could be beneficial. The outcome is a detailed execution roadmap for harmonizing AI with strategic goals.

With the strategy and direction for implementation in place, the active participation of frontline business units becomes crucial. These groups, which comprise the end-users of AI systems, can offer valuable insights. Involving them in collaborative workshops enables them to provide input on decisions AI could facilitate and challenges it could solve based on their practical experience. This engagement ensures that the AI systems are grounded in the practical realities of the business. The involvement of these leaders is vital to ensuring buy-in and smooth adoption. Additionally, by including a cross-functional perspective, AI opportunities can be identified and leveraged across all organizational activities.

This layered approach to AI strategy development ensures that the AI initiatives are comprehensive, pragmatic, and in sync with the organization's broader business strategy. By involving all levels of the organization, businesses can achieve a high degree of buy-in, facilitate a smoother implementation process, and enhance the likelihood of successful AI integration.

BUILDING AI STRATEGY WITH THE SENIOR MANAGEMENT TEAM

Building an effective AI strategy with the Senior Management Team is a critical endeavor that demands substantial time and resources. It hinges on deeply understanding the business strategy and assessing the organization's data and AI maturity. The primary objective is pinpointing and prioritizing the most beneficial areas for data and AI efforts, gauging their potential business value.

The first step in this process hinges on a comprehensive analysis of the organization's readiness to implement AI – assessing your "AI iQ." This examination spans several dimensions, including organizational readiness, architectural readiness, data readiness, AI readiness, GenAI readiness, and compliance readiness. Evaluating these aspects both from a leadership and an organizational perspective is crucial.

Following this assessment, the Senior Management Team must engage in extensive working sessions with line-of-business leaders to co-create a high-level AI strategy. This strategy must align closely with the overall business strategy and goals. These sessions analyze short- and long-term business objectives and assess the organization's existing data assets and AI capabilities. The outcome of these sessions, which typically require 4–8 hours of strategic analysis and planning, is a vision statement or North Star, a value proposition, priority focus areas, and success metrics rooted in the business strategy. This high-level strategy provides clear guidance on the AI direction, ensuring alignment between AI efforts and business goals.

The next phase involves identifying and prioritizing specific opportunities to apply data and AI across all business functions. Data/AI leaders collaborate with division heads and their teams to identify potential use cases where AI could deliver tangible business value. These use cases are evaluated and prioritized based on the potential value they could generate. The outcome is a prioritized list of data/AI opportunities, forming the foundation of the AI decision portfolio. This portfolio focuses on initiatives that are likely to have the most significant enterprise-wide impact and advance the strategic vision set by the C-Suite.

Engaging the Board is a critical step in this process. Data/AI leaders must prepare a comprehensive briefing to update the Board on the AI strategy, focusing on how AI initiatives support and accelerate current business goals and objectives. Establishing a regular cadence of updates, such as quarterly briefings, is essential to maintain urgency and ensure ongoing board involvement. This engagement helps the Board guide the AI strategy in alignment with evolving business priorities.

A best practice in AI strategy implementation is establishing a dedicated board committee for AI oversight or expanding the role of an existing committee. This governance structure allows leadership to concentrate on practical and ethical AI strategy implementation. The committee ensures AI initiatives align with business goals, monitors value delivery, and guides adjustments as market conditions change. It also reviews audit findings to guarantee rigorous execution and risk mitigation.

The Senior Management Team can develop a comprehensive, practical, and business-focused AI strategy by following these steps. This strategy aligns with the Board's strategic vision and considers the realities and opportunities identified by managers closer to day-to-day operations. This approach ensures that the AI strategy is strategically sound and pragmatically valuable, establishing a robust governance and reporting structure for effective implementation and desired results.

AI STRATEGY AND LINES OF BUSINESS

After achieving alignment between the Board and the Senior Management Team, the next crucial step involves the lines of business with the highest priority use cases. These lines of business must dig deeper to define and scope these use cases precisely. This process typically requires a one-to-two-day workshop involving key stakeholders, including the head of the lines of business (preferably the Senior Management Team member), relevant direct reports, necessary data experts, and technical experts.

1. **Define and Refine Use Cases:** The first step is to define and refine the use case in detail. This involves outlining the specific problems to be addressed, the proposed AI solutions, and the expected outcomes and benefits. This step ensures the use case is clearly defined and aligned with the senior management team's objectives. This ensures that everyone involved understands the goals and expectations.

2. **Understand the State of the Required Data:** The next step is to evaluate the state of the required data. This includes assessing the availability, quality, and relevance of the data used to train and implement the AI solutions. Any data gaps or issues should be identified at this stage – opportunities to augment gaps in data and existing data through procuring third-party or synthetic data.

3. **Identify Talent Gaps:** Understanding the gap between the needed and available talent is also crucial. This involves assessing the current team's skills and expertise and identifying areas where additional training or recruitment may be required. The development of an upskilling and talent acquisition plan should begin now.

4. **Break Down Use Cases**: Finally, most use cases at this level generally comprise a collection or ensemble of models. For this reason, the use cases should be broken down into parts. This detailed breakdown should be executed to a level that allows the technical teams to take the output and build a sprint plan for execution on six-week sprints. The lines of business can develop a detailed and practical plan for implementing the highest-priority AI use cases by following these steps. This approach ensures that the AI strategy is implemented effectively. It delivers the desired results while providing the necessary resources and expertise.

Implementing AI to drive business value requires strategic alignment, inclusive planning, and cultural change. Success stems from sustained commitment across the organization. The Board and Senior Management Team must set the overarching vision and priorities for AI adoption. Their high-level strategic direction focuses efforts on AI opportunities with the most significant potential impact based on business objectives. Bridging strategy to on-the-ground execution then falls to senior management. Drawing on their operational expertise, they define tactical applications of AI capabilities to enhance targeted decisions and processes. Frontline insights ensure initiatives address real-world pain points. Cross-functional collaboration provides a comprehensive perspective on AI opportunities across the enterprise.

With an expansive list of possibilities, management must re-prioritize initiatives based on potential value generated versus simply technology appeal. This stage warrants transparency. Any significant priority differences compared to the board's strategic direction require open dialogue to understand reasoning and realign on focus.

For top initiatives, intensive scoping sessions with stakeholders in impacted lines of business are essential to crystallize objectives, assess enablers like data and talent, and break execution into achievable sprints. Ongoing governance maintains alignment as strategic plans become operational reality. But even the most thoughtful strategy will only succeed with cultural readiness across the organization. AI adoption involves significant change that inevitably meets resistance without sufficient leadership commitment and employee buy-in. A combination of top-down leadership push and bottom-up involvement pull is critical to driving change. Providing training, clearly communicating benefits, and giving employees a voice in shaping AI plans counters skepticism. Empower people to experiment, take risks, and learn from mistakes rather than punishing failure.

With a supportive culture and inclusive planning, AI can transform operations, interactions, decisions, and business performance. However, strategic success requires a coordinated effort across the enterprise. Incremental progress builds capabilities and momentum. The time for tentative experimentation is over; AI mastery is now essential to thrive amid constant change.

IMPLEMENTING AI GOVERNANCE

Building a practical AI governance framework is essential for organizations leveraging AI technologies responsibly and ethically. This complex framework spans several dimensions, including ethical standards, legal compliance, data management, and technology oversight, aiming to address the multifaceted risks associated with AI, such as potential biases, lack of transparency, and privacy concerns.

At the heart of AI governance lies establishing clear ethical guidelines that reflect an organization's core values and commitment to responsible AI use. These principles serve as the foundation, guiding all AI-related decisions and actions. However, setting these guidelines is just the beginning. Ensuring regulatory compliance is equally crucial. Organizations must navigate a landscape of data privacy laws, industry-specific regulations, and emerging AI-specific legislation to ensure their AI systems operate within legal parameters.

Risk management is another critical aspect of AI governance. Organizations need to identify, assess, and mitigate risks related to AI deployments, focusing on the potential impact of AI decisions and understanding biases in AI models. This is closely tied to the governance of data, which ensures the quality, integrity, and privacy of data used in AI systems. Effective data governance involves careful management of data sources, storage, and usage, adhering to ethical and legal standards.

Transparency and explainability in AI systems are vital for building stakeholder trust and understanding. When AI decisions are transparent and their rationales are explainable, it enhances accountability and fosters deeper trust in AI technologies. Engaging stakeholders is also a part of this process, as involving employees, customers, and external experts in AI governance processes ensures diverse perspectives are considered, fostering inclusivity.

However, AI governance is not a set-and-forget process. It requires continuous monitoring and evaluation to maintain compliance, uphold ethical standards, and ensure the AI systems perform as intended. This ongoing process can be supported by establishing a dedicated AI ethics board or committee, which can provide oversight and guidance on the ethical use of AI. This body should ideally include cross-functional representatives from various departments, ensuring a holistic approach.

Developing and enforcing AI-related policies is another core strategy. These policies should cover AI use, data management, and ethical considerations and be communicated clearly to all relevant stakeholders. In addition, training and awareness programs are crucial. Employees need to understand the ethical use of AI, data privacy, and related risks to ensure the effectiveness of the governance framework.

Leveraging technology for governance is also becoming increasingly important. AI governance software tools can automate compliance checks, risk assessments, and reporting, offering real-time insights and facilitating decision-making. Collaboration with external organizations and industry groups can provide additional insights into best practices and emerging trends in AI governance.

Regular audits and assessments of AI systems are necessary to ensure they function as intended and adhere to governance standards. These assessments can help identify areas for improvement and potential risks, contributing to the overall effectiveness of the governance framework.

AI governance is a multidimensional endeavor requiring commitment and active participation from all levels of an organization. By establishing a comprehensive AI governance framework, organizations can ensure their AI initiatives are ethical, compliant, and aligned with broader business objectives. This proactive approach mitigates risks, builds trust, and enhances the overall value of AI initiatives.

BUILDING ORGANIZATIONAL CAPACITY THROUGH EDUCATION

In the rapidly evolving landscape of AI technologies, particularly GenAI, organizations face the challenge of adapting to and excelling in this new era. A key strategy in this adaptation is building organizational capacity through education, focusing on upskilling the workforce and equipping them with the skills necessary for practical use and development of GenAI capabilities. The burgeoning potential of AI technology has highlighted a growing skills gap within organizations. Bridging this gap requires a strategic, comprehensive educational initiative beyond mere technical training.

Upskilling for GenAI requires a holistic educational approach that includes understanding AI's nuances, ethical implications, and data literacy and applying this knowledge in practical, business-relevant contexts. The first step in this upskilling journey is identifying specific skills and knowledge areas essential for working with GenAI. These skills range from basic AI literacy for non-technical staff to advanced programming and data science skills for IT professionals.

Creating an effective learning ecosystem within the organization is crucial for this educational initiative. This ecosystem should offer varied learning opportunities tailored to different roles and skill levels, such as online courses, workshops, seminars, and hands-on projects. Collaborations with educational institutions and AI technology providers can enrich this ecosystem with external expertise and insights.

Encouraging a culture of continuous learning within the organization is vital. Critical in AI, where developments occur rapidly, this culture fosters curiosity and a willingness to experiment. Incentivizing learning through recognition, career advancement opportunities, and linking skill development to business outcomes can motivate employees to learn continuously.

Training in the ethical use of AI is a critical component of this educational initiative. As GenAI can significantly impact society, it's essential for training to cover understanding biases in AI models, the importance of data privacy, and the broader implications of AI technologies on society. Ethical training equips employees to make informed decisions and consider the broader consequences of AI deployments.

Applying theoretical knowledge in real-world scenarios through projects, hackathons, and problem-solving sessions solidifies the skills learned and encourages innovative thinking and problem-solving. These activities are essential skills for working with AI technologies.

Developing in-house training and mentorship programs, in addition to external training programs, can be particularly effective. Experienced AI professionals within the organization can mentor and guide less experienced staff, fostering a knowledge-sharing environment. This approach builds AI capabilities and strengthens team collaboration and knowledge transfer.

Regular evaluation of the education strategy ensures its effectiveness and alignment with organizational goals. Feedback mechanisms and skill assessments can provide insights into training programs' effectiveness and identify improvement areas. The education strategy should be adaptable to the changing AI landscape and evolving business needs.

In conclusion, investing in upskilling the workforce in GenAI is a strategic imperative for modern organizations. This process involves creating a comprehensive learning ecosystem, fostering a culture of continuous learning, and ensuring that ethical considerations are at the forefront of AI education. By investing in their workforce's education, organizations can harness the full potential of GenAI, driving innovation and maintaining a competitive edge in an AI-driven world.

FINAL THOUGHTS

As this chapter draws to a close, we are left with a profound understanding of integrating AI into business strategies as a transformative force. This chapter emphasized the necessity of a deep-rooted cultural shift within organizations, highlighting the critical role of leadership in driving this transformation. As delineated in this chapter, an effective AI strategy's essence hinges on adopting technology, starting with the strategic alignment with the organization's overarching goals. This approach ensures AI's role as a catalyst in reshaping business models and driving value.

We explored the dynamic interplay between AI and business strategies, underscoring this relationship's need for agility and adaptability. AI is not an isolated technological venture but a critical component in achieving specific business objectives. This chapter also stressed the importance of ethical considerations and regulation compliance in an era where AI's impact is increasingly pervasive.

Transitioning to Chapter 4, we focus on organizational culture's vital role in harnessing AI's power. Chapter 4 is poised to provide leaders and decision-makers with actionable insights for creating an environment where AI is deeply integrated into the organization's ethos. We will delve into developing a culture of innovation, upholding ethical standards in AI applications, and fostering enthusiasm for AI across all organizational levels.

Chapter 4 will explore how to instill an innovative spirit within teams, advocate for ethical governance in AI, and inspire a passion for AI throughout the organization. Chapter 4 promises to be a practical guide filled with actionable insights for creating a culture ready to adapt and excel with AI. The ultimate goal of Chapter 4 is to guide organizations in creating an AI-ready culture, ensuring that they are not just prepared for AI but thriving in its dynamic presence, leveraging its capabilities for innovative solutions, ethical progress, and sustained organizational growth.

KEY TAKEAWAYS AND ACTIONS

DEEPER UNDERSTANDING OF AI STRATEGY

- **Actionable Steps:** Align AI initiatives with business objectives.
- **Implementation:** Conduct thorough market and operational analysis to tailor AI solutions that address specific business needs.

INTERPLAY OF BUSINESS STRATEGY AND AI STRATEGY

- **Actionable Steps:** Ensure agility and adaptability in aligning business and AI strategies.
- **Implementation:** Regularly review and modify strategies in response to market changes and AI advancements.

AI STRATEGY AND ORGANIZATIONAL CULTURE

- **Actionable Steps:** Foster a culture that embraces AI and innovation.
- **Implementation:** Provide training and support for employees to adapt to AI-enhanced workflows; encourage risk-taking and learning from failures.

BUILDING AI iQ

- **Actionable Steps:** Develop a clear AI strategy initiated at the Board and C-Suite levels.
- **Implementation:** Engage various organizational tiers in AI strategy development, ensuring alignment with the company's mission and objectives.

AI STRATEGY WITH THE SENIOR MANAGEMENT TEAM

- **Actionable Steps:** Develop a business-focused AI strategy with senior management involvement.
- **Implementation:** Conduct in-depth readiness assessments and create high-level AI strategies aligned with business objectives.

AI STRATEGY AND LINES OF BUSINESS

- **Actionable Steps:** Implement AI strategies at the line-of-business level.
- **Implementation:** Define detailed use cases, assess data requirements, identify talent gaps, and break down use cases for effective execution.

IMPLEMENTING AI GOVERNANCE

- **Actionable Steps:** Establish comprehensive AI governance frameworks.
- **Implementation:** Develop ethical guidelines, ensure regulation compliance, manage risks, and promote transparency and stakeholder engagement.

BUILDING ORGANIZATIONAL CAPACITY THROUGH EDUCATION

- **Actionable Steps:** Upskill the workforce in GenAI.
- **Implementation:** Create varied learning opportunities, foster a culture of continuous learning, and focus on ethical AI training.

CHAPTER 4

AI-Ready Culture

INTRODUCTION

As we embark on the transformative journey detailed in Chapter 3, we delve into the critical role of organizational culture in harnessing the power of artificial intelligence (AI) and generative AI (GenAI). This chapter is designed to equip leaders and decision-makers with the insights and strategies necessary to create an environment where AI is not just implemented but is deeply integrated into the very ethos of the organization.

We explore the intricacies of developing a culture optimized for AI, focusing on fostering an environment of innovation, upholding ethical standards in AI applications, and igniting a pervasive enthusiasm for AI across all organizational levels. This chapter is not merely a theoretical exposition; it's a practical guide filled with actionable insights.

Innovation drives AI readiness, going beyond creativity to include a mindset that continuously challenges conventional practices and embraces AI's transformative potential. We will examine how to instill this innovative spirit within your teams, encouraging a culture where experimentation, learning from failures, and turning visionary ideas into practical solutions are part of the daily ethos.

Ethics in AI is another cornerstone of an AI-ready culture. This chapter will explore how organizations can embed ethical considerations into their AI strategies, ensuring that AI technologies are developed and utilized with accountability, fairness, and transparency. We address the importance of ethical governance in AI and guide the establishment of frameworks that ensure AI benefits all stakeholders without bias or discrimination.

DOI: 10.1201/9781003486725-5

Finally, we discuss how to foster enthusiasm for AI throughout the organization. We explore strategies to transform skepticism into advocacy and fear into a fascination with AI. This transformation requires leaders to communicate a compelling vision for AI, engage employees in AI experiences, and create a workplace culture that encourages exploration and learning.

By the end of this chapter, readers will have a comprehensive understanding of the essential components of an AI-ready culture and how to cultivate these within their organizations. This journey requires patience, persistence, and a nuanced appreciation of the potential and challenges of AI. The ultimate goal is to create an organization that is not just ready for AI but thrives in its presence, leveraging AI's capabilities for innovative solutions, ethical progress, and sustained organizational growth.

INFUSING INNOVATION, ETHICS, AND ENTHUSIASM INTO YOUR CULTURE

One fundamental truth stands out in the rapidly evolving landscape of AI and GenAI: technology alone will not enable transformation. The true power of AI is unleashed only when it is deeply embedded in the fabric of an organization's culture. This realization brings us to an essential aspect of AI readiness – cultivating a culture equipped to embrace AI and agile enough to thrive amidst its transformative influences.

This section delves into the intricate process of cultivating an AI-ready culture. Here, we explore the three pivotal cultural pillars – innovation, ethics, and enthusiasm – that form the cornerstone of a successful AI integration. This chapter is not just about understanding these elements in isolation; it's about weaving them into the very DNA of an organization.

Innovation in this context goes beyond mere creativity. It's about fostering a mindset that continuously challenges the status quo, embraces the possibilities of AI, and turns visionary ideas into tangible value. But innovation without a moral compass is directionless. Hence, the emphasis on ethics is not just a compliance requirement but a fundamental approach to ensuring AI benefits all, devoid of bias and discrimination.

Lastly, the pillar of enthusiasm speaks to the heart of change management. It's about igniting a passion for AI across the organization, transforming skepticism into advocacy, and fear into fascination. This transformation requires proactive leadership, effective communication, and a deep understanding of the human aspect of technological change.

As we navigate this section, we aim to provide leaders and decision-makers with practical insights and strategies to cultivate these cultural traits. It's a journey that requires patience, persistence, and a nuanced understanding of AI's potential and challenges. The ultimate goal is clear: to build an organization not just ready for AI but one that thrives on AI, leveraging its capabilities for innovative solutions, ethical progress, and sustained growth in an AI-augmented future.

Innovation is the lifeblood of AI readiness. It is challenging the status quo and viewing AI not as a threat but as an opportunity to reinvent and elevate business processes and offerings. The key lies in nurturing a mindset that thrives on creative thinking and embraces the transformative potential of AI.

Organizations must cultivate environments where experimentation and risk-taking are tolerated and encouraged. This means moving away from cultures that penalize failure, instead fostering spaces where deliberate and intelligent risk-taking and learning from failures are seen as pathways to innovation. Regular brainstorming sessions, forming cross-functional "innovation squads," and providing employees with "innovation time" are practical steps in this direction.

Physical and digital collaboration spaces are crucial in fostering serendipitous encounters and idea exchanges. Internal AI accelerator programs and AI-focused startup competitions can act as catalysts, driving innovation through hands-on skill development and incentivizing novel AI applications.

While fostering creativity, it's crucial to ensure that innovation aligns with the organization's strategic priorities. This alignment ensures that efforts are creative and contribute meaningfully to the organization's goals. Governance is critical here, ensuring that innovations adhere to architectural, policy, compliance, and ethical standards.

Ethics in AI ensures that AI systems are developed and used responsibly, with accountability, fairness, and transparency. This involves setting up oversight committees and ethical review boards to govern AI systems, conducting impact assessments before deployment, and implementing inclusive design principles to avoid biases.

Ethics must be integrated throughout the AI development lifecycle. This includes training all involved parties to recognize and mitigate biases, conduct third-party algorithmic audits, and incorporate ethical considerations into every AI development and deployment stage.

The responsibility for ethical AI cannot be delegated solely to oversight bodies; it must permeate the entire organizational culture. Leaders must set the tone by leading by example and fostering a culture of transparency and awareness. Regular training, communication, and the implementation of ethical metrics and incentives can shape behaviors organization-wide, ensuring that ethics become an integral part of the AI culture.

Generating enthusiasm for AI is essential for its adoption and effective utilization. Leadership must communicate a compelling vision for AI, highlighting its transformative potential for products, services, and processes. Leaders can actively motivate teams to embrace AI by connecting AI initiatives to meaningful outcomes.

To demystify AI and make it more accessible, organizations should engage in immersive AI demonstrations and workshops. These activities allow employees to experience the benefits of AI firsthand, thereby reducing intimidation and building comfort with AI technologies.

AI should be seamlessly integrated into the organizational culture. This can be achieved through targeted promotional campaigns, ambassador programs, and creating an environment that encourages the exploration of AI's possibilities. Participation incentives, change management support, and events focused on AI can further deepen engagement and enthusiasm.

The journey doesn't end with initial adoption. Sustaining momentum requires continuous efforts in celebrating achievements, promoting the benefits of AI, and showcasing tangible improvements brought about by AI initiatives. Transparent communication about successes and failures is essential in building a culture comfortable with experimentation and continual learning.

Creating a culture ready for AI and GenAI is more than technological readiness; it encompasses preparing the entire organization to adapt, evolve, and thrive in an AI-augmented future. Integrating innovation, ethics, and enthusiasm creates a fertile ground for AI to flourish, transforming business processes and the fabric of organizational culture. As we journey through this era of unprecedented digital transformation, the organizations that successfully cultivate these cultural traits will not only survive but thrive, unlocking the full potential of AI for their benefit and that of society at large.

LEADERSHIP COMMITMENT

This section explores the multifaceted role of leadership in guiding organizations toward AI readiness. Leadership in this context is not just about making decisions; it involves crafting a vision, aligning AI with strategic goals, fostering innovation, and ensuring ethical AI practices. Integrating AI into business processes is complex and requires a transformative approach from leaders. This discussion covers various aspects of leadership commitment, including crafting a compelling vision, aligning AI initiatives with broader organizational goals, enhancing efficiency, igniting innovation, and the ethical considerations of AI integration. Additionally, it delves into the importance of breaking down silos, fostering inclusivity, balancing innovation with operational stability, managing external partnerships, and maintaining a long-term commitment to AI integration.

In the transformative journey toward AI readiness, leadership occupies a pivotal role akin to a master chef orchestrating a gourmet kitchen. Their vision, expertise, and guidance are indispensable ingredients that shape the organization's path. Leaders in AI readiness must assume a role that goes beyond conventional decision-making; they must become the guiding light, illuminating a path toward a future where AI is not just an add-on but an integral and transformative element of the organization's strategic framework.

The foundation of leadership in AI readiness is the ability to craft and articulate a compelling vision. This vision is the guiding star, directing the organization's AI journey. It aligns with the broader strategic goals, emphasizing how AI can amplify efficiency, ignite innovation, and unlock new opportunities. Much like a master chef envisions a delightful culinary experience, leaders must imagine a future where AI and human expertise fuse seamlessly to create a dynamic, responsive, intelligent organization.

Leadership's commitment to AI readiness is reflected in its alignment with strategic goals. AI is not a standalone endeavor but a strategic enabler seamlessly integrated into the organization's overarching strategy. Leaders must ensure that every AI initiative, whether it's enhancing customer experiences, optimizing operations, or driving revenue growth, is in sync with the strategic compass of the organization. This alignment ensures that AI doesn't operate in isolation but contributes significantly to attaining broader objectives.

Efficiency lies at the heart of AI's transformative power. Leaders must emphasize how AI can streamline processes, automate repetitive tasks, and augment decision-making. Beyond replacing human capabilities, AI enhances them. Leaders should illustrate how AI can be the organizational sous chef, working with human talent to deliver efficiency gains that elevate performance and productivity.

Innovation thrives in an environment where creativity and exploration are encouraged. Leaders in AI readiness must foster a culture that tolerates and celebrates experimentation. This involves creating a safe space where teams can explore novel AI applications, take calculated risks, and learn from failures. It's akin to a master chef experimenting with new ingredients and techniques to craft innovative dishes that captivate the palate. Leaders should champion AI as the catalyst for innovation, sparking creativity across departments and inspiring teams to push the possible boundaries.

Leaders must also demonstrate the path to new opportunities that AI can unlock. This starts with identifying uncharted territories where AI can create value, whether through personalized customer experiences, data-driven insights, or novel revenue streams. Leaders should be the visionaries who recognize and communicate how AI can create previously untapped opportunities, propelling the organization into new frontiers.

One of the most profound aspects of leadership in AI readiness is demonstrating how AI and human expertise can coalesce harmoniously. It's not a choice between one and the other; instead, it's about harnessing the strengths of both to create a dynamic and responsive organization. Much like a master chef balances various ingredients to craft a symphony of flavors, leaders must showcase how AI augments human capabilities, enabling employees to focus on higher-value tasks. At the same time, AI handles the repetitive and data-intensive aspects. This synergy between AI and human expertise forms the core of an intelligent and adaptive organization.

Leadership transcends mere endorsement or passive support in creating a culture ready for AI. It embodies active advocacy and a dynamic approach toward cultivating a culture rich in innovation and collaboration. This multifaceted advocacy demands a shift from traditional management styles to a more vibrant, agile, and forward-thinking mindset. Leaders in this space must embrace AI technology and champion the cultural change necessary for successful integration.

The journey toward AI readiness requires more than technological adoption; it necessitates a cultural transformation. Leaders must cultivate an environment where experimentation is not just tolerated but celebrated. This involves breaking down the silos that often inhibit cross-functional collaboration and creating teams that bring together diverse perspectives and skills. In this environment, innovative ideas are not only encouraged but also rewarded. It's about creating a safe space where taking calculated risks and learning from failures are essential to innovation.

One of the critical strategies in fostering an AI-ready culture is the formation of cross-functional teams. These teams act as incubators for AI applications, bringing together expertise from various departments – from IT and data science to marketing and customer service. Such collaboration ensures that AI solutions are not developed in isolation but are rooted in a deep understanding of diverse business needs and customer experiences. This blend of varied insights and expertise drives innovation, making AI solutions more relevant, effective, and impactful.

For an AI initiative to succeed, it requires more than just a visionary leader; it needs the backing of human and technological resources. Strategic investment in AI research and development is crucial. Leaders must ensure the organization is equipped with the latest AI technologies and infrastructure. This commitment goes beyond financial investment; it's about investing in people. Building a team with the proper skill set, from AI specialists to data analysts, is crucial in creating a robust AI ecosystem. Moreover, continuous training and development programs are essential in keeping the team updated with AI advancements and methodologies.

Creating a sustainable AI ecosystem within an organization is a strategic initiative that requires thoughtful planning and execution. It involves the integration of AI into the company's DNA, where AI-driven decision-making becomes a part of the everyday workflow. Leaders must ensure that AI is not perceived as a distant, complex technology but as a tool that is accessible and useful for all employees. This means simplifying AI applications, making them user-friendly, and ensuring they add tangible value to the user's daily tasks.

Ultimately, the success of AI in an organization hinges on how well its people embrace it. Leaders play a crucial role in driving this adoption. By embodying the principles of innovation, risk-taking, and continuous learning, leaders can inspire their teams to explore the possibilities of AI. Leading by example shows genuine enthusiasm for AI and its potential to transform the organization.

Leadership in AI readiness extends beyond mere endorsement; it requires active engagement, understanding, and a demonstrated commitment to participation. Leaders should exemplify their dedication by rolling up their sleeves and getting directly involved in AI initiatives. This hands-on approach sends a resounding message about the significance of AI within the organization. It reinforces the message that AI is not an abstract concept but a tangible and vital part of the future.

Leaders should be visible advocates for AI within the organization. This means actively participating in AI training programs, collaborating with data science teams, and becoming integral parts of decision-making processes related to AI projects. By doing so, leaders set a precedent that AI is not an isolated or peripheral activity but a core aspect of the organization's operations.

AI can sometimes seem like a complex and distant opportunity, especially for those not directly involved in technical roles. Leaders play a crucial role in bridging this gap by demystifying AI concepts and making them accessible to everyone. Much like a mentor in a kitchen who guides aspiring chefs, leaders should provide guidance and support to employees who are exploring AI for the first time.

Building AI literacy across the organization is paramount. Leaders must champion the cause of AI education and ensure that employees at all levels have access to training and resources to understand and leverage AI effectively. This involves not only technical aspects of AI but also awareness of its ethical implications, potential biases, and the importance of data governance.

Leaders should ensure that their teams have access to the necessary resources for AI education. This includes investing in training programs, providing access to AI tools and platforms, and fostering a culture where learning and development are valued. Just as a master chef equips their kitchen with the finest ingredients and equipment, leaders should provide their teams with the tools and knowledge needed to thrive in an AI-driven environment.

Leaders should cultivate a culture of continuous learning and curiosity within the organization. This involves encouraging employees to explore AI concepts, experiment with AI applications, and share their learnings with others. It's about creating an environment where asking questions and seeking answers are accepted and celebrated.

Leaders must be at the forefront of AI education, setting an example for others. They should actively participate in AI training programs, engage in discussions about AI ethics, and showcase their commitment to building AI literacy. This instills confidence in their teams and demonstrates that AI education is an ongoing journey that even leaders must embark upon.

Leaders should also focus on nurturing the organization's next generation of AI talent. This involves identifying high-potential employees and providing them with opportunities for growth and development in AI. By doing so, leaders ensure that the organization has a steady pipeline of AI expertise to drive future initiatives.

ETHICAL LEADERSHIP AND GOVERNANCE: NAVIGATING AI's MORAL COMPASS

Integrating AI into business processes brings a set of ethical considerations and governance challenges that leaders must proactively address. As AI becomes more pervasive, its impact on society, privacy concerns, ethical use, and potential biases become increasingly important. Leaders must be honest stewards, ensuring their AI initiatives align with broader societal values and moral norms.

Leadership commitment to ethical AI begins with setting clear and comprehensive ethical frameworks for AI use within the organization. These frameworks should outline privacy, fairness, transparency, accountability, and bias mitigation principles. Leaders must ensure that AI aligns with ethical standards that guide its development and deployment.

Privacy is a fundamental concern in the age of AI. Leaders must advocate for robust privacy protections and ensure that AI systems are designed with privacy in mind. This involves establishing policies and practices safeguarding customer and employee data, obtaining informed consent for data usage, and adhering to data protection regulations. Leaders should also promote transparency in collecting, using, and storing data.

AI systems are susceptible to biases, which can lead to unfair outcomes. Leaders must champion fairness and bias avoidance as foundational principles in AI development. This includes conducting bias assessments on AI algorithms, addressing biases in data, and regularly auditing AI systems for fairness. Leaders should also encourage diversity in AI teams to mitigate biases in algorithm development.

Leaders must promote accountability and transparency in AI decision-making. This involves establishing mechanisms for auditing AI systems, tracking decisions made by AI algorithms, and ensuring that these decisions can be explained and justified. Leaders should advocate for developing explainable AI models to provide transparency into AI's decision-making processes.

Establishing mechanisms for ongoing monitoring and auditing of AI systems includes regular assessments of AI performance, identifying and addressing potential biases or ethical concerns, and conducting third-party audits when necessary. Monitoring and auditing ensure that AI systems align with ethical standards and do not deviate from their intended purposes.

Actively engaging in ethical discussions related to AI, both within and outside the organization, is a requirement. This involves participating in conversations about AI ethics at industry events, policy discussions, and public forums. Leaders should advocate for responsible AI and contribute to developing ethical AI guidelines and standards.

Leadership commitment to ethical AI extends beyond organizational boundaries. Leaders should ensure their AI initiatives align with societal values and moral norms. This includes advocating for AI policies and practices that contribute positively to society, address societal challenges, and avoid harm.

Leaders should also be the face of their organization's ethical AI initiatives in external forums. This involves speaking at industry events, participating in policy discussions, and engaging with the media. Through these external communications, leaders can position their organizations as thought leaders in the ethical AI space, influencing broader industry trends and standards.

Measuring progress and adapting strategies are indispensable components of leadership commitment in the transformative journey toward AI readiness. Leaders must establish mechanisms to gauge the advancement of AI initiatives and be willing to adjust their strategies based on feedback and outcomes. This iterative process ensures a dynamic strategy that evolves with the organization's growing understanding of AI, ultimately leading to AI success.

Leaders play a crucial role in setting clear benchmarks for AI initiatives. These benchmarks serve as key performance indicators (KPIs) that define what success looks like. Benchmarks should align with the organization's strategic goals and the specific objectives of AI projects. For example, benchmarks could include improvements in operational efficiency, cost reduction, or customer satisfaction. Setting clear and measurable benchmarks provides a roadmap for progress.

Regular reviews of progress are essential to track the advancement of AI initiatives. Leaders should establish a cadence for progress reviews, which could be monthly, quarterly, or annually, depending on the project's complexity and timeline. During these reviews, leaders should evaluate whether the project meets its benchmarks and is on track to achieve its goals. Progress reviews also provide an opportunity to identify challenges or roadblocks that may require intervention.

Leaders should encourage a culture of feedback and data-driven decision-making within the organization. This involves collecting data and insights related to AI initiatives and using this information to make informed decisions. Feedback can come from various sources, including employees, customers, and stakeholders. Leaders should establish feedback mechanisms and ensure teams can access the data and tools needed for analysis.

One of the hallmarks of effective leadership in AI readiness is the willingness to pivot when necessary. Not all AI initiatives will proceed as planned, and some may face unexpected challenges or changing circumstances. Leaders should be open to adjusting strategies, reallocating resources, or discontinuing projects that no longer align with the organization's goals. The ability to pivot demonstrates agility and adaptability.

Leaders must foster a culture of continuous learning and improvement regarding AI. This involves learning from both successes and failures. When an AI initiative succeeds, leaders should analyze what contributed to that success and how those lessons can be applied to other projects. Similarly, when an initiative falls short, leaders should conduct a post-mortem analysis to understand the reasons behind the failure and how to avoid similar pitfalls in the future.

Measuring progress and adapting strategies often require cross-functional collaboration. Leaders should ensure that different departments and teams are aligned in their approach to AI initiatives. This collaboration enables sharing insights and expertise, making identifying opportunities for improvement and course correction easier.

Leaders should invest in technology and tools facilitating progress measurement and adaptation to strategy. This includes implementing data analytics platforms, project management software, and reporting tools that provide real-time insights into AI initiatives' performance. Access to the right technology can streamline the measurement process and enable data-driven decision-making.

When strategies are adjusted based on progress measurement, leaders should communicate these adaptations clearly to all stakeholders. This includes employees, customers, and partners who may be affected by the changes. Clear and transparent communication helps manage expectations and ensures everyone is aligned with the revised strategy.

While measuring progress and adapting strategies are essential in the short term, leaders must maintain a long-term vision. AI readiness is not a destination but an ongoing journey. Leaders should emphasize the importance of sustained commitment to AI integration and convey that the organization's AI strategy will evolve and grow over time.

In the transformative journey toward AI readiness, one of the critical roles of leadership is breaking down silos of all kinds and fostering inclusivity to ensure that AI permeates throughout the organization. Leaders must actively encourage and facilitate inputs from all levels of the organization, fostering a sense of ownership and ensuring that AI solutions are grounded in real-world scenarios and challenges. This holistic approach is essential for successfully integrating AI into the organizational fabric.

Leadership in AI readiness demands a concerted effort to dismantle departmental silos that often exist within organizations. These silos can impede the flow of information and collaboration, hindering the effective use of AI. Leaders must take proactive measures to break down these barriers, promoting open communication and cooperation between departments. This involves creating cross-functional teams that bring together individuals with diverse skill sets and perspectives.

Cross-functional collaboration is at the heart of breaking down silos. Leaders should encourage and facilitate collaboration between departments that traditionally operate independently. For example, marketing and data science teams can leverage AI for personalized customer experiences, while HR and IT departments can collaborate on AI-driven talent acquisition and management initiatives. Leaders should actively promote initiatives that involve multiple departments, ensuring that AI is viewed as a cross-cutting enabler.

Ensuring inclusivity is not limited to the executive level but extends to all levels of the organization. Input from employees at all levels is invaluable for identifying AI use cases and understanding different departments' specific challenges. Inclusivity fosters a sense of ownership and empowerment among employees, making them active participants in the AI journey. Leaders should create channels for employees to share their ideas and feedback related to AI initiatives.

AI solutions should be rooted in real-world problem-solving. They emphasize the importance of AI in addressing practical challenges the organization faces. This approach ensures that AI is not seen as a nebulous concept but as a tool that can directly impact and improve day-to-day operations. Leaders can encourage teams to identify pain points and bottlenecks that AI can help alleviate, fostering a problem-solving mindset.

Effective communication and education are essential components of breaking down silos and fostering inclusivity. Leaders should communicate the organization's AI vision and objectives to all employees. This includes explaining how AI initiatives align with broader strategic goals and how they can benefit different departments. Additionally, leaders should provide training and educational resources to employees at all levels, ensuring they have the knowledge and skills to engage with AI effectively.

Recognizing and celebrating success stories related to AI integration can motivate employees and reinforce the importance of inclusivity. Leaders should highlight instances where cross-functional collaboration and inclusivity led to successful AI implementations. By showcasing these examples, leaders inspire other departments to embrace AI and actively contribute to its adoption.

Leadership in breaking down silos and fostering inclusivity requires agility and adaptability. Leaders should be willing to adjust their approaches based on feedback and changing circumstances. They should also be receptive to new ideas and innovative approaches from employees at all levels. An agile leadership style promotes a culture of continuous improvement and ensures that AI integration remains dynamic and responsive.

Balancing innovation with operational stability poses a significant leadership challenge in the journey toward AI readiness. As organizations embark on AI initiatives, disruptions in established processes and workflows are almost inevitable. This disruption can generate uncertainty and apprehension among the workforce, making it essential for leaders to act as stabilizing forces during innovation. Leaders must address these concerns through clear communication, unwavering support, and reassuring their teams. Open and transparent communication is critical, as leaders need to explain the goals and objectives of AI initiatives and their alignment with the organization's long-term strategy. Additionally, investing in training and upskilling programs is crucial to ensure employees have the skills to work effectively alongside AI technologies.

Emphasizing AI's value to the organization is another aspect of leadership in balancing innovation and stability. Leaders should highlight how AI can automate repetitive tasks, reduce errors, and free employees to focus on more creative and strategic aspects of their work. Moreover, leaders should actively listen to the concerns and feedback of their employees, addressing individual worries and providing practical solutions. Building trust and confidence among teams is essential to navigate the disruptive effects of AI.

While fostering innovation, leaders must also safeguard the stability of core operations. This involves careful planning and execution. Leaders can opt for phased implementation of AI initiatives, allowing teams to adapt gradually to changes and minimizing disruption. Continuous monitoring of AI implementations is essential, and leaders should establish feedback mechanisms to identify and resolve issues promptly. It's also prudent to have fallback plans in case of unexpected challenges, with leaders prepared to revert to previous processes while addressing any problems temporarily.

Involving employees from various departments in AI projects can be highly beneficial to ensure that operational considerations are considered. Cross-functional teams can identify potential disruptions and devise strategies to mitigate them effectively. Leaders play a pivotal role in guiding these teams and facilitating collaboration.

Leading by example is a cornerstone of effective leadership in AI-driven innovation. Leaders demonstrate their commitment and willingness to adapt by actively participating in AI initiatives. This sets a powerful precedent for the rest of the organization, encouraging employees at all levels to embrace change and innovation.

Acknowledging and celebrating small wins along the AI journey can boost morale and demonstrate the positive impact of AI. Leaders should highlight success stories that showcase how innovation and operational stability coexist harmoniously.

Leadership in AI readiness requires a delicate balancing act. Leaders must champion innovation while ensuring operational stability. They should provide support, training, and reassurance to their teams, listen to concerns, and maintain open lines of communication. Leading by example and celebrating success, leaders guide their organizations through the uncertainties of innovation and emerge more robust, agile, and fully prepared for the AI-driven future.

Managing external partnerships and navigating the ethical implications of AI are integral aspects of leadership in AI readiness. Organizations often rely on external vendors, consultants, and academic institutions to advance their AI initiatives in an interconnected world. Leaders are pivotal in managing these external collaborations, ensuring they align with the organization's vision and values.

Effective leadership in managing external partnerships begins with selecting the right partners. Leaders must exercise acumen in choosing partners who share the organization's goals and are committed to ethical AI practices. Collaborative relationships should extend beyond transactional interactions and evolve into strategic partnerships where external expertise complements internal efforts.

One crucial consideration in external partnerships is data privacy and security. Leaders must ensure that external partners adhere to stringent data protection protocols and ethical standards. This involves clear agreements and contracts specifying data handling procedures, security measures, and compliance with relevant regulations such as The European General Data Protection Regulation (GDPR), The California Consumer Protection Act (CCPA), etc. Leaders should also establish mechanisms for ongoing monitoring and auditing of data practices to maintain the integrity of AI systems.

Ethical considerations loom large in AI. Leaders must be at the forefront of advocating for responsible AI usage. This includes addressing societal concerns about job displacement, privacy, fairness, and bias. Leaders should actively engage in discussions within and outside the organization to shape ethical AI practices.

Internally, leaders need to establish ethical guidelines and frameworks for AI use. These guidelines should encompass fairness, transparency, accountability, and bias avoidance principles. Leaders should promote a culture of responsible AI by communicating these principles throughout the organization and integrating them into AI development processes.

Leadership in ethical AI extends to external forums and industry-wide discussions. To shape AI standards, leaders should represent their organizations in policy discussions, industry events, and collaborations. By actively participating in these conversations, leaders can influence broader industry trends and advocate for ethical AI practices that align with societal values.

Transparency is another essential element of leadership in managing ethical implications. Leaders should ensure that their organizations are transparent about how AI is used and its impact on stakeholders. Open communication with employees, customers, and the public fosters trust and helps demystify AI technologies.

Leaders should also prioritize ongoing education and awareness within the organization. This involves providing training and resources to employees on ethical AI practices and implications. Employees at all levels must deeply understand the ethical considerations surrounding AI and be equipped to make ethical decisions in their work.

Leadership in AI readiness encompasses the management of external partnerships and the responsible handling of ethical implications. Leaders must choose partners who align with the organization's vision and values while ensuring robust data privacy and security measures. They should champion responsible AI practices within and outside the organization, advocating for fairness, transparency, and accountability. By actively engaging in ethical discussions and promoting a culture of responsible AI, leaders can guide their organizations toward a future where AI is a force for good, aligned with societal values and ethical norms.

Leadership in AI readiness extends beyond internal messaging to external advocacy and communication. Leaders must champion AI initiatives within their organizations and represent them on a broader stage. This external engagement is crucial for positioning the organization as a thought leader in AI and influencing industry trends.

One facet of external advocacy is participation in industry events and conferences. Leaders should actively engage with AI-related events, where they can share insights, best practices, and the organization's experiences with AI integration. Speaking at such events showcases the organization's expertise and contributes to the broader knowledge sharing within the industry.

Policy discussions and engagements with regulatory bodies are another vital aspect of leadership in AI. As AI technologies evolve, policymakers seek input and expertise from industry leaders to shape regulations and standards. Leaders should actively participate in these discussions, offering insights on the potential impact of AI and advocating for laws that foster innovation while ensuring ethical use and data privacy.

Engaging with the media is also a strategic approach to external communication. Leaders can use media platforms to discuss their organization's AI initiatives, share success stories, and address misconceptions or concerns about AI. This not only raises the organization's profile but also helps in demystifying AI for the general public.

In addition to these external engagements, leaders should foster collaborations with academic institutions and research organizations. These partnerships can lead to valuable insights, innovations, and access to cutting-edge research in the field of AI. It's an opportunity for leaders to stay at the forefront of AI developments and leverage academic expertise to drive AI initiatives within their organizations.

Moreover, leaders should consider publishing articles, white papers, or reports on AI-related topics. This contributes to knowledge dissemination and establishes the organization as a credible source of information in the AI domain. Thought leadership through publications can attract talent, potential partners, and collaborators.

Effective external advocacy also involves engaging with the broader community. Leaders should seek opportunities to participate in AI-related initiatives to address societal challenges. Whether it's promoting AI for social good, addressing biases in AI algorithms, or contributing to AI ethics discussions, leaders can play a significant role in advancing AI technologies for the benefit of society.

Furthermore, leaders should actively engage with industry associations and organizations dedicated to AI. These associations often provide platforms for collaboration, networking, and advocacy. By participating in such groups, leaders can stay updated on industry trends, contribute to shaping industry standards, and advocate for AI's responsible and ethical use.

Leadership commitment to the long-term journey of AI integration is a pivotal aspect of achieving AI readiness. In the dynamic landscape of technology and business, AI is not a destination but an ongoing voyage, and leaders must exemplify unwavering dedication to this journey.

One of the core elements of long-term commitment is the readiness to evolve with technological advancements. AI is a rapidly changing field, with breakthroughs and innovations emerging regularly. Leaders must stay informed about the latest developments in AI and assess how these advancements can benefit their organization. This involves monitoring emerging technologies like machine learning, natural language processing, and computer vision and evaluating their potential organizational applications.

Adaptability is another critical component of long-term commitment. As the organization's understanding of AI deepens and its needs evolve, leaders should be prepared to adjust their AI strategies accordingly. This may involve revisiting the organization's AI vision, realigning it with changing business goals, and reevaluating resource allocation. Leaders should foster a culture of flexibility, where the organization can pivot and adapt its AI initiatives to meet new challenges and opportunities.

Continuous learning is integral to leadership commitment in the long-term AI journey. Leaders should actively seek AI education and skill development opportunities, staying up-to-date with AI's latest trends, best practices, and ethical considerations. This commitment to learning extends beyond technical knowledge; leaders should also deepen their understanding of AI's societal and ethical implications to make informed decisions and advocate for responsible AI usage.

In addition to learning, leaders should promote a culture of continuous improvement within their organizations. This involves regularly assessing the progress of AI initiatives, measuring their impact, and identifying areas for enhancement. Leaders should encourage a data-driven approach, where decisions about AI integration are based on evidence and results. By fostering a culture of continuous improvement, leaders ensure that AI remains aligned with the organization's evolving goals and needs.

Leaders must also consider the scalability of AI initiatives in the long term. As AI adoption grows within the organization, leaders should plan for scalability, ensuring that AI systems can handle increased data volumes and user demands. Scalability may require infrastructure, technology, and talent investments to support the organization's AI growth.

Furthermore, long-term commitment entails effective risk management. Leaders should be prepared for potential challenges and setbacks in the AI journey. This includes addressing issues related to data quality, algorithm biases, and cybersecurity threats. Leaders should have mitigation strategies and be ready to adapt and learn from these challenges to strengthen the organization's AI capabilities.

Leadership commitment to AI readiness is a dynamic and comprehensive endeavor. It starts with leaders crafting a vision for AI that aligns with the organization's strategic goals, emphasizing efficiency, innovation, and new opportunities. Leaders must also foster a culture that celebrates innovation and adaptability while ensuring ethical AI practices that respect privacy, fairness, and transparency.

Key actions include breaking down departmental silos, encouraging cross-functional collaboration, and promoting inclusivity at all levels within the organization. Leaders must also balance the disruptive nature of AI with the need to maintain operational stability, providing support and reassurance to their teams. Additionally, they should manage external partnerships focusing on ethical AI practices and data privacy.

Externally, leaders need to advocate for their organization's AI initiatives, participate in industry events and policy discussions, and engage with the media to establish their organization as a thought leader in AI. Internally, they must nurture the next generation of AI talent, fostering a learning culture that embraces continuous improvement and adaptability.

Finally, leadership commitment to AI readiness is a long-term journey that requires adaptability, continuous learning, scalability planning, and effective risk management. Leaders must navigate the evolving landscape of AI technology and business needs, focusing on building a sustainable and resilient AI ecosystem for the future.

FINAL THOUGHTS

As we conclude this chapter, it is evident that the journey to AI readiness is deeply intertwined with how an organization is shaped and functions. The foundational pillars laid down in this chapter – from fostering a culture of innovation and accountability to harnessing diverse talent and empowering grassroots mentors – are crucial in building an environment conducive to AI advancement. The emergence of roles like the Chief AI Officer (CAIO) underscores the strategic importance of AI in the modern enterprise.

This chapter has highlighted the multifaceted nature of preparing an organization for AI, stressing the need for a solid infrastructure, ethical AI development, and a culture that embraces continuous learning and innovation. These elements are essential for any organization aiming to thrive in an AI-enhanced future. By laying a solid foundation, structuring for innovation and accountability, and continuously nurturing talent and engagement, organizations can ensure that their AI initiatives are successful, sustainable, and ethically sound.

As we transition to Chapter 5, the focus shifts to exploring AI's practical applications and real-world impacts within the organizational framework. Chapter 5 delves into how AI solutions are implemented across various business domains, examining case studies and success stories illuminating AI's transformative power in action. From optimizing operational efficiencies to driving customer engagement and innovation, Chapter 5 will showcase the tangible benefits of AI integration and how it is reshaping the landscape of business strategy and execution.

Chapter 5, therefore, builds upon the foundational principles outlined in this chapter, offering a window into the practical implementation and real-world impact of AI in the corporate sphere. Through this exploration, readers will gain insights into how AI can be leveraged to enhance existing processes, create new opportunities, and drive business growth in an increasingly digital world.

KEY TAKEAWAYS AND ACTIONS

FOSTERING A CULTURE OF INNOVATION

- **Actionable Steps:** Encourage a mindset that embraces AI as a transformative tool. Facilitate environments where experimentation and intelligent risk-taking are the norms.
- **Implementation:** Establish cross-functional innovation squads, dedicate resources for "innovation time," and create spaces for idea exchanges.

EMBEDDING ETHICS IN AI

- **Actionable Steps:** Integrate ethical considerations into AI strategies, focusing on fairness, accountability, and transparency.
- **Implementation:** Set up oversight committees, conduct impact assessments, and implement inclusive design principles.

IGNITING ENTHUSIASM FOR AI

- **Actionable Steps:** Transform skepticism into advocacy by communicating the potential of AI effectively and engaging employees in immersive experiences.
- **Implementation:** Organize AI workshops, create ambassador programs, and integrate AI seamlessly into company culture.

LEADERSHIP COMMITMENT

- **Actionable Steps:** Craft and articulate a compelling AI vision that aligns with strategic goals. Balance innovation with operational stability.
- **Implementation:** Engage in continuous learning, adapt feedback-based strategies, and maintain a long-term commitment to AI integration.

BREAKING DOWN SILOS

- **Actionable Steps:** Promote open communication and collaboration across different departments to ensure AI permeates the entire organization.
- **Implementation:** Create cross-functional teams and provide platforms for sharing ideas and feedback.

EXTERNAL ADVOCACY AND COMMUNICATION

- **Actionable Steps:** Represent the organization's AI initiatives in industry events, policy discussions, and media engagements.
- **Implementation:** Collaborate with academic institutions, publish thought leadership pieces, and participate in community initiatives.

ETHICAL LEADERSHIP AND GOVERNANCE

- **Actionable Steps:** Ensure responsible AI usage by setting comprehensive ethical frameworks and promoting a culture of ethical AI.
- **Implementation:** Participate in ethical AI discussions, establish ongoing monitoring and auditing systems, and engage with industry bodies.

LONG-TERM AI INTEGRATION

- **Actionable Steps:** Embrace the evolving nature of AI technology, focusing on scalability, adaptability, and risk management.
- **Implementation:** Invest in technology and tools for progress measurement, foster a culture of continuous improvement, and prepare for challenges.

Organizational Structure

INTRODUCTION

This chapter delves into the organizational structure as pivotal in the journey toward artificial intelligence (AI) readiness. The organizational structure is the backbone for the creativity, development, and deployment of AI solutions, necessitating leaders craft an environment conducive to AI advancement. This journey involves laying a solid foundation, fostering innovation, ensuring accountability, harnessing talent, and defining critical roles within the organization, particularly the emergence of the Chief AI Officer (CAIO). Each element is crucial in how an organization adapts and thrives in an AI-enhanced future.

LAYING THE FOUNDATION FOR AI

Laying the Foundation for a successful AI strategy is critical. The significance of this foundational stage cannot be overstated, as it sets the tone and direction for how AI will be developed, implemented, and integrated into the various facets of the organization. This multifaceted process involves establishing foundational platforms that support and enable AI initiatives to flourish. These platforms serve as the backbone of AI development, offering a stable and robust framework upon which innovative AI solutions can be built.

A critical aspect of laying this foundation is facilitating easy collaboration. AI development is inherently collaborative, requiring inputs and insights from diverse fields and expertise. Therefore, the organization's structure must be designed to encourage and simplify this collaborative effort. This involves the physical architecture of the workspace and the

DOI: 10.1201/9781003486725-6

virtual and digital tools that enable seamless communication and data sharing. By fostering an environment where collaboration is not just possible but effortless, organizations can harness their teams' collective skills and knowledge, leading to more innovative and effective AI solutions.

Establishing oversight guardrails is equally vital in this process. As AI systems and algorithms are developed, it's crucial to have mechanisms that ensure accountability and safety, especially when these systems are iterated rapidly. This oversight ensures that AI applications perform as intended, adhere to ethical guidelines, and do not inadvertently cause harm. This oversight mechanism acts as a failsafe, ensuring that the rapid pace of AI development does not outstrip the organization's ability to control and understand the implications of these technologies.

Creating an environment that encourages intuitive interactions with AI systems is another important aspect of laying the foundation. The goal is to make AI tools and applications as user-friendly and accessible as possible. This includes designing interfaces that are easy to navigate and understand, regardless of the user's technical expertise. By doing so, organizations can ensure that their AI solutions are robust and widely accessible to all employees, maximizing their impact and utility.

Tailoring training to different organizational roles is an essential part of this process. AI technologies and applications vary widely, so the training required for various roles will also vary. For instance, the training needed for data scientists will differ significantly from that required for sales or marketing professionals. By providing role-specific training, organizations can ensure that their employees are familiar with AI technologies and can leverage these tools effectively in their respective domains.

Structuring for innovation, especially in AI, is a complex yet pivotal task for any organization aiming to stay at the forefront of technological advancement. The challenge lies in creating a structure that supports and actively promotes creative freedom while maintaining high operational efficiency. This balance is crucial; without it, organizations may either stifle innovation or grapple with inefficiencies that hinder their progress.

FOSTERING A CULTURE OF INNOVATION

Central to fostering an innovative environment is the empowerment of teams. This empowerment is not merely about granting permission to explore new ideas; it's about cultivating a culture where experimentation and creative risk-taking are the norms. Such a culture encourages individuals and teams to think outside the box, question the status quo, and envisage solutions that transcend traditional boundaries. However, for this culture to thrive, it must be supported by an organizational structure conducive to innovation.

Access to the right tools and resources is critical in this structure. In the context of AI, this means providing teams with the latest software, hardware, and datasets needed to develop and test new AI algorithms and applications. It also involves ensuring that teams have the necessary computational power and data storage capacity to handle the demands of AI development. Without these tools and resources, even the most creative and innovative ideas may never come to fruition, as teams would lack the means to execute them effectively.

Leadership is vital in ensuring that the organizational structure aligns with these needs. Leaders must be proactive in creating and maintaining an environment that nurtures innovation. This involves providing the necessary resources and tools and fostering a mindset that values and rewards innovative thinking. Leaders must also be adept at managing the inherent risks of innovation, balancing the pursuit of new and untested ideas with the organization's overall operational stability.

In practice, structuring for innovation may involve establishing dedicated teams or departments focused on AI research and development. These teams would operate semi-autonomously, allowing them to explore new ideas while still aligning with the broader goals and strategies of the organization. Cross-functional collaboration should be encouraged, as innovation often occurs at the intersection of different fields and disciplines. Such collaboration can lead to a cross-pollination of ideas, further enhancing the organization's innovative capacity.

STRUCTURING FOR ACCOUNTABILITY IN AI OPERATIONS

Structuring for accountability in AI operations is critical to responsible AI implementation and management. In an era where AI's impact on various sectors is profound and expanding, ensuring that AI systems are developed and used ethically is not just a regulatory requirement but a moral imperative. Organizations must, therefore, establish and rigorously enforce clear protocols and controls that govern every stage of AI development and deployment.

Establishing robust model risk management frameworks is at the core of this accountability structure. These frameworks are designed to identify, assess, and mitigate risks associated with AI models. They are pivotal in ensuring AI systems do not inadvertently cause harm or produce biased outcomes. Effective risk management in AI involves a comprehensive approach, encompassing everything from the initial design of the model to its final deployment and ongoing maintenance. It requires continuous vigilance and adaptation as AI systems evolve and new risks emerge.

Setting standards for testing methodologies is another crucial element of structuring for accountability. AI systems, by their nature, can be complex and unpredictable. Therefore, standardized testing protocols are essential to validate the performance of AI models under various conditions and ensure that they meet the intended objectives. These methodologies should be rigorous, transparent, and reproducible, allowing for consistent assessment of AI systems' efficacy and safety. Regular testing and validation help identify potential issues before deployment and maintain the trustworthiness of AI systems throughout their lifecycle.

Implementing performance monitoring systems is also essential. Once an AI system is deployed, it is imperative to monitor its performance to ensure it operates as intended continuously. Performance monitoring systems should be capable of detecting any deviations from expected behaviors and flagging potential issues for immediate review. This ongoing surveillance helps quickly identify and rectify problems, preventing long-term negative impacts.

Documentation is a vital part of ensuring accountability. Comprehensive documentation of AI systems – from design principles and development processes to operational protocols and performance metrics – is crucial. This documentation provides a transparent record of how AI systems are built and managed, which is essential for accountability. It allows stakeholders, including regulators, to understand how decisions are made and can be used as a basis for audits and reviews.

Access controls are equally important in structuring for accountability. These controls ensure that only authorized personnel can access AI systems, preventing unauthorized use or modifications that could compromise their integrity. Access controls should be stringent and regularly reviewed to adapt to changing personnel and technological landscapes.

Human oversight is an indispensable part of this structure. While AI systems can operate autonomously, human oversight ensures that ethical considerations are always at the forefront. It provides a crucial check on the systems' operations, ensuring that decisions made by AI are fair, unbiased, and aligned with ethical norms and organizational values.

HARNESSING TALENT AND BUILDING AI SKILLS

The successful implementation of AI within an organization is intrinsically linked to the talent it harnesses. This talent transcends beyond the realms of specialized AI professionals like data scientists and AI experts. It encompasses a broader spectrum of the workforce, where employees across various roles possess an understanding and capability to leverage AI effectively in their respective domains. The synergy between specialized AI expertise and broader workforce proficiency in AI applications forms the bedrock of an organization's AI success.

Leaders play a pivotal role in cultivating this talent ecosystem. Their focus must extend to nurturing internal AI skill sets, which involves a strategic approach to training and development. This training should not be limited to technical staff alone. Still, it should also encompass other employees, enabling them to understand the basics of AI, how it impacts their work, and how they can use AI tools to enhance efficiency and effectiveness. Such widespread AI literacy within the organization is critical to unlocking the full potential of AI technologies.

The development programs must be carefully designed to cater to different levels of AI proficiency and varying organizational roles. Advanced courses on AI methodologies, data analytics, and machine learning (ML) algorithms are essential for technical staff. For others, introductory courses that demystify AI and provide a basic understanding of how AI can be applied in different business contexts are crucial. By ensuring that employees at all levels have a foundational understanding of AI, organizations can foster a culture of innovation and collaboration, where AI initiatives are not siloed but part of the broader organizational strategy.

In addition to building internal capabilities, attracting external AI expertise is equally important. External talent brings fresh perspectives, new ideas, and specialized skills that might not be present internally. This infusion of external knowledge can accelerate AI initiatives, bringing cutting-edge practices and innovative approaches. The challenge for leaders here is attracting this external talent and seamlessly integrating them into the organization's culture and workflow.

This integration requires a thoughtful approach where external experts are not seen as outsiders but as valuable team members. Their expertise should be leveraged to mentor internal staff, fostering a knowledge-sharing environment where skills and ideas are exchanged freely. Such collaboration not only enhances the AI capabilities of the existing workforce but also ensures that the organization stays at the forefront of AI advancements.

NECESSARY ROLES FOR AI DEVELOPMENT

Successfully executing impactful data science projects requires thoughtfully assembling a complementary team with specialized expertise across several vital roles. While each member focuses intensely on their niche abilities, maintaining an integrated culture of collaboration and general understanding across disciplines enables the group to work synergistically. This diversity of perspectives unified into a cohesive unit multiplies capabilities, uncovering powerful insights beyond isolated efforts that can profoundly transform organizations.

The optimal data science team structure entails delineating clear responsibilities for each role while promoting information sharing across areas of specialization. Here is an overview of core focus areas:

The product owner is the foremost subject matter expert regarding business needs and domain knowledge. They will possess extensive immersion within the specific industry, competitive environment, organizational history, and strategic priorities. Ideally, the product owners will come from the lines of business where AI will impact workflows and processes.

A crucial duty involves the product owner working closely with leadership and operating teams to clearly define the specific business challenges, opportunities, and desired outcomes to be addressed through data science approaches. They distill vague notions like "improve customer retention" into concrete objectives like "reduce subscriber churn by 10% within six months."

The product owner then collaboratively translates these goals into technical problem statements, success metrics, testable hypotheses, and implementation requirements that data scientists can incrementally iterate on. For example, what available metrics indicate progress on the target? What internal and external data sources connect to those metrics?

Maintaining constant engagement across the organization and directly interfacing with end users, the product owner gathers invaluable context and feedback on whether data science solutions deliver meaningful business value upon deployment. They become a trusted advocate for data science priorities.

Data engineers provide the crucial data foundation enabling downstream science through expertise in sourcing, integrating, preparing, and engineering reliable data streams from dispersed systems into accessible analytical formats. This requires proficiency across a diverse toolkit, including APIs, message queues, data pipelines, transformation scripts, databases, and more.

An essential duty involves collaborating with stakeholders and the product owner to develop architectures efficiently, consolidating relevant data sources into a well-managed centralized data lake location. Data engineers build and maintain connective services, APIs, schemas, trusts, and databases, powering downstream data accessibility at scale. They integrate mechanisms to keep datasets current.

Data engineers play an instrumental role in instrumenting operational systems to capture high-quality data that may fuel predictive models. They apply quality assurance practices like monitoring, profiling, testing, and optimization to ensure the delivery of accurate, timely data. Cross-team coordination helps tailor outputs optimally for the use case.

The ML engineer focuses on architecting, developing, monitoring, and maintaining the predictive models that extract patterns and actionable insights from prepared data. This entails the iterative application of statistical, algorithmic, and coding skills spanning prototyping to production deployment.

Collaborating closely with the product owner and data engineer, the ML engineer identifies the most appropriate input features and labels that exhibit predictive relationships correlated to the target business objective. They design robust pipelines ingesting quality training data for modeling.

Applying statistical and ML fundamentals, the ML engineer selects, fine-tunes, and evaluates the performance of different modeling techniques to maximize predictive power. Models are repeatedly tested and improved before controlled deployment. The ML engineer tracks models in production, monitoring for drifts in accuracy that may necessitate retraining on new data.

While heavily overlapping with ML, the decision optimization engineer leverages predictive models to empower actionable simulations, scenario forecasting, and prescriptive recommendations optimized for business objectives. Their solutions weigh alternative actions based on critical parameters, uncertainties, and constraints to identify optimal course-balancing trade-offs.

Decision optimization engineers represent the problem context mathematically, incorporating predictive model outputs as inputs to probabilistic simulations. Techniques like Monte Carlo sampling help assess outcome distributions across decision paths evaluated. Optimization algorithms filter for choices, maximizing desired targets.

These interactive simulations allow adjusting assumptions and weights in real time to build intuition around quantified trade-offs. By modeling uncertainties, simulations identify options likely to optimize outcomes despite unpredictability. Such guidance leads organizations to make evidence-based decisions.

The data journalist role focuses on distilling complex model outputs and mechanics into intuitive formats and narratives for business leaders. They adeptly translate technical details into plain language and contextualize insights around the objectives and questions that motivate an initiative.

Data journalists closely collaborate with scientists to validate explanations of modeling methodologies, results, and implications. They parse models, code, and documentation to identify how outputs trace back to original goals. Key points become synthesized data stories, presentations, and visuals, rendering insights intuitive yet meaningful.

Programming abilities aid data journalists in wrangling results into clarifying statistical summaries and interactive visualizations. Their data fluency and communication skills are invaluable in transforming opaque techniques into compelling insights that persuade and guide decisions.

Prompt engineers specialize in translating business needs into crisp problem statements, sample inputs, and follow-up questions that optimally guide GenAI systems like large language models to provide relevant, compelling outputs.

This emerging role combines a deep understanding of AI model capabilities and limitations with creativity in incisively framing requests configured to draw on specialized knowledge. Prompt engineering unlocks the immense potential of AI investments through expertise in clarifying systems' objectives.

Prompt engineers closely partner with product owners to absorb contexts and goals. They research available training data and model strengths to craft prompts strategically aligned with desired responses. Iterative refinement identifies interpretation difficulties and expands prompts to reduce repetition and improve coherence.

Strong communication, logic, design thinking, and synthesis skills help prompt engineers to distill complex issues into simple prompts that efficiently steer AI solutions to address business needs with high relevance. Their artful prompting maximizes value.

Each role entails deep specialization, enabling seamless collaboration across the team and multiplies impact. A "T-shaped" skills model helps bridge gaps, with depth in one's primary expertise and enough breadth to communicate across disciplines.

Ongoing availability for inquiries builds empathy, while periodic rotations or informal seminars strengthen well-roundedness. Consistent status updates and documentation keep the team in sync. Leadership sets an open, collaborative tone across the group.

Optimizing the team structure involves clearly defining responsibilities for efficiency while facilitating frequent cross-functional interactions to share insights. Bringing complementary specialties into a cohesive team aligned under shared goals allows jointly unlocking success beyond isolated capabilities.

The foundation of AI readiness lies not just in the technology itself but in an organization's culture. A culture that embraces AI views it as a strategic enabler, transforming organizational operations and decision-making. This chapter underscores the importance of nurturing an environment where AI is integral to the corporate ethos.

Effective AI integration begins with a meticulously crafted workflow centered around collaboration and clear objectives. The product owner is pivotal, bridging business leadership and technical teams. This individual ensures that AI initiatives are technically feasible and strategically aligned with the organization's goals.

Engineers, including prompt and data engineers, convert these strategic objectives into focused problem statements, ensuring the AI systems are fed with accurate and relevant data. This step is critical for bridging the gap between theoretical goals and practical data requirements.

ML engineers then turn this data into actionable insights. Their expertise goes beyond technical skills; they must understand how their models can drive business decisions. These insights must be actionable, influencing decision-making that aligns with the organization's strategic goals.

Data journalists bring these insights to life for non-technical stakeholders, translating complex data into compelling narratives and visualizations. This translation is crucial for ensuring the insights are understood and persuasive enough to drive action.

The workflow concludes with a return to the product owner, who verifies that the results deliver tangible business value. This iterative process of refinement and validation ensures continual alignment of AI initiatives with business priorities.

A successful AI initiative also depends on integrating critical operational components. Centralized data management through a data lake or warehouse is crucial for accessible and analyzable data. Automation of model development, evaluation, deployment, monitoring, and retraining through machine learning operations (MLOps) pipelines streamlines processes and ensures reliability.

Collaborative tools like GitHub and Slack facilitate rapid communication and transparency, fostering a collaborative environment. Scalable cloud computing resources are vital for modeling and deployment flexibility. Experiment tracking maintains accountability and understanding of AI model evolution.

Microservices and APIs transform monolithic systems into modular, scalable capabilities. Real-time dashboards provide visibility into critical metrics and model behavior, which is essential for ongoing monitoring and decision-making.

The culmination of AI readiness is the harmonious blending of people, processes, and tools within an organization's culture. It involves creating a supportive environment that promotes development, transparency, controlled experimentation, and a purpose-driven approach, all guided by ethical standards.

When these elements are synergistically aligned, the impact on the organization is substantial. A diverse range of expertise, unified toward a common objective, can drive significant transformation, leveraging the power of data science and AI to reshape enterprises. This synergy accelerates AI efforts, leading to transformative outcomes that exceed the capabilities of isolated teams.

In essence, quantifying AI readiness transcends technical preparedness. It requires a holistic approach that weaves people, processes, technology, and culture together. This integration is not just about assembling components; it's about creating a cohesive entity that reflects the organization's commitment to innovation, ethical practices, and strategic growth through AI. By focusing on these elements, organizations can prepare for and excel in the AI era, turning challenges into opportunities for growth and innovation.

BUILDING DATA SCIENCE TEAMS WITH DIVERSITY AND INCLUSION

In an era where the digital landscape is rapidly evolving, the role of data science teams becomes increasingly crucial. These teams, often the bedrock of innovative solutions and strategic insights, are pivotal in shaping the trajectories of businesses. Yet, a glaring gap persists in this field: the lack of diversity. This issue isn't just a matter of representation; it's a bottle-neck that stifles innovation, creativity, and business growth. Addressing this gap isn't merely a moral imperative; it's a strategic necessity for organizations that aim to remain competitive and relevant.

The current state of diversity in data science is concerning. Globally, women represent only about 15% of data scientists, with their presence in technical leadership roles even more sparse. Ethnic minorities, the LGBTQ+ community, and other underrepresented groups also find themselves on the fringes of this field. This imbalance isn't just a statistic; it reflects untapped potential and overlooked perspectives.

The business case for diversity in data science is robust and well-documented. Research consistently shows that diverse teams are more innovative, better at problem-solving, and have a higher likelihood of financial outperformance. This isn't surprising, considering diverse teams bring various experiences, viewpoints, and approaches. They are better equipped to understand and cater to a diverse customer base, leading to products and solutions that resonate more broadly.

However, achieving diversity in data science isn't just about rectifying numbers. It's about cultivating an environment where different perspectives are valued and everyone can contribute and grow. This starts with the hiring process. Traditional hiring practices often inadvertently favor candidates who fit a specific mold – typically mirroring those already in the organization. This leads to a cycle of homogeneity, reinforcing the status quo and sidelining diverse talent.

To break this cycle, organizations must adopt a more intentional approach to hiring. This means re-evaluating job descriptions, recruitment strategies, and interview processes to ensure they are inclusive and unbiased. For instance, simplifying job requirements to focus on essential skills can broaden the pool of applicants, bringing in more diverse talent. Structured interviews and diverse interview panels can help minimize unconscious biases, ensuring a more fair and objective evaluation process.

Beyond hiring, fostering an inclusive culture is critical. An environment where diverse voices are heard and valued, where employees feel supported and included, is essential for retaining diverse talent. This involves regular training on diversity and inclusion, mentorship programs, and policies that ensure equity and respect for all employees.

Organizations must also look beyond their walls to build diversity. This includes partnerships with educational institutions, professional organizations, and community groups that work toward increasing diversity in

STEM fields. Internship and training programs can also guide underrepresented groups to enter and thrive in data science roles.

The path to building diverse and inclusive data science teams is not straightforward. It requires a sustained and multifaceted effort involving changes at every level of the organization. But the rewards are clear. Diverse teams are not only more creative and practical, but they are also a better reflection of the world we live in. In a field fundamentally about understanding and leveraging data to drive decisions, overlooking the value of diverse perspectives is not just a lost opportunity; it's a strategic misstep. As we move forward, the success of data science initiatives will increasingly depend on our ability to embrace and nurture diversity. This isn't just about doing the right thing; it's about doing the smart thing for our businesses and society.

GRASSROOTS MENTORS

The role of grassroots mentors in AI has become increasingly pivotal. These mentors play a crucial role in disseminating AI knowledge across organizations. They stand at the forefront, not just as transmitters of information but as catalysts of transformation, shaping the understanding and application of AI at a fundamental level.

The journey of a grassroots AI mentor begins with their advancement. After acquiring a deep understanding and proficiency in AI, these mentors, often respected internal advocates, take on the mantle of guiding their peers. Their role is to adapt AI knowledge to local needs, ensuring that the implementation of AI is not just theoretical but practical and relevant to their organization's specific requirements.

The structure of this mentorship is both formal and informal. Traditional mentorship programs involve structured engagements spanning several months, where mentors and mentees collaborate closely. These mentors guide their mentees through various stages of learning – from ideating applications of AI and understanding and interpreting model behaviors to responsible oversight and hands-on skill-building. This process is not a one-size-fits-all approach; it is highly personalized, considering each mentee's unique domain and learning objectives. Regular sessions, tailored to fit into busy schedules, and shadowing experiences are integral to this journey, enabling mentees to gain skills and the confidence to mentor others in the future.

In addition to these formal pairings, the role of grassroots mentors extends to fostering a broader learning environment through communities of practice and networking events. This informal mentoring includes hosting "office hours" for ad hoc questions, demonstrations to showcase AI capabilities, and workshops or hackathons where mentors lead groups through common challenges, offering an immersive learning experience.

The selection of these mentors is a critical process. It's not just about their technical skills in AI but also their aptitude for mentorship. Qualities such as patience, effective communication, and a commitment to service are essential. These mentors undergo extensive training to standardize their coaching methods and internalize diverse skills. Shadowing seasoned mentors is a part of this learning process, ensuring the development of effective mentoring techniques.

Once equipped, these mentors become the torchbearers of AI knowledge within the organization. Their credibility and personalized approach play a significant role in earning the trust and interest of teams that might otherwise be hesitant about AI adoption. They adapt use cases and methodologies to local contexts, overcoming resistance and fostering a culture of openness and innovation.

However, it is essential to acknowledge that not every skilled AI practitioner is cut out for mentorship. The ability to mentor effectively is a unique skill set in itself. Organizations must be discerning in identifying individuals who not only have technical expertise but also the interpersonal skills to guide and inspire others.

Through their contextual guidance and trust-building, Grassroots mentors unlock the potential for widespread AI adoption. They transform passive resistance into active engagement and enthusiasm, effectively democratizing AI knowledge within the organization. Organizations can empower these mentors to facilitate a peer-to-peer spread of AI literacy, turning each mentee into a potential future mentor. This creates a virtuous cycle of knowledge sharing and capability building.

Establishing grassroots mentors is a strategic imperative for organizations aiming to harness the full potential of AI. It's about moving beyond acquiring technology to embedding it into the organization's fabric. This approach goes a long way in ensuring that AI adoption is not just a top-down directive but a shared journey of learning and growth. Therefore, developing these mentors is an investment in individuals and the organization's future.

TAILORING MULTIFACETED TRAINING

In the fast-evolving landscape of AI, practical training is paramount, yet traditional one-size-fits-all methods fall short. Modern organizations must instead adopt a multifaceted approach, catering to diverse learning styles and fluency levels across various roles. This approach, encompassing online modules, taught classes, hands-on workshops, simulations, rotations, and forums, ensures a comprehensive understanding and practical application of AI within the organization.

The foundation of this training approach lies in introductory overviews. These overviews are designed to provide leadership and non-technical employees with a baseline understanding of AI's capabilities, applications, oversight practices, and ethical considerations. Utilizing engaging short video modules and interactive quizzes, these overviews facilitate a basic yet essential grasp of AI, enabling informed decision-making in strategic roles.

Building upon this foundation, role-specific courses target professional groups, such as analysts, marketers, and product managers. These courses are meticulously designed to equip individuals with the tailored fluency to ideate and implement AI solutions in their respective domains. Through contextualized examples and hands-on scenarios, these courses enable practical application of AI concepts, solidified by proficiency assessments that validate readiness for real-world application.

For technical staff and developers, the training strategy includes immersive boot camps. These bootcamps delve deep into programming toolkits, model building and validation, deployment automation, monitoring, and algorithmic fairness. Intensive coding labs embedded within these boot camps reinforce technical proficiency, while certifications upon completion serve as a testament to the mastery of these advanced skills.

Another critical element of this training framework is mentor-guided workshops. In these workshops, participants engage in hands-on learning tailored to their specific roles and work on building real prototypes that address actual business challenges. This collaborative approach fosters peer coaching and results in tangible, applicable AI solutions for the organization.

Design simulations add an experiential dimension to this training model. These simulations offer firsthand experiences with AI applications, enabling participants to build intuitional fluency in AI usage. Virtual reality simulations, in particular, provide an immersive interaction with model-powered scenarios, allowing users to understand AI applications from an end-user perspective, highlighting key insights and nuances.

An innovative aspect of the training strategy is incorporating rotational residency programs. These programs allow team members from various functions to embed within AI units, gaining skills through direct observation and active contribution. The short-term nature of these rotations ensures minimal productivity trade-offs while allowing for a broadened understanding of AI across various organizational functions.

The training model includes community forums, seminars, and hackathons to enhance learning and collaboration further. These events build technical capabilities and strengthen organizational culture through shared experiences and achievements. They serve as platforms for disseminating knowledge and fostering a community of AI practitioners within the organization.

Continuous optimization of these training programs is essential. Proficiency assessments, user feedback, and organizational analysis inform this optimization. Such a dynamic approach ensures the training remains relevant and practical, empowering broad contributions across the organization.

AI training in the corporate world must be diverse and multifaceted, meeting the unique needs of different organizational roles. Organizations can foster collective fluency and mastery of AI capabilities through tailored knowledge transfer mechanisms. This enables the workforce to shape the AI future and actively contribute informed solutions.

As technology continually evolves, so too must the workforce. Continuous training is essential to sustain readiness amidst technological advances and personnel changes. This ongoing development encompasses rotational programs, certification pathways, alum networks, conferences, hackathons, and design summits, offering a comprehensive framework for skill enhancement and capability alignment.

Rotational programs are crucial in this ongoing learning process. They enable team members to embed temporarily across different units, fostering cross-training and knowledge diffusion. This approach transfers experiential learning through real-world collaboration, broadening perspectives, and enhancing skill sets.

Structured certification pathways are another integral component, offering continuous education through milestone credentials in various domains such as data engineering, MLOps, applied AI, and ethics. These pathways maintain fluency and guide professional progression, with alums recognized as field experts.

Alum networks extend the learning beyond the organization, sharing external best practices, technologies, and use cases. Participation in conferences, workshops, and studio tours builds connections with the broader AI ecosystem. Alums returning to brief teams on emerging innovations and responsible practices observed externally ensure a continuous infusion of fresh ideas and methodologies.

Immersive training experiences, such as hackathons and design summits, drive continuous growth through hands-on creativity and teamwork. These events co-develop solutions under mentor guidance, fostering a culture of innovation and collaboration. Design summits, in particular, create actionable roadmaps, while conferences share advances through workshops and plenaries, embedding experiential learning within the organizational fabric.

In environments where time constraints often limit formal training opportunities, microlearning through brief online modules fills knowledge gaps just in time. Simulations exercise nuanced concepts experientially, allowing for a deeper understanding of complex AI applications. Training assistants identify knowledge deficits, ensuring that training balances efficiency with depth.

Prioritizing continuous development is essential to keep pace with evolving technologies and changes in personnel. Renewed capabilities enable organizations to realize new value and maintain a competitive edge.

Organizations ensure that their teams progress in lockstep with advances in the field by fostering a culture of learning and growth through rotational programs, structured certifications, alumni networks, and immersive experiences. Continuous investment in training translates into compounding capabilities, driving innovation, and maintaining relevance in an ever-evolving digital landscape.

CELEBRATING MILESTONES

Organizations embarking on the transformative journey of integrating AI must prioritize celebrating milestones. Acknowledging progress at various stages builds a collective identity and serves as a beacon during challenging times. Through strategic communications, organized events, and thoughtful recognition, organizations nourish the commitment and morale of their teams.

Leaders play a pivotal role in spotlighting key milestones. These include successfully delivering new AI capabilities, reaching user adoption targets, and achieving specific accuracy or revenue generation goals. It is essential to quantify these benefits, as this makes the abstract progress of AI tangible for stakeholders. Compelling storytelling is a powerful tool here, as it connects individual and team accomplishments to the organization's shared mission, fostering a sense of unity and purpose.

Major launches present opportunities for communal celebration. These events not only recognize achievements but also foster a sense of camaraderie and shared success. Similarly, reaching prototyping milestones offers a creative outlet to acknowledge and reward the innovators pushing the organization's boundaries.

Celebrating anniversaries, such as deploying the first models, forming AI teams, or launching strategic AI initiatives, is equally important. These anniversaries serve as reminders of the originating visions and aspirations. Founder's Day events, for instance, can effectively link current progress to the organization's history, featuring stories from veterans and showcasing archive exhibits that illustrate the evolution of AI efforts.

Another impactful approach is to create rotating exhibitions in office spaces. These exhibitions can highlight the challenges faced in specific projects, the prototypes developed, and the outcomes achieved. By doing so, they familiarize all employees with the AI journey, irrespective of their direct involvement. Creative installations that convey AI concepts experientially can further enhance this immersion, building intuition and interest in AI across the organization.

While internal celebrations are crucial, organizations must also maintain a balance with external modesty, particularly when considering the societal impacts of AI. Acknowledging and celebrating incremental achievements frequently is critical to sustaining teams through the nonlinear progress typical of AI initiatives.

Celebrating milestones is more than a mere acknowledgment of progress. It is about reinforcing the organizational momentum, particularly during setbacks. It demonstrates the tangible impact of the team's efforts, serving to energize and motivate. It solidifies a communal identity, aligning everyone around the shared mission of leveraging AI for organizational success.

It is vital for organizations to enthusiastically recognize the contributions of individuals and teams and to collectively commemorate achievements through various forms of communication, events, and experiences. Integrating AI into organizational processes and cultures is a marathon, not a sprint. Regularly celebrating small wins together is fundamental to sustaining progress and fostering a resilient, united workforce. This unity and shared sense of achievement lies in the strength to navigate AI's complex and evolving landscape. With a spirit of celebration and recognition, organizations can navigate this journey with vigor and purpose.

MEASURING ENGAGEMENT

In AI, gauging and enhancing user engagement is akin to how a chef values diner feedback to refine culinary creations. This essential process involves various methodologies like regular pulse surveys, skills assessments, values evaluations, interviews, and real-time input channels. These tools are vital in optimizing AI user experiences and guiding continuous improvement.

Pulse surveys are a primary tool for assessing user satisfaction with AI systems. They focus on the utility of the systems, ease of interfaces, accuracy of models, and their overall business impact. Monitoring trends over time in these surveys offers insights into areas of progress and those needing attention. Importantly, segmenting feedback by user persona and use case reveals differential needs, helping to target development priorities more accurately.

Alongside these surveys, skills assessments play a crucial role. Understanding and addressing growing user fluency needs become essential as AI offerings expand. These assessments evaluate users' proficiency in explaining models, bias mitigation, and oversight practices, among other areas. Insights from these assessments inform the creation of personalized training programs, aiming to close skill gaps and bolster AI system utilization.

Ethical alignment is another critical consideration addressed through values surveys. These tools evaluate the congruence of AI systems and practices with ethical standards such as fairness, accountability, and transparency. Dips in these values signal a need for a thorough examination of potential harms and controls, ensuring that AI systems remain trustworthy and ethically sound.

Interviews and focus groups provide qualitative insights to add depth to quantitative data. These discussions delve into users' pain points, desired capabilities, and adoption barriers. Emerging themes from these interactions offer invaluable insights into friction points in integrating AI innovations and ideating new applications.

Further enhancing engagement measurement is the use of real-time feedback mechanisms. Embedded directly in AI systems, these tools enable users to provide immediate feedback on model performance and behavior, helping log issues, highlight unseen biases, and improve system explainability. Given its contextual nature, this real-time feedback provides targeted insights for more effective improvements.

While continuous user feedback is essential, balancing the feedback collection process with the user participation burden is crucial. Surveys should be concise, relevant, and beneficial for users, with analytics employed to monitor and address survey fatigue. Reciprocating users' time and effort in providing feedback is critical to maintaining high engagement levels.

Regularly gathering user feedback is a cornerstone of sustaining the value delivery of AI systems as needs evolve. This practice ensures that AI systems are not static but dynamic, evolving continuously with user input. By employing a mix of surveys, interviews, focus groups, and real-time input channels, organizations empower users to shape the AI tools they use actively. This responsive, user-centered development approach is fundamental to unlocking the full potential of AI innovations, ensuring they remain relevant and valuable in meeting the evolving needs of users and delivering substantial business impact.

FINAL THOUGHTS

As we wrap up this chapter, focusing on the integral aspects of organizational structure in achieving AI readiness, we've journeyed through the multifaceted approaches essential for a successful AI implementation. This chapter stressed the importance of a conducive environment for AI development, emphasizing leadership, collaboration, talent development, and critical roles within an organization, particularly highlighting the emergence of the CAIO. From laying the groundwork for AI integration to fostering innovation and ensuring accountability, this chapter comprehensively covered the strategic measures needed for an organization to embrace AI and excel in its deployment and application.

This chapter also delved into the nuances of building a cohesive data science team, underscoring the value of diversity and inclusion for fostering innovation and productivity. The role of grassroots mentors was highlighted, illustrating the importance of hands-on guidance and peer-to-peer learning in AI adoption across an organization. Furthermore, this chapter emphasized the need for multifaceted training programs tailored to meet an organization's diverse learning styles and professional requirements.

As we transition to Chapter 6, the focus shifts from the organizational structure to the very bedrock of AI implementation – the underlying infrastructure. This upcoming chapter will explore the critical considerations across core infrastructure domains, including computing, data, networking, orchestration, and analytics. It aims to provide insights into optimizing and unifying capabilities across both on-premises and cloud environments, establishing a reinforced support system ready for the immense possibilities of AI.

Chapter 6 will address the growing demands for specialized computing acceleration, scalable data platforms, capable networking, and automated orchestration, which are essential for developing and deploying advanced AI systems. Chapter 6 promises to equip executives with the knowledge to optimize infrastructure readiness, confidently supporting innovative AI applications. With robust infrastructure, transformative AI systems can be rapidly constructed, securely and responsibly, to drive breakthrough value.

In essence, Chapter 6 will underscore the necessity of having a solid and adaptable infrastructure as the foundation upon which AI solutions can be effectively built and scaled. It will guide readers through the strategic planning and execution required to evolve infrastructure holistically, ensuring that organizations are well-prepared to embrace and exploit the vast potential of AI technologies. As the future beckons, Chapter 6 aims to lay out the core considerations for building a resilient infrastructure poised to support the immense potential of AI in the years ahead.

KEY TAKEAWAYS AND ACTIONS

LAYING THE FOUNDATION FOR AI

- **Actionable Steps:** Establish foundational platforms for AI, facilitate easy collaboration, provide necessary resources, and ensure ethical AI development.
- **Implementation:** Develop physical and digital infrastructure for collaboration, provide access to computational resources, and establish oversight guardrails for ethical AI.

FOSTERING A CULTURE OF INNOVATION

- **Actionable Steps:** Create an organizational structure that supports and promotes innovation in AI.
- **Implementation:** Empower teams, provide access to tools and resources, adopt modular AI architectures, and encourage a culture of creative risk-taking.

STRUCTURING FOR ACCOUNTABILITY IN AI OPERATIONS

- **Actionable Steps:** Implement protocols and controls for ethical AI development and deployment.
- **Implementation:** Establish model risk management frameworks, standardized testing methodologies, performance monitoring systems, comprehensive documentation, and human oversight.

HARNESSING TALENT AND BUILDING AI SKILLS

- **Actionable Steps:** Develop internal AI skill sets and attract external AI expertise.
- **Implementation:** Create tailored training programs, hire external AI experts, and integrate them into the organization's culture.

BUILDING A COHESIVE DATA SCIENCE TEAM

- **Actionable Steps:** Assemble a team with specialized expertise across critical roles, such as Product Owner, Data Engineer, ML Engineer, and Data Journalist.
- **Implementation:** Define roles clearly, promote cross-disciplinary cohesion, and establish an effective data science workflow.

EMPOWERING GRASSROOTS MENTORS

- **Actionable Steps:** Develop mentors within the organization to coach peers in AI applications.
- **Implementation:** Set up formal mentorship programs, encourage informal mentoring, and select capable mentors through assessments and nominations.

TAILORING MULTIFACETED TRAINING

- **Actionable Steps:** Provide diverse and comprehensive AI training programs.
- **Implementation:** Offer introductory overviews, role-specific courses, immersive boot camps, and workshops tailored to different learning styles.

ONGOING TRAINING AND DEVELOPMENT

- **Actionable Steps:** Sustain workforce readiness through continuous training programs.
- **Implementation:** Implement rotational programs, certification pathways, alum networks, and immersive training experiences.

CELEBRATING MILESTONES AND MEASURING ENGAGEMENT

- **Actionable Steps:** Recognize achievements in AI and continuously gauge user engagement.
- **Implementation:** Spotlight AI milestones, conduct regular pulse surveys and skills assessments, and foster a culture of feedback.

CHAPTER 6

Infrastructure Readiness

INTRODUCTION

Constructing adaptive systems that safely unlock immense opportunities from artificial intelligence (AI) necessitates establishing robust underlying infrastructure to support these towering capabilities.

Specialized computing acceleration provides the essential muscle to train powerful AI models. Highly scalable data platforms offer repositories of enterprise knowledge. Capable networking prevents bottlenecks that could hamper possibilities. Automated orchestration streamlines immense pipelines to boost productivity. Unified analytics generate invaluable visibility, enabling continuous improvement.

Together, these compounding elements form a crucial foundation upon which AI solutions can be built to reach remarkable new heights. But realizing this potential requires evolving infrastructure holistically, not in fragmented silos. Strategic cross-domain planning and execution are imperative.

This chapter will explore considerations across core infrastructure domains, including computing, data, networking, orchestration, and analytics. We will discuss optimizing and unifying capabilities across on-premises and cloud environments to establish reinforced support that is ready for immense possibilities.

With robust infrastructure, transformative AI systems can be constructed rapidly, securely, and responsibly to drive breakthrough value. But first, these indispensable foundations must be championed and strengthened. Executives play a vital role in this progress.

Leadership must pave the path forward as AI grows exponentially. The heights achievable tomorrow depend directly on the groundwork laid

DOI: 10.1201/9781003486725-7

today. This chapter will equip executives to optimize infrastructure readiness to confidently support immense innovations ahead.

The future beckons those laying robust foundations now. With reinforced infrastructure secured, remarkable possibilities await through AI. But first, essential bedrock must be established stone upon stone. The time to begin building is now. Let us explore core considerations to prepare infrastructure for the immense potential ahead.

COMPUTING POWER

Specialized computing accelerators like Graphics Processing Units (GPUs), Tensor Processing Units (TPUs), and hardware provide the essential capabilities enabling modern AI techniques to extract immense insights from vast datasets through massively parallel processing.

Their streamlined architecture, with thousands of tiny cores tailored for matrix math and model graph computations, allows efficient execution of the immense workloads of neural network training and real-time inference execution.

Selecting the right accelerator technology and optimally configuring deployments establishes a crucial foundation empowering significant improvements in capability. With robust computing power, even the most demanding workloads become tractable.

Initially designed for graphics rendering, GPUs have become the primary accelerators providing indispensable acceleration for AI workloads. Their throughput-optimized architecture containing thousands of tiny specialized processing cores excels at the types of parallel workloads in machine learning, like matrix multiplications.

This allows the massive distribution of computational graphs across many concurrent threads to optimize and train deep neural networks much faster than what traditional CPUs could achieve alone. Leveraging this innate parallelism dramatically reduces model training cycles by efficiently exploiting many simultaneous operations.

Public cloud services like Amazon Web Services (AWS) and Google Cloud Platform (GCP) allow provisioning thousands of GPUs on-demand for massively parallel training jobs, then releasing capacity when finished. This elasticity avoids purchasing idle resources upfront since workloads fluctuate. Together, these capabilities make GPUs the primary driver of extensive AI acceleration.

However, realizing full benefits requires optimizations to maximize GPU utilization and throughput. Monitoring usage identifies underutilized resources to consolidate workloads. Scaling deployments aligns capacity to workload demands, avoiding over-provisioning.

Load balancing distributes jobs among GPUs evenly. Memory-heavy workflows benefit from GPUs with more significant onboard memory. Multi-instance GPUs share resources across tasks. Hybrid CPU + GPU computing boosts efficiency by offloading only parallel segments. Together, these techniques optimize GPU clusters.

Upgrading to the latest-generation GPU architectures maintains momentum as efficiency improves exponentially between versions. For example, moving from Nvidia's Volta to Ampere GPUs doubled tensor teraflops. This added performance directly accelerates training and inference.

On-premises deployments must weigh capital acquisition costs versus configurable cloud access. However, modernizing resources prevents legacy inertia. GPUs provide versatile acceleration.

Cloud TPUs are custom chips purpose-built by Google to accelerate machine learning workloads by maximizing execution efficiency. Their streamlined matrix multiply units and high-speed interconnections between cores help TPU pods achieve high optimization, especially for models like TensorFlow.

This squeezes latency while maximizing throughput, resulting in higher performance efficiency on supported workloads than the latest GPUs. Their tight integration and optimization for Google's services offer ideal acceleration at hyper-scale.

However, TPUs impose programming constraints given their custom architecture. Their adoption to date has trailed GPU ubiquity. Most organizations standardize on versatile GPUs first for broad applicability, with TPUs reserved for specific use cases where their specialized efficiencies maximize returns like transformer-based language models. But when applicable, TPUs excel by focusing exclusively on machine learning.

While powerful GPUs and TPUs efficiently accelerate training complex models, specialized inference processing chips purpose-built to execute deployed models provide optimized performance during low-latency real-time serving.

Chips like Nvidia's TensorRT apply model optimizations and run on dedicated Inference GPUs built for low-power efficient inferencing. Google's Edge TPU packs ML acceleration into small Inferencing Processing Units operating without a host server. Edge silicon focuses entirely on efficient execution.

Specialized inferencing improves response latency and throughput while minimizing costs and power consumption relative to leveraging full desktop GPUs. Accelerating demanding techniques like computer vision, voice recognition, and natural language understanding directly at the point of use allows the deployment of real-time AI while minimizing server overheads and data movement. Efficient inferencing enables new possibilities.

While convenient access to GPUs, TPUs, and inference chips via public cloud services has accelerated adoption by removing upfront capital costs, integrating acceleration within on-premises environments enables localized training on sensitive data, tighter governance controls, and optimized economics depending on workloads.

Solutions like NVIDIA DGX servers, Supermicro GPU servers, or Lenovo ThinkSystem servers provide cloud-style capabilities internally through appliances containing the latest generations of GPUs and networking. This allows scaling parallel training capacity within firewalls rather than moving data externally.

However, governance practices must ensure equitable access and queueing for shared internal resources. Refresh cycles should maintain hardware parity with the cloud to prevent inertia. When applicable, purpose-built inferencing deployed close to data sources can improve performance, privacy, and cost efficiency versus excessive server expenses for real-time edge services.

Combining cloud elasticity with governed on-premises resources provides flexibility to fulfill surging, specialized AI computing demands across diverse workloads and use cases while balancing agility, control, and spending. However, fragmented approaches quickly introduce complexity.

In summary, rapidly advancing machine learning techniques are creating demand for specialized computing power – massively parallel capacity for training and optimized silicon for efficient inferences. Modern GPUs, TPUs, and purpose-built ASICs deliver this essential capability, enabling significantly higher performance versus legacy hardware.

But fully benefiting requires adopting accelerators comprehensively across architecture, workflows, culture, and talent strategy. Refresh cycles must maintain cutting-edge access. Monitoring and optimization maximize utilization. Hybrid cloud and on-premises infrastructure balance strengths while minimizing data movement. Updated networks prevent bottlenecks.

These considerations establish AI computing readiness, providing the robust foundation to unlock immense potential. However, isolated, ad hoc additions yield minimal impact. With executive alignment on long-term roadmaps, cross-functional collaboration, and talent development, organizations can confidently build this capability as demands grow.

Computing readiness ultimately serves larger business goals – not as an end, but as a means to enable immense possibilities previously out of reach. With surging workloads showing no signs of slowing, radical performance improvements from modern accelerators offer the essential capacity to achieve greatly expanded outcomes through AI. But strategy must guide adoption. With computing power in place, the path ahead opens to reach remarkable new heights through AI.

While convenient access to GPUs and TPUs via public cloud services has accelerated adoption by removing upfront capital costs, integrating acceleration hardware within on-premises environments enables localized training on sensitive data, tighter governance controls, and optimized economics depending on workloads.

Solutions like NVIDIA DGX servers, Supermicro GPU servers, or Lenovo ThinkSystem servers provide cloud-style capabilities internally through appliances containing the latest generations of GPUs and networking. This allows massive scaling parallel training capacity within firewalls rather than moving data externally to the cloud.

However, governance practices must be established to ensure equitable access and queueing for shared internal resources. Refresh cycles should be managed to maintain hardware parity with cloud infrastructure to prevent legacy inertia as new generations emerge.

Combining public cloud services' elasticity and global reach with the security, control, and governed access of on-premises resources provides excellent flexibility to fulfill surging, specialized AI computing demands across diverse workloads and use cases. However, fragmented, ad hoc approaches quickly introduce unnecessary complexity.

Organizations should evaluate several key factors when assessing on-premises AI infrastructure readiness. Susceptible applications like healthcare may require hardened on-prem security isolation, which is unavailable in public cloud-shared infrastructure. Strict data governance also often favors internal environments. They keep data movement between storage and computing to an absolute minimum and favor processing within or very close to on-premises data lakes when feasible to reduce latency. Localized inferencing also minimizes lag.

Steady production workloads with predictable capacity requirements suit on-premises environments for cost efficiency and control versus fluctuating experimentation better suited for cloud elasticity. Cloud innovations like AI accelerators and managed services offer leading-edge capabilities on-demand, advantageous for exploratory projects. On-prem requires more internal skills. Strict governance requirements around regulations, data residency restrictions, or client mandates may necessitate on-premises or private cloud placement, where multi-cloud can help.

For organizations that require absolute control over hardware access and infrastructure configuration for security or compliance reasons, on-premises and private clouds allow customization. For high-volume predictable workloads with steady utilization, owning on-prem resources can minimize variable public cloud expenses in the long term if capacity is right-sized. By weighing these key factors, organizations can determine optimal workloads for on-premises infrastructure versus cloud based on their specific use cases and requirements. But integrated data and identities are crucial to avoiding silos.

Once the decision is made to deploy AI infrastructure on-premises, thoughtful architecture is critical to maximize accelerators and avoid bottlenecks. Modernizing networks with high throughput network interface cards (NICs), low latency switches, and ample bandwidth prevents communication from becoming a constraint during data parallel training. Shared high-speed storage like all-flash arrays, parallel filesystems, or Hadoop Distributed File Systems (HDFS) enhances accessibility from GPU clusters for model and dataset consumption.

Adding dedicated GPU servers like NVIDIA DGX or integrating GPU blades into existing servers provides a massively parallel modeling capacity rivaling the cloud. Workflow schedulers like Kubernetes efficiently queue, monitor, and dynamically allocate GPU-intensive jobs across shared clusters. Containerization frameworks like Docker allow packaging-trained models for standardized deployment across environments. Interfaces for identity, security, access controls, auditing, and compliance must align with cloud standards where possible.

With robust on-premises infrastructure, enterprise-specific enhancements can further optimize performance and economics. Interconnecting on-prem GPU clusters to cloud storage adds burst capacity while minimizing egress fees. Multi-instance GPUs balance cost and flexibility by dynamically allocating fractional resources.

Inference appliances place optimized silicon near deployment endpoints to improve real-time service latency, throughput, power efficiency, and privacy. To optimize provisioning, comprehensive monitoring provides visibility into utilization, data flows, and workload performance.

Together, these best practices maximize the performance, efficiency, and rapid adaptability of on-premises AI infrastructure. But seamless integration and governance remain critical to avoiding fragmented silos across cloud and internal systems. With thoughtful architecture and implementation, on-premises environments can provide optimized venues for the most demanding, regulated, steady-state AI workloads.

The blend of cloud agility and on-prem control provides ideal symbiosis. But cultural changes are equally vital to preventing inertia. With cohesive adoption, on-prem GPU clusters unlock localized possibilities minus cloud data egress. Internal resources retain advantages when strategically governed, refreshed, and integrated – but should complement cloud capabilities, not operate in isolation.

When thoughtfully modernized, on-premises infrastructure is integral in fueling AI progress across the entire pipeline from development to training to deployment. Yet, it remains only one element of comprehensive AI readiness. Its purpose must ultimately serve larger business aims and opportunities previously out of reach. With prudent upgrades and governance, on-prem systems provide a robust venue tailored for the most demanding workloads. Combined with cloud and edge, infrastructure is fortified to support immense potential.

OPTIMIZING SPEED AND LATENCY

The surging data and compute appetites of rapidly advancing AI necessitate optimizing networking performance, storage access, workload portability, and seamless orchestration. Massive datasets must flow with minimal latency between diverse environments during training and inference. Automation and abstraction must streamline immense pipelines. Containers empower portability across venues. Together, these techniques remove friction and bottlenecks to accelerate the exploration, development, and delivery of transformative AI capabilities.

Realizing the immense potential of AI requires moving extraordinary volumes of data between distributed sources, processors, accelerators, storage, and endpoints with great speed and immediacy. The unprecedented computing capacity in modern data centers must be fully fed and utilized by efficiently shuttling vast datasets wherever they are needed to power algorithms and insights. Training complex neural networks and executing real-time inferences demand flexibility to consume and analyze petabytes of structured and unstructured data on demand across disparate systems with minimal delay. Latency directly hampers potential.

They are surging data volume, velocity, and variety of pressure network capacity. Transferring enormous datasets and model checkpoints rapidly between cloud and on-premises environments stresses bandwidth. Real-time streaming data for online inferences and IoT endpoints necessitates excellent responsiveness even under heavy loads with usage spikes. Exponentially growing models require repeatedly moving terabytes of training data across accelerators. Together, these needs strain legacy networking, initially designed for more static traffic patterns.

Preemptively scaling up connectivity using link aggregation, higher-throughput cables, and more capable switch hardware maintains speed and capacity as demands escalate. Intelligently balancing data locality and movement minimizes transfers through thoughtful caching strategies and keeping processing within or very close to databases where feasible to avoid roundtrips. Expanding raw bandwidth with larger pipes prevents bottlenecks that could slow productivity and iteration speed. Holistic connectivity stitches diverse environments together to enable unified workflows. With integrated networking, data pipelines flow freely between venues to accelerate possibilities without introducing chokepoints. Frictionless flows fuel AI progress.

Equally important, manually configuring, deploying, and managing immense distributed machine learning pipelines across heterogeneous cloud, multi-site, and edge environments introduces enormous complexity. Role-based access controls must enforce security across tools. Dynamic provisioning of specialized accelerators is imperative. Workloads shift continually. Monitoring job status, data provenance, model lineage, and billing requires integration. Without robust orchestration, complexity hampers experimentation and operationalization.

AI-focused workflow orchestration engines like Kubernetes address these needs by efficiently scheduling and monitoring training jobs across distributed GPU clusters while dynamically provisioning cloud resources on demand via infrastructure-as-code techniques. This automation and abstraction built atop underlying infrastructure accelerate experimentation and iteration by removing manual bottlenecks at scale. Dashboards provide visibility into real-time status and resource utilization to optimize provisioning that is aligned to workload needs. Pre-built helm charts simplify the deployment of new tools. Role-based access built on Lightweight Directory Access Protocol (LDAP) or Security Assertion Markup Language (SAML) integration enforces security. Together, these capabilities simplify operations immensely.

Containerization frameworks like Docker further complement orchestrated infrastructure by empowering packing complete application environments into transportable images that run uniformly on any supporting platform, encapsulating models, frameworks, packages, binaries, and dependencies into self-contained units. This enables predictable portability of workflows across diverse on-prem, multi-cloud, and edge environments without modifications, avoiding configuration drift or conflicts. Docker images are instantiated as lightweight containers share just the app layer, minimizing resource overhead. Dynamic orchestration scales instances up or down to meet evolving demands, adjusting billing accordingly. Together, containerization and orchestration modernize development and deployment, accelerating the delivery of AI innovations.

Yet realizing these benefits at the enterprise scale requires integrating holistic data gravity, security, access, and technology strategies. Simply bolting on new tools invites brittleness. Application Programming Interfaces (APIs) propagate across systems reliably. Talent must blend infrastructure and machine learning domains. With patient alignment across domains, modern orchestration and containerization combine to streamline immense pipelines, empowering data science teams to focus efforts on maximizing predictive value. The tools fade to the background, accelerating discovery.

Surging data volumes and exponentially escalating model complexity mandate optimizing network throughput, storage access, and compute provisioning while streamlining intricate workflows for productivity. High-speed interconnected data pipelines prevent bottlenecks. Containerizing workloads boosts portability across environments. Dynamic orchestration scales resources just in time while automating repetitive tasks. Together, these techniques remove friction, empowering unhindered exploration, development, and delivery of potentially transformative AI capabilities. But holistically integrating considerations across technology, security, data, and talent strategies remains imperative to avoid ad hoc brittleness. Organizations can unlock immense productivity with robust networking, orchestration, and containerization, complementing hardware acceleration and data platforms. The path forward must secure reliable pipelines.

UNIFIED ANALYTICS PLATFORMS

Collating and analyzing immense volumes of structured and unstructured data, monitoring metrics, logs, and traces while tracking lineage and metadata requires unified analytics platforms. These must ingest diverse data streams and empower actionable insights through dashboards, visualizations, alerts, and collaborative investigation capabilities. Analytics solutions yield tremendous value from underlying infrastructure and data, optimizing development, training, deployment, and oversight of intricate AI systems.

Out-of-the-box services are available, providing integrated environments that collect and structure machine data at scale, build and compare models using techniques like machine learning and statistical analysis, generate interactive visualizations and dashboards, configure threshold-based alerts for proactive monitoring, and enable collaborative investigation using shared notebooks and other tools. These platforms aim to provide a single solution covering the entire pipeline, from ingestion to training to monitoring and troubleshooting.

Scaling to immense data volumes across metrics, logs, metadata, and analytics platforms enables deriving maximum insight from AI and infrastructure operations. Generating visualizations conveys interrelationships and patterns. Statistical methods and machine learning aid predictive analysis and classification. Proactive alerting based on threshold spot anomalies in real-time. Rapid collaborative investigation using integrated tools accelerates root cause analysis and issue resolution.

These techniques empower leveraging infrastructure telemetry and AI model behavior data to optimize reliability, spending, security, and performance continuously. Analyzing model lineage, hyperparameters, and metrics identifies incremental improvements. Monitoring data flows highlights bottlenecks for remediation. Correlating trace events speeds diagnosis. Forecasting usage patterns optimize provisioning. This data-driven insight streamlines operations and delivery.

Yet realizing these full benefits requires prudent data governance and strategic design. Capabilities must integrate cohesively, avoiding fragmented tools and data silos. Presenting interrelated observability signals together conveys coherent stories rapidly. Skill building ensures technical teams understand how to leverage analytics platforms fully. With patient alignment, analytics yield immense value.

Constructing and operating towering AI solutions that can withstand turbulent business environments requires laying a robust bedrock foundation across processing, storage, networking, orchestration, and analytics. Holistic design coordinates these components for seamless interoperation, maximizing collective capabilities while minimizing bottlenecks. Hybrid models thoughtfully balance the strengths of cloud services and on-premises environments. Compounding scalability and efficiency unlocks significant performance gains and cost savings at scale.

With well-architected infrastructure, organizations can construct adaptive data-driven systems that can withstand whatever competitive threats emerge. But this necessitates preparing the underlying foundation prudently based on strategic roadmaps. The path forward must evolve infrastructure holistically before embarking on transformative AI initiatives.

While convenient access to on-demand infrastructure via the public cloud provides a strategic launchpad for experimentation through global reach and managed services, on-premises environments retain advantages around security, regulatory compliance, control, and optimized economics depending on workloads and use cases. An integrated hybrid approach aims to maximize these combined strengths.

Yet legacy on-premises data centers designed for traditional applications often struggle to meet the surging demands of AI workloads without modernization. Optimizing internal infrastructure readiness is vital to complementing cloud agility. High-speed NICs and GPUs establish localized acceleration while scale-out network-attached storage improves accessibility for data-intensive modeling. Orchestrators like Kubernetes enable dynamic resource allocation. Refreshing outdated hardware prevents stagnation. Together, these upgrades transform static legacy resources into agile on-premises environments that fuel AI exploration beyond the cloud.

But holistic preparation remains imperative, as piecemeal additions in isolation have minimal impact. Cross-functional collaboration and executive alignment on long-term roadmaps allow smoothly evolving on-premises infrastructure while cultivating complementary skillsets across cloud and legacy technologies. With robust preparation, integrated on-premises data centers can provide well-governed venues tailored for the most demanding, data-sensitive applications – unlocking localized possibilities beyond the cloud's reach.

As data volumes, model complexity, and computing power continue rapidly escalating, the public cloud's virtually unlimited on-demand capacity, constantly upgrading infrastructure, worldwide footprint, and usage-based spending provide indispensable acceleration for the exploration, development, and delivery of AI systems at a global scale. Cloud elasticity offers freedom from legacy constraints that limit potential.

However, integration with on-premises environments aims to maximize mutual strengths while minimizing risks. This involves aligning specific workloads to the ideal venue based on security, data gravity, usage patterns, regulatory needs, and economics. On-premises infrastructure suits steady production, security-sensitive data, and predictable workloads. The cloud facilitates dynamic experimentation, worldwide reach, and absorbing demand spikes.

Cloud and on-premises infrastructure enables exploring immense possibilities if strategically unified through architecture, workflows, controls, and culture. Organizations gain a robust foundation for constructing industry leadership with cloud-fueling momentum and on-prem providing balance. But success depends on cohesive adoption and aligning incentives to prevent organizational silos. With prudent design, cloud and on-premise environments forge a symbiotic balance, enabling previously unreachable heights.

Holistically designed infrastructure combining cloud innovation and integration strengths with governed on-premises environments establishes a robust bedrock upon which adaptive AI solutions can be constructed to drive transformative value. Optimized networking minimizes latency, while container orchestration streamlines immense pipelines. Unified analytics generate insights enabling continuous improvement. These compounding elements allow efficient powering of intensification data and compute-driven systems even amidst exponential change.

However, realizing these full benefits requires cross-disciplinary collaboration and cohesive adoption. The path forward must secure reliable pipelines through governance, culture, and architecture. With a robust underlying infrastructure set, organizations can then unlock immense productivity from AI while upholding ethics. The heights achievable depend directly on the reinforced support below. Leadership must champion strengthening these indispensable foundations.

FINAL THOUGHTS

This chapter comprehensively explores the intricate infrastructure layers essential for supporting and advancing AI initiatives. This chapter highlighted the critical importance of specialized computing acceleration, scalable data platforms, effective networking, automated orchestration, and unified analytics platforms. Each element forms a crucial foundation upon which AI solutions are built, enabling organizations to achieve remarkable heights in AI applications. The strategic cross-domain planning and execution, essential for evolving infrastructure holistically, have been emphasized, illustrating how robust infrastructure underpins transformative AI systems, fostering rapid, secure, and responsible growth.

In transitioning to Chapter 7, the focus shifts from the foundational infrastructure to the pivotal aspect of data readiness in analytics and AI. Chapter 7 will delve deep into the essence of establishing an environment where data is available, deeply valued, and effectively utilized. Data readiness in this context involves creating a robust data culture, ensuring high-quality data, effective data governance, and seamless data accessibility and integration.

Chapter 7 will discuss the transformative process of developing a data culture, where data is seen as an invaluable asset crucial for informing decisions. Leadership's role in demonstrating the power of data and the importance of investing in data literacy programs will be highlighted. Chapter 7 will emphasize empowering employees with the necessary tools and training for independent data access, analysis, and interpretation, fostering a culture that celebrates data-driven success and nurtures curiosity.

A significant focus will be on the criticality of data quality for effective AI and analytics. Organizations often face challenges in maintaining consistent data quality, and Chapter 7 will explore the components of a sustainable data quality program, including establishing quality parameters, continuous measurement, identifying problem patterns, executing remediation strategies, integrating quality into governance, and fostering a culture that values data excellence.

Data governance, another crucial component of modern business strategy, will be addressed, highlighting how it transforms data from a potential liability into a strategic asset. Chapter 7 will discuss the integration of automation and accountability in governance, paving the way for structured and scalable data management. The various components of comprehensive data governance, including policies, standards, processes, roles, controls, and lifecycles, will be explored.

Furthermore, Chapter 7 will emphasize the importance of data accessibility and integration. It will outline strategies for enabling safe and scalable democratizing data access across the enterprise, managing access requests, implementing tiered data security, enriching metadata for discovery, providing self-service analytics, and launching data literacy initiatives.

Chapter 7 presents a comprehensive overview of the different facets of data readiness, which is crucial for leveraging data as a powerful tool for digital transformation. It will provide practical insights and strategies for organizations to harness the transformative power of AI and analytics effectively, ensuring they are well-prepared for the challenges and opportunities of a data-driven future.

KEY TAKEAWAYS AND ACTIONS

COMPUTING POWER

- **Actionable Steps:** Invest in specialized accelerators like GPUs and TPUs for AI workloads.
- **Implementation:** Optimize deployments of these technologies, considering cloud services for scalability and on-premises solutions for sensitive data.

OPTIMIZING SPEED AND LATENCY

- **Actionable Steps:** Improve networking performance and storage access.
- **Implementation:** Scale up connectivity, implement efficient data transfer strategies, and balance data locality with movement.

UNIFIED ANALYTICS PLATFORMS

- **Actionable Steps:** Utilize platforms like Splunk and Databricks for data analysis and insight generation.
- **Implementation:** Integrate these platforms to manage data collection, model building, and monitoring in a unified environment.

CLOUD AND ON-PREMISES INTEGRATION

- **Actionable Steps:** Blend the agility of cloud services with the control of on-premises infrastructure.
- **Implementation:** Determine the optimal workload distribution between cloud and on-premises based on security, regulatory compliance, and cost considerations.

ON-PREMISES INFRASTRUCTURE

- **Actionable Steps:** Upgrade on-premises data centers to meet AI demands.
- **Implementation:** Integrate modern hardware like high-speed NICs and GPUs and employ orchestrators like Kubernetes for dynamic resource allocation.

CLOUD INFRASTRUCTURE UTILIZATION

- **Actionable Steps:** Leverage the cloud for scalability and global reach.
- **Implementation:** Utilize cloud services for AI experimentation and development, especially for dynamic and globally scaled workloads.

CULTIVATING A HOLISTIC INFRASTRUCTURE STRATEGY

- **Actionable Steps:** Develop a comprehensive infrastructure strategy that combines the strengths of both cloud and on-premises environments.
- **Implementation:** Ensure cross-functional collaboration and executive alignment on long-term infrastructure roadmaps.

LEADERSHIP'S ROLE

- **Actionable Steps:** Secure commitment from top leadership for infrastructure development.
- **Implementation:** Leaders should drive the strategic vision for infrastructure development, ensuring alignment with AI goals and business objectives.

CONTINUOUS IMPROVEMENT AND ADAPTATION

- **Actionable Steps:** Regularly assess and update infrastructure to keep pace with technological advancements.
- **Implementation:** Implement a continuous improvement process for infrastructure, staying abreast of technological developments and adapting accordingly.

CHAPTER 7

Data Readiness

INTRODUCTION

Data readiness is a cornerstone for successful analytics and artificial intelligence (AI) initiatives in modern business. This chapter delves into the essence of establishing an environment where data is not just present but deeply valued, which encourages and fosters data-driven decision-making.

Developing a data culture is a transformative process that enhances decision-making, operational efficiency, and innovation. It's about instilling a mindset that views data as an invaluable asset for informing decisions. This chapter explores the crucial role of leadership in demonstrating the power of data and the importance of investing in data literacy programs. It emphasizes empowering employees with the necessary tools and training to access, analyze, and interpret data independently. The objective is to create a culture that not only celebrates data-driven successes but also nurtures curiosity and recognizes the vital role of quality information in generating actionable insights.

As we venture into the future, where AI is set to revolutionize every aspect of our lives, the significance of data readiness cannot be overstated. It's not just about having data; it's about ensuring it is high-quality, well-governed, accessible, and integrated. It's about nurturing a culture that values data and understands its transformative power to drive insights and innovation.

This chapter also addresses the criticality of data quality. High-quality data is essential for effective AI and analytics. Many organizations need help maintaining consistent data quality, not due to a lack of tools or

DOI: 10.1201/9781003486725-8

technologies but due to the absence of rigorous processes and culture actively monitoring and resolving data quality issues.

Establishing a comprehensive data quality management practice is essential to harness the power of AI and analytics. Poor data quality can significantly impede the potential of advanced technologies by depriving them of the necessary fuel to deliver accurate insights and trusted automation. This chapter explores the components of a sustainable data quality program, including establishing quality parameters, continuous measurement, identifying problem patterns, executing remediation strategies, integrating quality into governance, and fostering a culture that values data excellence.

A vital aspect of any data quality initiative is establishing a shared understanding of what data quality means within the organization. This involves considering the inherent qualities of data, such as accuracy, completeness, consistency, and timeliness, and evaluating its quality in the context of its intended use. This chapter discusses how quality benchmarks vary across different use cases, influenced by factors like output requirements, compliance controls, consumption scenarios, and the criticality of the decisions based on the data.

Furthermore, the chapter delves into data governance, highlighting its emergence as a crucial component of modern business strategy, particularly as organizations grapple with burgeoning data volumes and diverse use cases. Data governance transforms data from a potential liability into a strategic asset, enabling organizations to derive insights at scale, build trust, manage risks, and fuel a data-driven digital transformation.

The foundation of data governance lies in its framework, designed to extract maximum value from data while effectively managing associated risks. This chapter discusses how governance involves the integration of automation and accountability, paving the way for structured and scalable data management. It also highlights the various components of comprehensive data governance, including policies, standards, processes, roles, controls, and lifecycles, all working in concert to enable broad access to data while managing risks effectively.

Finally, this chapter emphasizes the importance of data accessibility and integration. It stresses the transformative power of data in guiding decisions, optimizing processes, and creating competitive advantages unleashed when data is accessible. This chapter outlines strategies for enabling safe and scalable democratizing data access across the enterprise, highlighting managing access requests, implementing tiered data security, enriching metadata for discovery, providing self-service analytics, and launching data literacy initiatives.

This chapter presents a comprehensive overview of the different facets of data readiness, from data culture and quality to governance, accessibility, and integration. It provides practical insights and strategies for organizations to leverage data as a powerful tool for digital transformation, ensuring they are well-equipped to harness the transformative power of AI and analytics.

DATA QUALITY

High-quality data is the cornerstone for practical AI and advanced analytics. However, many organizations struggle to maintain consistent data quality over time. This challenge is often not due to a lack of tools or technologies. Still, it stems from the absence of rigorous processes and a culture of actively monitoring and resolving data quality issues.

For companies keen on harnessing the power of AI and analytics, establishing a comprehensive data quality management practice is not merely beneficial – it is imperative. Poor data quality will severely impede advanced technologies' potential, depriving them of the essential input to yield accurate insights and reliable automation.

This chapter delves into the essential components of a sustainable data quality program. It encompasses the establishment of clear quality parameters, the implementation of continuous measurement systems, the systematic identification of problem patterns, the execution of tailored remediation strategies, the integration of quality management into governance frameworks, and the fostering of a culture that places a high value on data excellence. Embedding robust data quality within the systems and culture of an organization equips it to confidently pursue AI and analytics initiatives, secure in the knowledge that its data foundation is solid and reliable.

The initiation of any data quality initiative starts with a shared understanding of what data quality means within the organization. Data has inherent qualities such as accuracy, completeness, consistency, and timeliness. However, evaluating its quality must also consider the context of its intended use. Quality benchmarks vary across use cases, influenced by factors such as output requirements, compliance controls, consumption scenarios, and the criticality of the decisions that rely on the data.

For instance, the level of precision required for models and reports that consume the data is a significant consideration. High-stakes decisions necessitate stringent accuracy standards. Compliance controls are crucial – whether regulations or contractual obligations dictate specific legal quality requirements. Data that supports critical decisions contains personally identifiable information or is financial and often has mandated quality levels.

The intended users of the data and their purposes also significantly influence the quality requirements. Different stakeholders may necessitate varying levels of data quality. The nature of business decisions informed by the data introduces additional layers of complexity. For example, data that supports low-risk decisions might allow for greater flexibility compared to data used for high-impact judgments.

Given these considerations – output requirements, compliance, consumption scenarios, and decision criticality – it is essential that quality expectations are collaboratively defined for each dataset by bringing together all key stakeholders. These include the creators of the data, those responsible for transforming and storing it, compliance officers providing oversight, and the analysts, applications, and decision-makers who use it.

This interdisciplinary team is responsible for defining quality standards and metrics tailored to the dataset, taking into account its intended use and business impact. The scrutiny required for transactional financial data, for example, is considerably higher than for informal customer feedback logs. The goal is to establish "fit-for-purpose" quality levels that align with the specific needs of its use.

Following the collaborative definition of quality dimensions, the next step involves the development of quantitative metrics and auditing processes to ensure adherence to these standards. These metrics turn the abstract concept of "good data" into measurable terms. Key metrics such as completeness, validity, accuracy, consistency, and timeliness, quantified in percentages, highlight areas needing attention. Thresholds are established to trigger alerts when these metrics fall below accepted levels.

However, relying solely on metrics is not sufficient. Audits add a qualitative layer by manually examining data to identify issues that metrics might overlook, such as incorrect categorizations, outlier values, and anomalies. These audits assess the relevance and logical integrity of the data, going beyond basic validity checks. An ongoing auditing process, which includes sampling and targeted investigation of issues, measures adherence to the tailored quality standards set for each dataset based on the needs of its downstream consumers. The dimensions requiring focus are guided by the intended use of the data in analysis, decision-making, and AI applications.

Effective measurement is critical to pinpointing where data quality issues exist. Common problematic patterns include errors in input data that propagate downstream, integration errors introduced during data processing, manual processing defects due to inconsistent human judgment, and gradual data drift over time that goes unnoticed without vigilant monitoring.

Profiling and metrics play a crucial role in diagnosing the root causes of these defects, revealing which systems and workflows are accumulating errors. This analysis informs the remediation strategies. Identifying the root causes of data issues is crucial for taking effective and decisive action.

Detecting data problems is only the beginning. Organizations must then act decisively to resolve these issues through tailored remediation strategies. Corrective tactics like data cleansing involve replacing, modifying, or deleting incorrect values based on predefined rules. Master data management can provide authoritative values for corrections. Data enrichment strategies fill in missing data through lookups and inferences. Migrating to new systems can leave behind quality issues while offering opportunities to restructure data for better management. Addressing defects in upstream processes is fundamental to preventing the introduction of errors into downstream systems.

Preventive measures are equally crucial. Aligning master data definitions ensures consistency across different systems. Training and educating staff improve the human handling of data. Tightening specifications and validation processes prevent the entry of poor-quality data. Utilizing monitoring tools fosters ongoing vigilance, while workflow automation reduces the likelihood of inconsistent manual interventions.

Organizations must blend targeted corrective actions with systemic preventive improvements for sustainable results. This approach should be tailored based on the identified issues' scale, severity, and variety. Sustainable data quality requires fixing current problems and enhancing processes to prevent new issues. This strategy builds resilient data assurance through corrective and preventive measures.

Embedding these practices into their systems and culture ensures that organizations maintain data quality not as a one-off initiative but as a continuous process. This approach fosters a culture where data excellence is the norm, characterized by vigilant monitoring, rapid response to issues, thorough investigation of root causes, and a collective commitment to maintaining high data standards. The foundation for leveraging AI and analytics becomes robust, resilient, and enabling in such an environment.

DATA GOVERNANCE

Data governance is crucial to modern business strategy, especially as organizations navigate the complexities of burgeoning data volumes and diverse use cases. In this evolving landscape, governance extends beyond its traditional role, becoming a strategic tool crucial for ensuring data accessibility, accuracy, and security. This chapter illuminates how data governance can transform data from a potential liability into a strategic asset. This enables organizations to extract insights at scale, build trust, manage risks, and propel a data-driven digital transformation.

The foundation of data governance lies in its framework, designed to extract maximum value from data while effectively managing associated risks. With data spread across multiple systems, the limitations of manual oversight become clear. Thus, governance necessitates the integration of automation and accountability, paving the way for structured and scalable data management.

Several aspects underline the necessity for comprehensive governance. Firstly, it plays a vital role in risk management by minimizing vulnerabilities and safeguarding sensitive data through robust policies and controls, thereby protecting stakeholders. Secondly, it balances the need for data accessibility with the potential risks of misuse, ensuring that data is used appropriately, facilitating discovery, and preventing fragmentation. Thirdly, governance is critical to optimizing the value of data, providing its fitness for intended purposes through lifecycle management, adding business context, and maintaining consistency through established standards.

Additionally, governance is instrumental in coordinating various stakeholders across teams, systems, and data ecosystems, fostering policy-driven alignment and collaboration that amplifies data's impact. It also addresses the challenge of managing complexity in diverse environments by introducing necessary automation and policy-driven frameworks. Moreover, governance enforces compliance by embedding required practices across data lifecycles, thus preventing potential sanctions. Lastly, it governs analytics and insights, ensuring that models use quality data aligned with business objectives, thereby maintaining data relevance and integrity.

Comprehensive data governance consists of various components, including policies, standards, processes, roles, controls, and lifecycles, all working in concert to enable broad access to data while managing risks effectively. Policies govern data usage, security, privacy rights, lifecycles, and compliance. Standards provide specifications for consistent data usage and exchange across systems. Processes define the workflows for data management, covering aspects like ingestion, integration, storage, access provisioning, quality management, and privacy. Clearly defined roles and responsibilities ensure accountability, while technical controls enforce policies, preventing unauthorized access and detecting vulnerabilities. Managing data lifecycles from ingestion to archival or deletion is also crucial.

When these components are integrated harmoniously, they facilitate scaling governance across heterogeneous data landscapes. Governance effectively bridges the gap between technical implementation and business oversight, enabling access to trusted data. The relationship between data governance, data quality, and metadata initiatives forms a comprehensive foundation for effective data management.

A consistent taxonomy and glossary are fundamental to effective governance. They establish a common language, eliminate confusion, and provide a framework for governance practices. Creating governance bodies aligned with this taxonomy ensures a balance between decentralized authority and centralized oversight. These bodies, including steering committees, domain-specific councils, and data stewardship programs, ensure domain-specific policies and standards are effectively implemented.

The codification of governance through comprehensive policies and procedures lays the groundwork for its practical application. These frameworks cover various areas such as security, privacy, lifecycles, quality, metadata, issue management, compliance, AI ethics, roles, and access governance. Regular policy reviews ensure alignment with evolving regulations, technologies, and business practices.

Operationalizing governance is achieved through data stewardship. Stewards enforce policies, maintain metadata, monitor data quality, manage compliance, and collaborate with peers. Providing them with the necessary training, tools, and support ensures decentralized but effective governance.

Issue management transforms incidents into opportunities for improvement. This process involves systematic approaches to issue intake, classification, investigation, resolution, monitoring, and feedback, collectively elevating governance maturity.

Scalable governance requires extensive automation. Tools such as metadata platforms, policy engines, data quality automation, data integration and modeling tools, and data democratization platforms are indispensable. Embedding controls into the technical data stack ensures preventative policy enforcement, which complements the cultural change.

However, technical automation alone is insufficient. Cultivating a culture of data governance requires effective communication, training, incentives, transparency, and leadership that models ethical practices. Demonstrating the value of governance in preventing misuse and risks while enabling insights is critical. Tailored training programs, rewards for compliance, transparency in issue management, and executive endorsement are essential in embedding governance thinking into the organizational fabric.

In summary, comprehensive governance is an ongoing journey. The backbone enables organizations to ethically leverage data's potential at scale while carefully managing risks. This convergence of people, processes, policy, and technology forms the bedrock of an effective data governance strategy.

DATA ACCESSIBILITY

Data's transformative power in guiding decisions, optimizing processes, and creating competitive advantages is unleashed when it is accessible. However, its potential remains untapped when locked away and inaccessible. This chapter focuses on enabling safe and scalable democratization of data access across the enterprise. It highlights managing access requests, implementing tiered data security, enriching metadata for discovery, providing self-service analytics, and launching data literacy initiatives. The guiding principle is to foster an ethical culture that shares information openly while protecting sensitive data, thus empowering individuals through expanded data accessibility.

Comprehensive data accessibility, underpinned by thoughtful data architecture, security, governance, and culture change, allows organizations to leverage their information resources fully. This unlocks collaboration, automation, and growth by making data readily available, thus accelerating insight generation and unlocking latent potential.

Data as a living asset must be activated across the organization rather than passively stored. Accessibility is crucial for several reasons. It quickens data-driven decision-making by enabling faster insights through self-service capabilities. It empowers more organization members to engage with data, fostering innovation and exploring new use cases. Controlled accessibility enhances transparency and democratic participation, granting access to a broader range of stakeholders. Seamless access improves productivity and collaboration by connecting people with the information they need for their roles. Thoughtful accessibility also maintains compliance by controlling sensitive data while making less risky datasets more accessible. Future-proofing data architectures, incentivizing metadata documentation, optimizing tiered storage, and powering automation initiatives are other critical aspects of accessibility.

Accessibility transforms data from a static resource into an active strategic asset. It becomes a crucial enabler of digital transformation, facilitating exponential gains as more individuals interact with data in well-governed and trusted environments.

The foundation for scalable data accessibility while managing risks involves several technological capabilities. It starts with identity and access management that authorizes users and enforces appropriate access levels. Data discovery is facilitated through curated metadata, cataloging, and search tools, helping users find relevant data effortlessly. Data inventory capabilities index key data attributes such as existence, location, and ownership. Optimized data storage balances cost, performance, and accessibility, while data lifecycle management policies manage data from ingestion through archival. Integration and Extract, Transform, Load (ETL) tools synchronize disparate data sources into accessible repositories. Ensuring data remains usable and accurate post-integration is crucial, as is maintaining referential integrity across data sources. Security controls like masking and encryption enable broad access to information products without exposing raw data. Compliance tools enforce data usage policies, and monitoring and auditing ensure appropriate access levels and detect misuse. These capabilities, integrated into a robust data governance framework, create an environment where data can be safely and efficiently accessed and used.

Structured processes for onboarding, off-boarding, and managing data access entitlements are vital. These processes, governed by documented policies, ensure access is aligned with business needs. Formal workflows for granting or revoking access, multistage reviews, tiered access levels, auditable logs, and proactive certification processes collectively promote accountable and compliant access. Automating these workflows adds efficiency.

Intuitive data search and location capabilities, backed by comprehensive metadata documentation, are essential for enabling discovery. This includes business definitions, technical specifications, data lineage, ownership details, lifecycle stages, and quality metrics. Centralized, searchable metadata catalogs, supplemented by AI, transform data into a dynamic, navigable library.

Self-service analytics platforms enable business teams to interact directly with data, increasing engagement and adoption. However, they require thoughtful controls like output masking and usage monitoring to prevent misuse. These platforms drive value while ensuring data security.

Beyond technical solutions, data literacy programs are crucial for fostering understanding and critical thinking around data. Training in data storytelling, problem framing, strategic application of insights, and data ethics empowers individuals to derive meaningful insights from data.

Cultural transformation, led by leaders advocating for ethical and transparent data usage, sustains data democratization. Transparent practices like publishing data dictionaries and sharing data usage case studies build a culture of trust and openness.

Balancing governance with innovation is essential. Governance should focus on need-based access, transparency, and ethical data application. This approach guides data usage toward positive outcomes while minimizing potential harms.

Data accessibility transforms data into an engine of innovation and insight. Data becomes a strategic asset driving collaboration, innovation, and growth by combining technological solutions, structured processes, and cultural transformation. This chapter underscores that the insights within an organization's data are immense, and by adopting a strategic approach to data accessibility, these insights can propel a more informed, innovative, and prosperous future.

DATA INTEGRATION

Data integration is synthesizing diverse data elements into a unified, meaningful whole. This involves extracting data from various sources, transforming it into a consistent format, and loading it into target systems like databases or data lakes. These integrated data sets become the backbone of enterprise-wide analytics, decision automation, and AI applications.

This chapter focuses on how organizations can enhance their analytical and AI capabilities through effective data integration strategies and governance. The discussion encompasses design approaches, execution methodologies, metadata management, data modeling, ETL pipelines, schema alignment, and master data management. Additional topics include integrating third-party data, achieving real-time integration, ensuring scalability, and effectively using data warehouses, data lakes, and data marts within cloud adoption.

The overarching aim is to methodically increase the complexity of data integration, establishing robust data provenance, automating execution, and enabling agility through modular architectures. The ultimate objective is to democratize access to integrated data, ensuring it is trustworthy and valuable, thus serving as a reliable source of fuel for digital transformation.

Data integration breaks down information silos and unlocks exponential value. For instance, integrating call center logs with customer transaction history and product data can provide a comprehensive understanding of customer interactions. Similarly, merging patient medical records with clinical trial data and public health statistics can lead to breakthroughs in precision medicine. Integrating supply chain data with sales, marketing, and demographic information can uncover optimization opportunities.

The benefits of thoughtfully executed data integration are manifold. It enables unified enterprise-wide analytics and reporting by consolidating diverse data sources. This integration fosters collaboration across business units by establishing common standards. It enhances automated decision-making and AI accuracy by providing high-quality data inputs. Analysts spend less time assembling data, allowing more time for high-value analytical tasks. Additionally, integration reduces redundancy, improves data quality, and enhances transparency through shared infrastructure and governance.

The journey toward comprehensive data integration is gradual and strategic. Organizations typically start with foundational use cases, progressively moving toward more complex integrations. This phased approach allows for competency development and incremental value delivery aligned with business priorities.

Effective data governance ensures integrated data security, compliance, and reliability. This involves establishing curation workflows for master data, formal change review processes, building reusable integration components, and setting explicit data usage and access guidelines. Data tagging for automated controls, compliance risk assessment, metadata management, usage monitoring, and data quality profiling are all part of robust data governance.

Data integration architecture is pivotal in translating business goals into technical solutions. This involves defining business requirements, adopting an iterative approach to deliver incremental value, designing for long-term scalability, and leveraging existing assets. Understanding source systems, balancing standardization with autonomy, selecting the proper extraction techniques, and continuously refining the architecture are critical aspects of effective data integration.

The technical framework includes pipelines, schemas, data models, storage solutions, compute resources, metadata management systems, and orchestration tools. The initial focus is extracting and loading data into staging areas, followed by transformation and cleansing to meet quality standards. The final step involves populating databases and data hubs for consumption.

Master data management is central to creating unified data structures from diverse sources, ensuring consistent and accurate decision-making. It involves identifying critical data domains, establishing data models, assigning stewardship, managing access, performing entity resolution, consolidating records, enriching data, and implementing automated governance.

Access and delivery of integrated data require careful consideration. This includes providing query interfaces, building connectors and pipelines, implementing security measures, and delivering self-service tools. Monitoring usage, managing resource consumption, and obscuring data structures are also important.

Accountable data governance, overseen by cross-functional leaders, stewards, and governance bodies, ensures balanced and ethical data utilization. This governance framework defines policies, encourages data ethics, monitors data quality, and fosters agile, iterative delivery methods.

Implementation involves orchestrated rollouts, leveraging existing strengths, deciding on deployment locations (cloud or on-premises), coordinating pipelines, choosing between ETL and ELT approaches, implementing change data capture, balancing custom code with configuration, providing master data context, thorough testing, and user-centric design.

Continuous user feedback is vital for ensuring the relevance of data integration efforts. Engagement mechanisms include observational studies, user groups, surveys, interviews, focus groups, support tracking, analytics, roadmap transparency, and open communication channels.

Integrating technical and cultural elements allows data integration initiatives to transform disparate data into actionable insights, fueling the digital enterprise's journey.

DATA CULTURE

Data culture, as the final pillar of data readiness, holds a paramount position akin to how a garden thrives under the care of a skilled gardener. A transformative shift occurs in an environment where data is acknowledged and deeply valued, opening doors to growth and practical utility. This chapter explores how fostering a robust data culture is fundamental in realizing the full potential of data, particularly in driving effective decision-making, enhancing operational efficiency, and fueling innovation.

Establishing a data culture is a deliberate process beyond mere appreciation of data. It's about ingraining a mindset where data-driven decision-making becomes habitual across the organization. Such a culture celebrates successes achieved through data insights, promotes transparency in data handling and usage, and encourages a mindset among employees where data is not just a tool but an integral part of the decision-making process. Employees are motivated to engage with data actively, to question, explore, and utilize these insights to guide their choices and actions.

Cultivating a data culture demands a concerted shift in perspective at every organizational level. Leadership plays a critical role in this paradigm shift. Leaders can spearhead this transformation by exemplifying the value of data, setting a tone that underscores its importance, and investing in comprehensive data literacy programs. They are the catalysts in demonstrating how data can be a formidable asset in strategic decision-making and daily operations.

Integral to nurturing a data culture is equipping employees with the necessary tools and training. This empowerment enables them to access, analyze, and interpret data effectively, fostering a sense of ownership and confidence in making data-driven decisions. Such empowerment aligns individual contributions with the organization's broader goals, thereby embedding data culture into the very fabric of daily operations.

The convergence of the five pillars of data readiness – data quality, governance, accessibility, integration, and culture – lays a robust foundation for successful AI implementation. As we stand on the cusp of a future dominated by AI, reshaping every facet of our lives, the significance of data readiness becomes increasingly pronounced.

In the realm of AI, the importance of data readiness extends far beyond the mere possession of data. It encompasses ensuring that data is of high quality, governed with precision, easily accessible, and integrated seamlessly. It's about fostering an environment that values data and comprehends its immense potential to drive insights, foster innovation, and guide strategic initiatives.

As we embark on this journey into the ever-expanding universe of AI, it's imperative to acknowledge the critical role of data as the driving force. Without adequate preparation and readiness, data remains an untapped resource, unable to unleash the full power of AI. Data readiness is not just about gearing up for the present challenges; it's about setting the stage for a future where AI and data synergies unlock uncharted potential. This synergy promises a future brimming with opportunities, challenges, and the potential for transformative advancements.

By strongly emphasizing data readiness, we can ensure that our AI systems are functional, reliable, and credible. It's a strategic approach that prepares us not just for the immediate horizon but for a future where AI and data work in tandem, unlocking possibilities we are just beginning to explore. In ensuring our data is primed and ready, we are laying the groundwork for the next exciting chapter in the evolution of AI – a chapter replete with immense possibilities, daunting challenges, and the promise of a brighter, more informed tomorrow.

FINAL THOUGHTS

As we close the comprehensive discussion in this chapter, we recognize the intricate framework that forms the backbone of successful AI and analytics initiatives. This journey, marked by a steadfast commitment to cultivating a robust data culture, echoes the importance of viewing data beyond mere numbers as a transformative force capable of driving informed decisions and innovative solutions.

As we transition to Chapter 8, we move from the foundational bedrock of data into the dynamic and evolving world of AI. This next chapter takes us deeper into AI, exploring how organizations can transition from data-ready to AI-ready. The leap from data readiness to AI readiness is not just a step but a strategic evolution, requiring a shift in mindset, processes, and culture.

In "AI readiness," we delve into the state of preparedness necessary for organizations to embrace AI responsibly. This encompasses assessing current capabilities, identifying gaps, and fortifying strengths across key dimensions like AI quality, governance, accessibility, integration, and culture. Chapter 8 promises to illuminate the path for organizations to navigate the complexities of AI adoption, ensuring that their journey is not only technologically sound but also ethically grounded and culturally attuned.

As we embark on this journey through Chapter 8, we anticipate a comprehensive exploration of AI's transformative potential, guided by pragmatic roadmaps, dedicated leadership, and organizational alignment. This exploration is crucial, as AI is not just another tool in the business arsenal; it represents a holistic transformation, reshaping the fabric of how decisions are made and operations are conducted. The insights and strategies laid out in Chapter 8 will be pivotal for organizations aiming to harness the full power of AI, turning its promise into a reality.

KEY TAKEAWAYS AND ACTIONS

DATA QUALITY

- **Actionable Steps:** Establish a data quality management practice, define data quality standards, implement metrics and audits, and identify and remediate data issues.
- **Implementation:** Collaborate across departments to define quality standards, routinely measure data against these standards, and ensure continuous improvement and adherence to data quality.

DATA GOVERNANCE

- **Actionable Steps:** Implement data governance frameworks encompassing policies, standards, roles, processes, and metadata management.
- **Implementation:** Establish clear data governance policies, define roles and responsibilities, and utilize metadata to improve data discovery and usage.

DATA ACCESSIBILITY

- **Actionable Steps:** Democratize data access across the organization while maintaining security and compliance.
- **Implementation:** Develop policies for data access, invest in technology for secure data sharing, and promote ethical data culture.

DATA INTEGRATION

- **Actionable Steps:** Integrate disparate data sources to provide a unified, meaningful, and accessible dataset.
- **Implementation:** Develop a phased approach to data integration, use metadata for data management, and ensure that data models and ETL pipelines are efficient and scalable.

DATA CULTURE

- **Actionable Steps:** Cultivate a data-driven culture within the organization.
- **Implementation:** Lead by example in using data for decision-making, invest in data literacy programs, and provide tools and training for employees to leverage data effectively.

CREATING A COHESIVE STRATEGY

- **Implementation:** Develop a comprehensive strategy encompassing all aspects of data readiness: quality, governance, accessibility, integration, and culture. Each element should be aligned with the organization's overall goals and objectives.

LEADERSHIP AND COMMITMENT

- **Actionable Steps:** Secure commitment from top leadership to drive a data-driven culture.
- **Implementation:** Leadership should actively use data in decision-making, allocate resources for data initiatives, and communicate the value of a data-driven approach.

EMPOWERING EMPLOYEES

- **Actionable Steps:** Provide employees with the necessary tools, training, and access to data.
- **Implementation:** Offer ongoing training and development opportunities in data analysis, ensure access to relevant data, and encourage employees to use data daily.

CELEBRATING SUCCESS

- **Actionable Steps:** Recognize and celebrate data-driven achievements within the organization.
- **Implementation:** Publicly acknowledge teams and individuals who successfully use data to drive improvements, fostering a culture that values data-driven insights.

CONTINUAL IMPROVEMENT

- **Actionable Steps:** Regularly assess and improve data capabilities.
- **Implementation:** Continuously monitor data practices, gather feedback, and implement improvements to ensure data remains valuable.

CHAPTER 8

AI Readiness

INTRODUCTION

Integrating transformative artificial intelligence (AI) requires fundamental shifts in thinking, processes, and culture across organizations. AI is not merely another technology tool bolted onto operations – it necessitates holistic transformation. This journey requires committed leadership, pragmatic roadmaps, and organizational alignment.

This chapter introduces the pivotal concept of AI readiness, which signifies the state of preparedness enabling organizations to adopt AI and unlock its benefits responsibly. Assessing readiness identifies priority gaps, strengths, and areas needing focus. The AI readiness framework examines five key dimensions: AI Quality, Governance, Accessibility, Integration, and Culture. Evaluating these interdependent pillars creates a strategic blueprint guiding organizations toward effective, sustainable AI adoption.

This chapter illuminates how organizations can elevate readiness across technology, policies, processes, and culture by exploring leading practices across each dimension. With commitment and wisdom, AI's immense possibilities can be actualized, elevating products, decisions, and lives. Our shared future relies on galvanizing efforts today to deploy AI responsibly to solve tomorrow's greatest needs.

AI QUALITY

AI Quality signifies the meticulous processes and diligent culture needed to deliver robust, accurate, and reliable AI systems that perform consistently over diverse conditions and timeframes. This requires extensive validation, rigorous testing methodologies, vigilant performance monitoring,

DOI: 10.1201/9781003486725-9

comprehensive data coverage, meticulous data curation, handling of outliers and missing values, bias detection, redundancy checks, transparency, and controls to detect deviations indicative of errors or performance drift rapidly.

Only consider deploying AI systems after first validating accuracy through substantive testing and establishing oversight protocols to monitor ongoing performance in the real world. AI Quality is the bedrock foundation on which all other dimensions of AI success depend. It entails far more than model development alone – organizations must shepherd models from conception through continuous improvement to become genuinely trustworthy.

This chapter delves into pragmatic strategies and leading practices enabling organizations to elevate AI Quality across the extended model lifecycle. We will explore a multifaceted approach encompassing data excellence, model development best practices, monitoring and maintenance, performance testing, explainability, scenario planning, documentation, iteration, evaluation, and cultural commitment. Embracing quality as an enduring journey rather than a one-time achievement unlocks lasting value.

But first, exploring why AI Quality warrants such extensive focus compared to more traditional software applications is prudent. Fundamentally, AI systems exhibit exponentially greater complexity with inherent uncertainties that necessitate a higher bar for trust and safety.

Whereas conventional linear software operates predictably based on programmed logic, AI systems dynamically learn patterns and behaviors from data that are impossible to predict before deployment. The known relationships morph in unpredictable ways as operating conditions change.

Furthermore, AI often drives semi-autonomous or fully autonomous decisions and processes affecting the physical world. Unlike bounded digital apps, errant physical-world output can risk human lives and livelihoods. Unreliable AI-controlling machinery, processes, recommendations, or predictions can yield catastrophic outcomes if not rigorously validated.

Lastly, the probabilistic nature of many advanced AI algorithms inherently allows small margins of prediction errors, unlike traditional deterministic logic, which demands 100% precision. Their performance profiles are characterized by precision-recall tradeoffs and confidence intervals, not binary correctness. However, designers must account for the real-world conditions where such statistical variability may exceed acceptable thresholds.

These distinctions necessitate extensive diligence validating that AI Quality stays within appropriate guardrails matching or exceeding human capabilities for reliability, accuracy, security, and safety across the full breadth of deployment conditions. Achieving this bar is far from automatic – it requires holistic lifecycle practices implemented with commitment. Only rigorous AI Quality paves the road for AI to progress responsibly.

With the pivotal importance of AI Quality delineated, how can organizations strategically build capabilities spanning technology, process, testing, and culture to elevate quality? Let's explore key focus areas enabling mastery:

High-quality training data with sufficient coverage of target scenarios, variability, global diversity, and combinations provides the essential raw material for quality AI. Data must encompass edge cases, anomalies, biases, security attacks, diverse operating conditions, temporal fluctuations, geographies, demographics, cultural contexts, languages, and potential scenario futures.

Data augmentation techniques like GenAI, simulation, synthetics, and perturbation bolster variability. Upstream data governance with monitoring, validation, and master data foundation enhances integrity. Industrial benchmark datasets aid model development while production data fine-tunes real-world performance. Ongoing data management aligns with AI's evolving needs.

Institutionalizing machine learning operations (MLOps) and modeling practices ensure consistent, auditable workflows for requirements tracking, version control, pipeline automation, explainability, iterative validation, human review, staging deployment, and continuous retraining. Cross-functional team collaboration provides multifaceted oversight spanning data, analytics, engineering, compliance, ethics, security, domain experts, and leadership. Development rigor prevents errors or misalignment.

Once operational, continuous model monitoring detects data drift, concept drift, skewed, stale, or unreliable outputs, indicating the need for retraining on new data or logic refinements. Automated pipelines retrain models on streaming data. Feature stores continually provision training datasets. APIs simplify monitoring integration and alert triggering.

Rigorously testing models on immense sample diversity across data combinations, security attacks, production volumes and rates, long-tail scenarios, operational conditions, explainability, and simulated deployments provide invaluable validation before launch. This builds justified confidence in reliability. Techniques include train-test splits, k-fold validation, canary releases, A/B trials, chaos engineering, adversarial simulations, and synthetic use cases.

With a strategic focus across these areas, organizations enhance AI quality from conception through real-world implementation. But this requires translating ambitions into execution. We will now traverse the extended journey from model inception to deployment while spotlighting tangible practices that actualize quality aspirations.

AI initiatives begin with a discovery phase defining the business context, goals, feasibility, and cross-functional team. This foundational stage involves clarifying the specific business needs through user research with target personas, quantifying current state baselines and success metrics through detailed business case analysis, inventorying available training data and infrastructure to create a data sourcing strategy, proactively identifying and mitigating ethics risks across dimensions like bias, fairness, transparency, privacy and security, and forming a complementary cross-disciplinary team encompassing data, AI, engineering, compliance, design, domain expertise, and project management.

In-depth user research, including interviews, journey mapping, surveys, and ethnographic observation, builds empathy and deeply understands problems from the user's perspective. Quantifying current state baselines and modeling success metrics provide concrete targets guiding requirements. Auditing available data and infrastructure uncovers strengths and gaps needing augmentation. Ethics reviews proactively flag potential risks early when mitigation is more feasible. Convening a team combining diverse skills establishes collaborative oversight for quality, transparency, and ethical diligence across the development lifecycle.

With vision, goals, data plan, ethical guardrails, and an integrated team aligned, the discovery phase provides a strategic foundation guiding all downstream efforts toward quality outcomes, optimizing value for users and the business.

With vision, goals, data strategy, ethics review, and a complementary team aligned, the next phase focuses on constructing robust model development and deployment pipelines, selecting optimal algorithms, iterating on model architectures, training models at scale on quality datasets, implementing explainability, and enabling extensive evaluation.

Architecting version-controlled pipelines supporting automation, experiment tracking, explainability methods, staging environments, and efficient retraining integrates foundational infrastructure to enable quality workflows. Carefully selecting candidate algorithms based on use case needs, data characteristics, accuracy and latency constraints, operating conditions, and team skills reduces risks from poor fit.

Iteratively exploring numerous model variations, adjusting architectures, tuning hyperparameters, comparing preprocessing techniques, and tracking performance through structured experiments provides empirical insights for sizing model complexity appropriately. Pipeline automation scales training on curated benchmark datasets partitioned into training, validation, and test subsets meeting requirements.

Implementing explainability using methods like Local Interpretable Model-agnostic Explanations (LIME), Shapley values, and saliency mapping provides transparency into factors influencing predictions. Extensive performance evaluation spanning edge cases, errors, outliers, adversarial attacks, long tail scenarios, and simulated production variability surfaces problematic biases, gaps, and weaknesses.

Cross-team collaboration focused on explainability, transparency, and rigorous evaluation uncovers issues early when remedies require lower effort. This stage converts conceptual models into high-quality trained artifacts ready for thorough validation.

AI GOVERNANCE

While foundational AI Quality principles prevent deviation through ingrained practices, thoughtful AI Governance provides the ethical compass guiding organizations safely through AI adoption. AI Governance encompasses the structures, accountabilities, procedures, and oversight processes implemented across the extended AI model lifecycle to align development, testing, deployment, monitoring, and retirement with organizational values, ethics, regulations, policies, and risk tolerance.

Effective AI Governance ensures projects thoughtfully balance innovation, efficiency, and compliance by reducing risks and providing organizational oversight at crucial checkpoints. It necessitates delineating team member roles to set expectations on ethical responsibilities and boundaries. Proactive risk planning, mitigation, and monitoring are imperative across dimensions like ethics, bias, regulatory compliance, user privacy, data security, safety, transparency, and vulnerability testing.

Vigilantly scanning for biases and ensuring fair, transparent, ethical AI practices are crucial to oversight. Legal and compliance input helps navigate relevant regulatory constraints while upholding security, privacy, and human rights. Lifecycle management protocols carefully track projects from conception, funding, and prototyping through testing, deployment, production monitoring, and eventual retirement or redesign.

With sufficiently mature, holistic AI Governance capabilities rooted across technology, policy, processes, and culture, organizations can steer initiatives safely, unlocking immense potential through accountable, ethical development and deployment over the extended model lifecycle. AI Governance provides ways to ensure the journey leads to broad benefits exceeding any costs to individuals or society. However, achieving this bar requires translating noble principles into consistent, diligent practices across diverse dimensions.

While rigorous AI Quality controls provide the bedrock for reliable and accurate systems, equally crucial guardrails come from comprehensive AI Governance capabilities aligning development, deployment, and monitoring with ethics, values, policies, and risk appetite. AI Governance oversees the structures, procedures, accountabilities, and oversight processes implemented across the AI model lifecycle to ensure initiatives balance innovation, efficiency, safety, and compliance. Mature governance guided by ethical principles steers organizations clear of preventable reputational, financial, and opportunity costs that result from a lack of foresight. It also unlocks lasting competitive advantages through accountable AI that accessibly provides broad value to stakeholders. This section explores pragmatic building blocks for establishing capable AI governance foundations.

Mature AI governance requires clearly defining granular team roles and responsibilities to eliminate ambiguity around ethical oversight expectations. Ethics and risk management obligations should be explicitly detailed per role. Cross-functional checks and balances through milestone reviews ensure accountability across technical, compliance, legal, domain experts, leadership, and external advisors. While intelligently applying automation, ultimate human accountability is imperative for overseeing AI development, testing, deployment, and monitoring at critical checkpoints.

Being proactive is crucial through identifying, planning mitigations for, and monitoring emerging risks across dimensions like ethics, bias, security, privacy, regulations, safety, system abuse, data quality, model drift, public perception, liability, and potential unintended impacts on individuals or groups. Envisioning possible downside scenarios facilitates assessing their likelihood and potential harms, enabling controls through system design rather than relying on optimistic assumptions.

Guidance and approval should come from diverse ethics and risk review boards at milestones based on beneficial outcomes, proportionality, human dignity, and justice principles. Convening external AI ethics boards provides impartial guidance on improving societal benefits and mitigating community risks based on reviewing goals, data, use cases, and safeguards.

Engaging compliance, legal, HR, security, finance, and public policy teams collaboratively in reviews is essential to address biases, privacy, regulations, individual rights, disclosures, restrictions, policies, and obligations. Implementing mechanisms throughout the lifecycle monitors for and mitigates risks like bias, discrimination, opacity, privacy violations, security holes, and other ethics or compliance breaches.

These practices establish capable foundations for AI governance to scale responsibly across the extended lifecycle. However, the pragmatic focus must continually enhance policies, processes, controls, and culture as AI capabilities progress into new frontiers.

Comprehensive lifecycle management is crucial for ingraining ethical development, diligent risk management, and thoughtful oversight across the AI model timeline from conception through retirement. This involves instituting stage gates requiring risk and compliance reviews before projects can proceed from proposals, pilots, development, testing, limited deployment, broad release, maintenance, enhancements, and eventual sunset. Maintaining meticulous version control and configuration management for all AI assets, including components, data, documentation, credentials, and dependencies, ensures full reproducibility, traceability, and accountability.

Once models are deployed, continuous monitoring against benchmarks identifies concept drift, emerging biases, quality deviations, or indicators of model staleness that may necessitate pausing usage or redeployment after root cause analysis. For models reaching the end of useful life, responsible decommissioning procedures cease usage, alert stakeholders, retain records, replace capabilities, migrate consumers per data retention policies, and thoughtfully purge artifacts.

While sound governance principles are crucial, pragmatic execution transforming aspirations into consistent behaviors and demonstrable risk reduction remains imperative. This requires granular documented procedures, embedded technical controls, rapid response protocols, continuous policy alignment with learnings, incentives promoting diligence, heightened oversight of increasingly capable systems, required ethics training, predictive risk modeling, risk knowledge bases, and grassroots cultural norms reinforcing workplace ethics and transparency.

These practices emphasize ethical human oversight, automated control, documented knowledge, aligned priorities, and shared commitment. With maturity across these dimensions, AI governance becomes an indispensable compass guiding organizations responsibly forward on the path to broad societal benefit.

AI ACCESSIBILITY

For AI to transcend isolated prototypes into transformative enterprise-wide capabilities, organizations must diligently ensure emerging solutions become accessible tools users actively employ daily rather than unused prototypes gathering dust. The immense potential of AI is realized when thoughtfully designed systems empower a spectrum of employees to incorporate capabilities seamlessly into their workflows, enhancing individual and collective performance.

Accessibility entails focusing holistically on usability, adoption, training, and multichannel delivery to make AI solutions available and beneficial for intended audiences across roles, locations, languages, devices, and sophistication levels. Success requires deeply understanding target users' needs, designing straightforward interfaces distilling complexity into intuitive interactions, integrating AI into familiar business platforms employees already use, providing comprehensive training resources scaled to different expertise levels, and delivering AI capabilities through employees' preferred omnichannel mix of desktop, mobile, voice, augmented reality, and embedded product experiences.

When made accessible through relentless user focus, AI solutions can evolve from siloed capabilities within technical teams into indispensable intelligent assistants, augmenting productivity across an enterprise's entire workforce. Thoughtful accessibility practices multiply the benefits of AI investments substantially by allowing more minds to safely and effectively apply AI, unlocking exponential value.

Let's explore leading strategies and pragmatic approaches to make AI accessible, enabling organizations to transition promising projects from functional prototypes into user-friendly tools that improve individual and collective outcomes:

At its essence, accessibility means intended users across the organization can easily understand, interact with, and adopt AI capabilities into their daily workflows in a way that meaningfully amplifies their potential. User experience design is pivotal in determining whether technically proficient AI prototypes leap into actively utilized tools – or fade into obscurity from user indifference.

While user experience principles are well known for their role in digital interfaces and mobile apps, they become even more pivotal for AI systems, given the inherent complexity users must navigate. Excellent user experience elevates ease of use as a primary driver shaping system design and AI implementation. Critical user experience success factors include:

Progressive disclosure carefully sequences interactions, only revealing advanced capabilities contextually when needed to prevent overload. Intuitive layout and visual hierarchy guide users through logical next steps aligned with goals. Simplified workflows distill multistep processes into streamlined paths for critical tasks. Embedded assistance provides in-context guidance and support to smooth adoption. Inclusive language and designs align with user sophistication levels. Continuous iteration via user input rapidly improves experiences.

Broad adoption flourishes when the interface becomes a transparent medium for users' goals, and AI seamlessly solves their pain points through empathetic design. User experience sets the stage for transitioning raw AI prototypes into responsive assistants users trust.

Successfully ushering employees through significant AI-driven workflow changes requires more than elegant technical design. Thoughtful change management increases adoption by seamlessly transitioning individuals and the organization from current working methods to new processes enabled by AI capabilities. This is achieved through proactive communication, training, and multichannel support.

Essential elements of effective AI change management include identifying all stakeholders affected, conducting impact assessments to mitigate challenges, ensuring executives visibly align messaging and participate in early pilots, creating phased transition roadmaps for coordinated rollout, fostering networks of AI power users across units as evangelists, closely tracking usage metrics, and providing ongoing support channels smoothing adoption barriers.

With rigorous planning and empathy for those experiencing change, AI capabilities shift from empty hype into active daily use, empowering employees to accomplish more. Managed well, AI-driven transformation can unlock immense value by accelerating and smoothing adoption across an enterprise.

Even the most elegant AI systems with executive solid sponsorship remain shelf-ware unless users develop sufficient proficiency to harness capabilities effectively. Developing robust training programs tailored to diverse needs across roles and sophistication levels proves crucial for accessibility.

While one-size-fits-all training fails, leading practices should train across modalities, blending virtual instruction, micro-learning, hands-on labs, self-paced modules, and expert coaching. Content tailoring to the needs of specific roles and tasks makes concepts relatable. Practically applied scenarios build tangible capabilities, improving outcomes. Communities reinforce the sharing of tips and tricks. Skills credentialing, micro-certifications, and coaching networks validate and reward proficiency milestones to motivate further progress through levels of mastery.

With continuous, immersive training empowering workers, AI usage flourishes. Knowledge unlocks access, transforming tentative exploration into confident adoption.

Accessibility relies on delivering AI capabilities through channels matching employees' context and preferences rather than forcing change. AI should span mobile apps, conversational interfaces, browser-based apps, tools embedded in familiar productivity software, Augmented Reality (AR)/Virtual Reality (VR) platforms, and offline modes.

This omnichannel approach weaves AI seamlessly into the daily fabric experienced by users rather than requiring them to switch contexts constantly. Meeting employees on their terms accelerates habitual usage and dependability across scenarios. AI adapts to user needs rather than demanding rigid adoption of proprietary platforms.

Long-term accessibility relies on participatory design mechanisms continuously evolving AI capabilities to meet users' changing needs through input, feedback, and enhancement suggestions. This empowers users to actively co-create their AI tools.

Strategies include continually soliciting user needs through interviews and research, engaging user communities in generative design workshops and focus groups, establishing customer advisory boards providing insights, implementing in-product feedback features, and incentivizing product teams to rapidly iterate based on user requests.

With relentless user focus spanning research, co-creation, and improvement, organizations transform inaccessible, isolated AI prototypes into responsive, trusted assistants that users actively adopt. AI's benefits compound when capabilities continuously adapt to user needs through participatory enhancement. Our collective future depends on empowering more minds to access AI's possibilities safely.

AI INTEGRATION

Transitioning AI capabilities from isolated prototypes into integral drivers of value necessitates comprehensive integration across systems, processes, and workflows. The most transformative AI solutions become embedded into the day-to-day operational fabric rather than remaining siloed tools adjunct from core operations.

Thoughtful integration weaves together data, systems, processes, and insights – enabling AI to interoperate bidirectionally with users and surrounding technologies. This manifests AI as an augmented intelligence enhancing nearly every function and user rather than an ancillary utility.

The benefits of seamless AI integration are immense, yet achieving this outcome requires diligent orchestration. Success demands collaboratively unifying data management, pipelines, platforms, interfaces, security protocols, monitoring, and iteration cycles across IT and business teams. With patient work addressing interdependencies, AI can synthesize previously disconnected signals and respond dynamically to emerging needs.

Let's explore leading integration strategies and pragmatic approaches allowing organizations to elevate AI from narrow standalone capabilities into intelligent services woven throughout operations:

Integration begins with data – providing models seamless access to comprehensive, high-quality datasets through modern data architecture. This enables training, prediction, and continuous learning without manual data wrangling and piecemeal transfer.

Modern data platforms provide AI solutions to read and query access to integrated, trustworthy data via APIs, pipelines, and feature stores. This connects models directly to data lakes housing unified enterprise datasets from transaction systems, operational databases, instrumentation signals, IoT feeds, and more. With accessible, automatically refreshed data, models operate with broad inputs, furthering accuracy.

Architectural integration empowers models to digest more signals and contexts, allowing ever-finer inferences and recommendations. It also enables predictive models to detect data quality issues and outdated training labels, recommending data governance enhancements over time. Thoughtful data integration lays a robust foundation.

On top of integrated data, MLOps platforms provide a robust springboard for scalable model development, deployment, monitoring, and governance. Leveraging proven platforms accelerates capability delivery while avoiding undifferentiated coding from scratch.

Industrialized MLOps platforms offer model hosting, version control, CI/CD pipeline automation, reproducibility, model monitoring, explainability tools, bias detection, model registries, and governance modules in ready-to-use packages. Built thoughtfully, these platforms encode leading practices while remaining adaptable to new techniques and use cases.

Rather than custom coding core model ops capabilities, leveraging robust platforms allows organizations to focus innovation on breakthrough techniques and creative business integrations. Platforms also facilitate collaboration across large, distributed teams of data scientists, engineers, and subject matter experts. With scalable MLOps systems underpinning models, the pace of sustainable integration accelerates.

Transitioning beyond platforms, integration further necessitates embedding AI capabilities into surrounding line-of-business tools, workflows, and legacy systems. This weaves AI seamlessly into the user experience while avoiding disjointed context switching.

Integration options range from light-touch API connections allowing systems to exchange data to deep customization plugging predictive intelligence into complex operational environments. Tactics include exposing models through prediction APIs, developing connectors to on-premise and cloud apps, embedding components into mobile experiences and containerization, and providing portable AI modules for varied deployment footprints.

Ideally, users engage AI intuitively through familiar interfaces rather than specialty portals. For example, supply chain AI could be infused into Enterprise Resource Planning (ERP) system order screens via dynamically generated insights panels. Predictive engagements would flow naturally rather than requiring disruptive system hopping. Thoughtful embedding delights users.

To sustain value, integrated AI solutions require ongoing monitoring, evaluation, and continuous improvement, adjusting to evolving conditions over time. This necessitates technical performance monitoring and user feedback flows to identify enhancements.

Monitoring techniques include canary deployments to detect deviations, A/B trials benchmark variant models, and blue-green phased rollouts sequence upgrades. Broad user feedback capture proactively surfaces User Experience (UX) refinements and feature needs. Insights fuel rapid iteration and deployment cycles, adapting models to changing needs and data without prolonged development bottlenecks.

With constant learning loops built across technical and user inputs, integrated AI capabilities maintain relevance over time. The integration enables AI to reinvent operations versus continually operating as fixed-point solutions. The monitoring, evaluation, and refinement cycle becomes the system's heartbeat.

Lastly, practical integration benefits profoundly from participatory design, engaging diverse cross-functional teams and user communities.

This mitigates integration blind spots through collaborative creativity, feedback, and collective accountability for solving adoption barriers.

Inclusive design workshops, hackathons, and implementation clinics allow contributors across IT, analytics, business operations, end users, management, and more to shape solutions transparently. Actively solicited feedback prevents isolation. Retrospective analyses empower blunt truths and growth through failures. With collective input shaping priorities, AI integration aligns sustainably with human needs.

The interplay of people, processes, and technologies makes or breaks successful AI adoption. With diligent orchestration, AI transitions from hype and isolated proofs of concept into intelligent services woven through routines and relationships, amplifying enterprise potential. The journey requires patience yet yields consequential payoffs when aligned with user needs.

AI CULTURE

While technical capabilities provide essential foundations, organizations cannot realize AI's full potential without complementary cultural evolution embracing new mindsets, values, and behaviors. Ultimately, cultural readiness will determine whether AI remains an isolated tool versus becoming intrinsically woven into the collective way of working.

Positive AI culture powers exponential results by catalyzing technology's potential through engaged users, grassroots enthusiasm, ethical application, seamless embedding into workflows, participatory design, continuous hands-on learning, and ubiquitous refinement. It breathes life into AI initiatives.

Conversely, negative AI culture impedes outcomes through indifference to training needs, lack of executive prioritization, siloed tool mentalities, disconnect from user difficulties, deficient transparency, uncoordinated governance, lone-wolf development habits, and ignorance of downside risks. An organization's culture profoundly shapes the difference between shallow AI adoption and truly embracing AI holistically.

Evolving collaborative mindsets and behaviors requires consistent leadership signaling, immersive training, incentives, community building, and rewards reinforcing desired cultural values. With commitment over time, AI can transform from a bolted-on novelty into an intrinsic way of organizational life.

Cultural transformation relies on authentic groundswell enthusiasm and viral peer-to-peer sharing, reinforcing AI's benefits. Top-down messaging alone falls flat without supporting grassroots energy. Tactics to spur organic momentum include cultivating internal influencers through early AI accelerator programs, hosting morale-building spirit weeks, encouraging grassroots meetups, empowering peer-to-peer teaching through AI clinics, and publicly recognizing adopters.

Visible curiosity, voluntary tinkering, and willingness to learn outside formal roles signal rising engagement. With sincerely cultivated grassroots excitement, AI's momentum feeds on itself into an autonomous movement.

While grassroots energy proves essential, visible leadership commitment provides urgency and resources catalyzing culture change. Executives must demonstrate commitment by dedicating meaningful budgets, personally participating in early capability pilots, visibly aligning messaging, and clearing adoption roadblocks.

Leaders can signal AI priorities by speaking regularly on its strategic importance, sponsoring high-potential projects, reviewing adoption metrics and costs, resolving resourcing gaps slowing progress, and enthusiastically engaging in capability pilots, hackathons, and training. When leaders prioritize AI in deeds more than words, urgency cascades through the organization.

Maximizing AI's benefits requires a culture encouraging adventure, creativity, flexibility, and lifelong learning. Employees should feel psychologically safe exploring new capabilities without fear of failure. Measured experimentation, intelligent risk-taking, and openly sharing learnings signal a growth mindset.

Tactics to catalyze continuous learning include providing microfunding for exploration projects, allowing time for self-directed learning, establishing innovation forums for idea sharing, and incentivizing capability building through credentialing programs. Frequent exposure to innovations spurs ongoing development. With a spirit of discovery fueled, curiosity becomes the cultural norm.

Without cultural incentives guiding developers and users toward responsible, ethical design and usage habits, well-intended AI risks unethical consequences. Instilling strong ethics requires establishing clear guidelines combined with accountability mechanisms.

Example incentives include incorporating responsible AI criteria into performance reviews, mandating ethics training for project participation, requiring diverse review boards, and embedding measured bias detection into model testing procedures. Celebrating outstanding ethics adherence reinforces principles organizationally. With both top-down guidance and peer reinforcement around ethical behaviors, employees make principled choices instinctually.

Organizations must democratize data access to multiply benefits through broad participation – dissolving restrictive monopolies. Providing strategic data-sharing platforms, self-service analytics tools, data fellowships for novices, and internal data marketplaces facilitates access. Sandboxes enable low-risk exploration. Grassroots literacy programs build viral enthusiasm. With data as a creatively shared public good, innovation can flourish bottom-up.

With AI solutions requiring ongoing refinement responding to user feedback and changing conditions, culture should incent rapid iteration over rigid, long development cycles. Empowering agile delivery, instant user input channels, automation streamlining updates, and failure-positive mindsets drawing learnings from each experience all accelerate continuous improvement. Normalizing constant incremental enhancements sustains relevance over time as needs evolve.

Cultural change is rooted in aligning priorities, building empathy, and strengthening shared accountability across data, technology, business, and user communities. AI solutions should enhance lives holistically across the organization. Establishing cross-boundary teams, mandating rotational assignments between areas, conducting empathy-building design exercises, and celebrating collaborative innovation reinforce shared mission. With collective orientation united around human needs, technology enables elevating potential. Our shared future relies on infusing AI transformation with a unifying collaborative spirit.

While foundational technical capabilities and data resources provide essential springboards, evolved culture determines the scope of advancement. Organizations cannot bolster AI superficially through skills and platforms alone – they must reignite curiosity, unite teams, actively model desired mindsets, and nurture grassroots passion. With time and consistency, the payoffs compound as AI becomes woven intrinsically into individual behaviors and collective identity. But culture only evolves through active commitment to lead people's hearts and minds toward purposeful growth. Our joint readiness hinges on cultural maturity.

AI ETHICS AND INCLUSIVITY

In the vast and intricate landscape of AI, cultivating an ethical and inclusive culture is paramount, akin to the meticulous care a master chef devotes to fostering a culture of excellence in a world-class kitchen. For AI to truly transform an organization, it must be embraced with an enthusiasm that transcends the sheer allure of technology, grounded firmly in human values and responsible application. This transformation demands an unwavering commitment from organizations to establish and uphold responsible AI policies, demonstrate leadership commitment, and engage in immersive training and literacy initiatives. These endeavors are not merely procedural but the lifeblood of aligning workforce skills with a broad, ethical, and inclusive vision.

Organizations embarking on this journey must first lay the groundwork with robust policies that codify expected behaviors and operational guidelines. These policies are the compass that guides ethical AI development and usage, encapsulating crucial aspects such as fairness, accountability, transparency, and privacy. They must articulate these principles clearly and provide actionable steps for their realization. However, the mere existence of these policies is not enough. Leadership commitment to these policies, demonstrated through consistent communication and strategic investments, is critical. It reinforces their importance, ensuring they are more than words on paper but principles ingrained in the organizational ethos.

Beyond policy formulation, immersive training programs play a pivotal role in embedding these ethical considerations into the very fabric of AI development. These programs should be experiential, offering hands-on experiences that vividly illustrate the real-world implications of AI decisions. Crucially, such training should not be confined to technical teams alone. It must encompass all employees, fostering a company-wide understanding and dialogue around AI ethics. This broad-based approach demystifies AI, making it a shared enterprise rather than the sole province of tech specialists.

Further amplifying this understanding are grassroots literacy initiatives. These initiatives cultivate a shared language and principles that guide every individual in the organization. They act as a bridge, connecting various departments and teams and facilitating a unified approach to AI development and application. The goal is to create an environment where AI is not just a tool but a collaborator, enhancing human capabilities ethically, responsibly, and inclusively.

In addition to these internal mechanisms, creating forums where practitioners from across teams can collaborate and share best practices is essential. These forums should be safe for open, honest discussion, allowing employees to voice concerns, propose solutions, and share insights related to responsible AI development, deployment, and monitoring. This collaborative approach fosters a culture of continuous learning and improvement, ensuring that AI practices evolve in response to emerging ethical challenges and opportunities.

The journey toward an ethical AI landscape is continuous and requires a multifaceted approach. It involves establishing and refining policies and nurturing an organizational culture that values ethical considerations as much as technical achievements. This culture is shaped through various means: consistently signaling priorities, celebrating behaviors that exemplify ethical AI practices, establishing feedback loops, and creating incentives that align with these values.

Key to this cultural shift is ensuring diverse voices are heard in the design and oversight of AI systems. Diversity here goes beyond demographic representation; it encompasses a diversity of thought, experience, and perspective. Multidisciplinary teams bring together varied viewpoints, which are instrumental in identifying potential biases and ethical pitfalls in algorithms and data. These teams act as the organization's moral compass, guiding AI development in a manner that considers its broad impacts.

Inclusive oversight committees also play a critical role. Comprising diverse internal and external stakeholders, these committees oversee AI standards and practices, providing the necessary checks and balances to ensure alignment with ethical principles. They offer transparency in operations and a platform for addressing and remedying potential conflicts or harms.

This holistic approach to AI ethics and inclusivity is not a one-time effort but a continuous process. It involves regularly revisiting and revising policies, staying abreast of the latest developments in AI ethics, and maintaining open communication channels across all levels of the organization. Only through such sustained and concerted efforts can organizations ensure that their AI initiatives are technologically advanced, ethically sound, and inclusive.

In conclusion, fostering an ethical and inclusive AI culture is a multifaceted endeavor that requires a concerted effort across policy formulation, training programs, internal forums, and cultural initiatives. The journey demands persistence, commitment, and a willingness to evolve continuously. By steadfastly nurturing these aspects, organizations can ensure their AI capabilities are innovative, trustworthy, and elevating for all stakeholders.

FINAL THOUGHTS

As we conclude this chapter, we've navigated the intricate landscape of preparing for a future deeply intertwined with AI. This journey has taken us through the pillars of AI readiness, emphasizing the need for robust quality, comprehensive governance, universal accessibility, seamless integration, and a supportive, ethical culture. We've seen how these elements are critical in shaping an environment where AI is not just a technological marvel but a transformative force across organizations.

As we transition to Chapter 9, we're stepping into an even more dynamic and burgeoning field of AI. GenAI, with its ability to create new, original content ranging from text to multimedia, represents a leap forward in AI's capabilities and potential impact. Chapter 9 aims to guide us through the nuances of preparing for GenAI, which extends beyond the realms of traditional AI applications.

Chapter 9 promises to dive deep into the nuances of generative AI, exploring how it differs from traditional AI and the unique considerations it brings. We will explore the need for holistic readiness across the familiar yet expanded dimensions of technology, governance, accessibility, integration, and culture, all tailored to the unique context of GenAI.

As we embark on this exploration, we'll uncover the practices and strategies necessary to harness GenAI responsibly and creatively. From ensuring the quality and reliability of generative content to governing its ethical use, from making these tools accessible and understandable to seamlessly integrating them into existing systems and processes and fostering a culture that embraces and drives innovation with GenAI – these will be our focus areas.

The journey ahead in Chapter 9 is not just about understanding GenAI but about mastering it to benefit humanity while responsibly navigating its challenges. It's about preparing ourselves to harness this powerful technology for good, ensuring we are ready to shape a future where GenAI amplifies human creativity and solves some of our most significant challenges.

As we turn this page, we stand at the brink of a new era in AI that holds immense possibilities and requires our thoughtful and strategic approach. Let's step into "Generative AI Readiness" with the insights and learnings from our journey through AI readiness, ready to embrace and shape this new frontier.

KEY TAKEAWAYS AND ACTIONS

AI QUALITY

- **Actionable Steps:** Focus on developing highly accurate and reliable AI systems.
- **Implementation:** Establish rigorous testing methodologies, monitor performance, and maintain comprehensive data coverage to ensure the AI systems are robust and reliable.

AI GOVERNANCE

- **Actionable Steps:** Implement structured governance to responsibly guide AI development and deployment.
- **Implementation:** Establish clear governance frameworks and procedures, focusing on ethical considerations, bias detection, and regulation compliance.

AI ACCESSIBILITY

- **Actionable Steps:** Make AI tools user-friendly and widely accessible within the organization.
- **Implementation:** Develop intuitive interfaces and comprehensive training programs. Integrate AI seamlessly into existing workflows and systems.

AI INTEGRATION

- **Actionable Steps:** Embed AI capabilities deeply into organizational processes and systems.
- **Implementation:** Focus on data architecture and machine learning operations platforms for efficient integration. Regularly update and refine AI solutions based on user feedback and changing requirements.

AI CULTURE

- **Actionable Steps:** Cultivate an organizational culture that supports and enhances AI adoption.
- **Implementation:** Foster a culture of continuous learning and ethical AI practice. Encourage leadership commitment and grassroots enthusiasm for AI.

AI ETHICS AND INCLUSIVITY

- **Actionable Steps:** Ensure ethical AI practices and inclusivity in AI design and decision-making.
- **Implementation:** Develop and enforce policies for ethical AI, set up diverse oversight committees, and engage in participatory design for diverse stakeholder input.

Generative Artificial Intelligence Readiness

INTRODUCTION

Artificial intelligence (AI) has spawned as a transformative capability, reshaping the contours of technology and innovation: Generative Artificial Intelligence (GenAI). This novel derivative of AI, capable of synthesizing new content dynamically – from text and images to audio, video, software code, and multimedia content – stands at the forefront of a technological revolution. By learning patterns from diverse training datasets, GenAI creates unimagined possibilities.

However, the path to effectively harnessing this technology extends beyond those traversed by traditional AI. It demands a comprehensive readiness strategy encompassing technological aspects, governance, accessibility, integration, and cultural adaptation. This chapter delves deep into these five essential pillars, delineating the pivotal distinctions between GenAI and traditional AI methods. It sheds light on how organizations can seamlessly and responsibly integrate generative models into their operations, augmenting human creativity and potential.

As we embark on this exploration, we recognize the extraordinary potential of GenAI as a catalyst for innovation, efficiency, and personalized solutions. Our approach to preparing for this technology today will significantly shape the future, steering GenAI as a force for good. It promises to address some of humanity's most pressing challenges, provided we lay a solid foundation across multiple dimensions – data, algorithms, governance, skills,

DOI: 10.1201/9781003486725-10

literacy, and ethical application. Through a meticulous understanding and mastery of these pillars, we can navigate the intricacies of GenAI, ensuring its safe, accountable, and positive contribution to society.

The journey through the subsequent sections – Quality, Governance, Accessibility, Integration, and Culture – remains unchanged, each meticulously crafted to guide you through the nuances of GenAI readiness. These sections will provide you with a comprehensive understanding and actionable insights, equipping you to navigate the transformative world of GenAI with confidence and foresight.

As we progress through this chapter, we stand at the cusp of a new era in AI. An era where the confluence of human intellect and GenAI's capabilities can redefine the boundaries of innovation and progress. Let us embark on this journey with a vision to harness this powerful technology, shaping a future that resonates with the aspirations of a rapidly evolving digital society.

GenAI QUALITY

In GenAI, the emphasis on quality is not just a technical requirement but a strategic imperative. Quality in GenAI encompasses a broad spectrum of attributes, including performance, reliability, robustness, and versatility, each playing a crucial role in successfully deploying and accepting these systems.

Performance is the bedrock upon which GenAI models are evaluated. The accuracy and precision of these models are critical, necessitating rigorous validation processes before deployment. This evaluation is not a static process but an ongoing commitment. It involves continuous testing and maintenance to adapt to the changing data and business requirements landscape, ensuring that GenAI models consistently deliver high-quality, accurate outputs.

Robustness in GenAI refers to the resilience of these models. A robust model can handle unexpected inputs or changes in its operational environment without significant degradation in performance. These models must be designed to manage missing or incomplete data and adapt to changes in data distribution. This robustness is paramount for maintaining the integrity and utility of GenAI across various applications and scenarios.

Reliability, another critical dimension, pertains to the consistent performance of GenAI models over time and across different input data sets. Consistency is essential for maintaining user trust in AI systems. Organizations must establish processes to sustain and enhance model quality over time, regularly updating models based on new data and evolving business needs. This ongoing process ensures that GenAI remains a reliable tool for decision-making and operations.

Versatility in GenAI is about the model's ability to operate effectively across different tasks or contexts. A versatile GenAI model can adapt to various problems or scenarios, maximizing the return on investment in AI technologies. This versatility is essential in today's fast-paced business environment, where pivoting and adapting to new challenges is a competitive advantage.

Furthermore, a robust mechanism to manage model failures, adversarial attacks, outliers, exceptions, biases, and data leakage is essential for maintaining the quality of GenAI. Addressing hallucinations or redundancies in model predictions is also crucial. These models must handle noise in inputs and anomalies in outputs efficiently, ensuring their interpretability and generalizability.

The impact of GenAI models on business outcomes should be a regular evaluation focus. This assessment goes beyond direct effects such as improved productivity or cost reduction. It should also consider indirect impacts like enhanced customer satisfaction or improved decision-making capabilities. Understanding these impacts helps fine-tune the GenAI models to align better with business goals and customer expectations.

In addition to technical robustness, it is imperative to consider the ethical implications of GenAI. Ethical considerations play a significant role in determining these technologies' long-term viability and acceptance. This includes ensuring that the data used for training these models is free from biases that could lead to unfair or discriminatory outcomes. Ethical governance frameworks should guide the development and deployment of GenAI, embedding principles of fairness, transparency, and accountability into these systems.

Moreover, the integration of GenAI into existing workflows and systems should be seamless and user-friendly. User experience (UX) plays a critical role in the adoption and effectiveness of these technologies. The more intuitive and integrated these solutions are, the higher their utility and acceptance among end-users.

The journey to realizing the full potential of GenAI involves a complex interplay of technical excellence, ethical considerations, UX, and business alignment. Organizations must adopt a holistic approach, focusing not only on the technical capabilities of these models but also on their ethical implications, integration into business processes, and the overall impact on stakeholders. By doing so, businesses can harness the power of GenAI to drive innovation, efficiency, and growth while upholding the highest standards of quality and ethical responsibility.

GenAI GOVERNANCE

Governance in GenAI presents a complex and nuanced challenge distinctively different from traditional machine learning. This difference stems from the innovative nature of GenAI and its potential impacts, necessitating a governance approach encompassing clear roles and responsibilities, sophisticated risk management, ethical considerations, and stringent compliance measures.

In the realm of GenAI, allocating roles and responsibilities transcends the typical boundaries seen in traditional machine learning. Here, stakeholders from various domains collaborate, bringing together a mix of creativity and technical expertise unique to GenAI projects. This interdisciplinary approach demands a governance structure that effectively manages diverse contributions and aligns them with the project's goals. Data scientists, engineers, domain experts, managers, executives, and external partners must clearly understand their roles, contributing to a cohesive effort that harnesses the full potential of GenAI.

Risk management in GenAI takes on a broader scope, encompassing technical and operational risks and ethical, reputational, and strategic risks. The ability of GenAI to create new, synthetic forms of data or content introduces novel risks. Issues such as generating realistic yet inauthentic data, the potential for misinformation, and concerns over intellectual property rights become paramount. Governance frameworks must, therefore, be robust and dynamic, capable of identifying, assessing, and mitigating these unique risks while also being adaptable to the continuously evolving nature of GenAI technologies.

The ethical landscape of GenAI is particularly complex. Issues of bias, fairness, transparency, and privacy are amplified in systems capable of generating entirely new data or content. Governance in this context must ensure that GenAI aligns with fundamental human rights and values, addressing the ethical implications of both the algorithms and their outputs. This requires ongoing ethical scrutiny integrated into every stage of the AI lifecycle, from design and development to deployment and use.

Compliance with organizational policies and legal regulations poses a dual challenge in GenAI governance. Navigating the intricacies of data protection, privacy laws, and industry-specific regulations becomes more challenging due to the novel outputs of GenAI systems. The rapid evolution of these technologies often outpaces existing regulatory frameworks, necessitating a governance approach that is both proactive and flexible, capable of adapting to new technological advancements and regulatory changes.

Governing GenAI demands reevaluating and adapting traditional governance models used in machine learning. The unique characteristics and implications of GenAI require a comprehensive and flexible governance framework that is multidisciplinary, risk-focused, ethically vigilant, and compliant with evolving legal standards. As the adoption of GenAI grows, organizations must prioritize developing governance structures that can effectively navigate these technologies' complexities and transformative potential. This involves a proactive and forward-thinking approach, ensuring that GenAI is leveraged responsibly, ethically, and effectively, aligning with the organization's and society's broader objectives and values.

GenAI ACCESSIBILITY

In the world of GenAI, accessibility emerges as a paramount consideration, distinctly different from traditional machine learning in scope and impact. This aspect of GenAI encompasses not just the physical availability of tools and resources but also extends to the proficiency and empowerment of staff across various organizational levels.

The challenge of ensuring accessibility in GenAI begins with the provision of tools, platforms, data, models, outputs, documentation, APIs, infrastructure, software, and hardware. Making these resources physically accessible to all relevant staff lays the groundwork for effective implementation. However, the concept of accessibility transcends physical availability. It includes ensuring that these resources are approachable and usable for staff, regardless of their technical background.

To fully leverage the potential of GenAI, team members need to be equipped with the necessary skills and knowledge. This requirement marks a significant departure from traditional machine learning, where the focus may be more on technical expertise. In the realm of GenAI, training programs, workshops, and seminars become essential tools for enhancing AI literacy. They need to cater to those directly handling AI tools and platforms and those in non-technical roles who will interact with or be impacted by AI outputs. This broad-based approach to training is crucial in creating a workforce aware of the capabilities and limitations of GenAI and capable of applying these technologies effectively and ethically.

Moreover, managing the user interface (UI) and user experience (UX) of GenAI systems is integral to accessibility. Given the complexity and novel nature of GenAI outputs, these systems require intuitive, user-friendly interfaces and are tailored to the needs and preferences of a diverse range of users. Special attention must be paid to the accessibility needs of individuals with disabilities to ensure inclusivity. This aspect of accessibility is critical in ensuring that GenAI tools are functional but also inclusive and equitable.

GenAI also necessitates a unique focus on inclusivity. The potential impact of GenAI extends beyond the technical teams to encompass various user groups both within and outside the organization. This broader impact requires a concerted effort to ensure that GenAI tools and systems are designed with inclusivity. It is about understanding and addressing the varied needs of different user groups, providing that these innovative tools and systems are as universally accessible as possible.

Accessibility in GenAI is a multifaceted and dynamic concept that requires a comprehensive approach. It involves ensuring the physical availability of resources, enhancing literacy across the organization, designing user-friendly and inclusive interfaces, and fostering a culture of inclusivity. As GenAI continues to evolve and permeate various aspects of business and society, prioritizing accessibility and inclusivity will be crucial in unlocking its full potential. Through this holistic approach, organizations can harness the transformative power of GenAI, not only as a driver of innovation and efficiency but also as an enabler of inclusive and sustainable growth.

GenAI INTEGRATION

Integrating GenAI into organizational structures presents unique challenges distinct from traditional machine learning. GenAI, by its very nature, requires a holistic approach to integration, ensuring that it becomes an integral part of an organization's systems, processes, and overall strategic framework.

GenAI's integration extends beyond merely embedding it within the organization's IT infrastructure. It demands seamless incorporation into business processes, data sources, other AI and non-AI systems, external systems, cloud services, and edge devices. This comprehensive integration is crucial for unleashing the full potential of GenAI, allowing it to leverage the organization's data and resources comprehensively. It facilitates the smooth flow of information and insights across various segments of the organization, breaking down silos, fostering collaboration, and enhancing the overall effectiveness of operations.

Incorporating GenAI into various systems such as social media platforms, customer relationship management systems, enterprise resource planning systems, human resources, financial, marketing, sales, supply chain, logistics, manufacturing, research and development, operations, legal, risk management, governance, and strategic planning systems is paramount. This wide-ranging integration ensures that the insights generated by GenAI are pertinent and actionable, enabling decision-makers to derive data-driven insights for informed decision-making.

A key challenge in this integration is ensuring that the insights and outputs of GenAI models are relevant and quickly assimilated into the organization's strategic and operational processes. Unlike traditional machine learning models, GenAI can produce novel and highly sophisticated outputs, necessitating a deeper understanding and a more nuanced approach to integration. Organizations must ensure their teams have the knowledge and skills to interpret and apply these insights effectively.

Furthermore, integrating GenAI requires careful consideration of ethical implications. Given its ability to generate new data and content, it's crucial to establish robust ethical guidelines and compliance measures to govern its use. This involves ensuring that the data is bias-free, the models are transparent and accountable, and the outputs align with the organization's ethical standards and societal norms.

Another challenge is the technical aspect of integration. GenAI systems require more advanced computational resources and specialized infrastructure than traditional machine learning models. Organizations must be prepared to invest in the necessary technology and infrastructure to support GenAI's advanced capabilities.

Integrating GenAI into organizational frameworks is a multifaceted endeavor. It requires strategic planning, investment in technology and infrastructure, up-skilling of teams, and a robust ethical framework. It's not just about technological implementation but about aligning GenAI with the organization's broader goals and values. Successfully integrated, GenAI has the potential to transform various aspects of an organization, driving innovation, efficiency, and growth while navigating the unique challenges it presents compared to traditional machine learning.

GenAI CULTURE

In the GenAI landscape, cultivating an organizational culture attuned to its nuances is as crucial as its technical and operational deployment. Unlike traditional machine learning, GenAI introduces unique challenges and opportunities necessitating organizational cultural shifts. This culture encompasses attitudes, beliefs, values, and behaviors associated with GenAI and is pivotal in harnessing its full potential.

The embrace of GenAI across all departments marks a significant departure from traditional machine learning. It involves valuing its role as a technological tool and a key driver in achieving business objectives. This requires fostering a culture of continuous learning and development specifically tailored to the field of GenAI. In this dynamic field, staying abreast of the latest developments and understanding their implications becomes essential for all levels of the organization.

Encouraging and rewarding the successful use of GenAI is fundamental. This goes beyond acknowledging technical achievements; it involves recognizing the innovative application of these technologies in solving complex business problems, driving innovation, and creating new opportunities. Promoting a culture of experimentation and innovation is vital in this context. It empowers teams to explore the capabilities of GenAI beyond conventional boundaries, leading to groundbreaking solutions and advancements.

Collaboration is more critical in GenAI projects than traditional machine learning. The interdisciplinary nature of GenAI demands cooperation between diverse roles – from data scientists and engineers to domain experts and decision-makers. This collaboration is fostered in an environment where transparency in the development and use of GenAI is the norm, and ethical considerations are at the forefront of every initiative.

A culture of diversity and inclusivity within GenAI teams is indispensable. The diverse perspectives a varied team brings enrich the development process, enabling the creation of more robust, innovative, and ethical AI solutions. Sharing knowledge and best practices in GenAI within and across organizations further strengthens this culture, creating a community that learns, innovates, and grows together.

GenAI's potential to transform customer experiences, operational efficiency, and business processes is immense. Its integration enables organizations to make data-driven decisions, automate repetitive tasks, improve product and service quality, reduce costs, and increase profitability. Moreover, it provides a competitive edge, enhances risk management, improves governance, and supports strategic planning. In addressing these multifaceted business aspects, GenAI contributes to immediate operational success and lays the groundwork for long-term, sustainable, and responsible business practices.

In conclusion, the comprehensive evaluation of GenAI within an organization encompasses assessing its quality, governance, accessibility, integration, and, crucially, its culture. Understanding and nurturing this culture is vital to unlocking the transformative potential of GenAI. It involves technological and operational readiness and a readiness to embrace change, foster innovation, and cultivate a forward-thinking mindset. Through this holistic approach, organizations can fully leverage the capabilities of GenAI, enhancing their competitive stance and paving the way for sustainable success in the digital era.

FINAL THOUGHTS

As we close this chapter, we reflect on the transformative journey through the realms of artificial and generative intelligence. This exploration has emphasized these technologies' technical prowess and broader implications, demanding a holistic approach to readiness. We have navigated through the essential pillars of ensuring quality, governance, accessibility, integration, and fostering a supportive culture, tailoring these elements to the unique context of GenAI.

As we transition to Chapter 10, the focus shifts to the intricate compliance landscape in the AI and GenAI world. This chapter marks a crucial pivot from the technical and creative aspects of AI and GenAI to the equally critical facets of regulatory frameworks, ethical considerations, and governance standards. It's about balancing fostering innovation and ensuring societal benefit, a balance that demands a proactive and informed approach to maintain public trust and compliance.

In Chapter 10, we will delve deep into the complexities of compliance in the rapidly evolving domain of AI. We will explore the nuances of regulatory frameworks like the EU AI Act, OECD Principles, and ISO/IEC standards, all of which are pivotal in shaping responsible AI practices globally. Chapter 10 will highlight the importance of ethical AI readiness, underscoring the need for documented ethical practices, independent oversight, and immersive workforce training to maintain the integrity and trustworthiness of AI applications.

Furthermore, Chapter 10 will examine the criticality of AI governance readiness. It will illustrate how robust documentation, change review processes, and model risk management can fortify AI applications against potential risks. Special attention will be given to the unique challenges and considerations surrounding GenAI, advocating for heightened vigilance and stringent oversight to harness its potential responsibly.

As we journey through Chapter 10, we will also investigate the role of standards and certifications in AI and GenAI. Recognizing them as markers of an organization's commitment to ethical and high-quality AI practices, we will delve into how engaging in these areas demonstrates compliance and contributes to the responsible evolution of AI technologies for the greater good of society.

In essence, Chapter 10 is about understanding the critical intersection of AI technology with the world of regulations, ethics, and governance. It's about preparing organizations to navigate this complex landscape, ensuring that the strides made in AI and GenAI are technologically advanced, ethically sound, and compliant with global standards.

As we enter Chapter 10, we are reminded that the journey is not just about mastering technology and navigating the broader societal and regulatory contexts that shape its development and deployment. It is a journey that requires vigilance, adaptability, and a deep commitment to upholding the principles that ensure AI's benefits are realized responsibly and equitably.

KEY TAKEAWAYS AND ACTIONS

GenAI QUALITY

- **Actionable Steps:** Focus on the performance, reliability, robustness, and versatility of GenAI.
- **Implementation:** Conduct regular testing and maintenance, ensure resilience to unexpected inputs, maintain performance consistency, and develop versatile models for various scenarios.

GenAI GOVERNANCE

- **Actionable Steps:** Implement clear governance structures for GenAI initiatives.
- **Implementation:** Define roles and responsibilities, manage risks, address ethical considerations, and ensure compliance with organizational policies and legal regulations.

GenAI ACCESSIBILITY

- **Actionable Steps:** Make GenAI tools and resources accessible to all relevant staff.
- **Implementation:** Offer training programs, ensure physical and knowledge-based access to AI tools, and manage UIs for inclusivity and ease of use.

GenAI INTEGRATION

- **Actionable Steps:** Seamlessly integrate GenAI into the organization's systems and processes.
- **Implementation:** Ensure connectivity with IT infrastructure, business processes, data sources, and other AI and non-AI systems for a unified operational approach.

GenAI CULTURE

- **Actionable Steps:** Foster a positive culture around using GenAI.
- **Implementation:** Encourage experimentation, reward successful AI applications, promote ethical practices, and support a diverse and inclusive environment for AI development and use.

CHAPTER 10

Compliance Readiness

INTRODUCTION

This chapter delves into the intricate landscape of artificial intelligence (AI) and generative Artificial Intelligence (GenAI), highlighting the imperative of comprehensive readiness across the evolving domains of regulations, ethics, governance, and standards. As these technologies rapidly advance, striking a balance between innovation and societal benefit becomes crucial, demanding a proactive approach to ensure public trust.

This chapter navigates the complexities of regulatory frameworks, such as the European Union's Artificial Intelligence Act (EU AI Act), Organization for Economic Cooperation and Development (OECD) Principles, IEEE, and International Organization for Standardization (ISO/IEC) standards, emphasizing their pivotal role in shaping responsible AI practices. We explore the essence of ethical AI readiness, underscoring the importance of documented ethical practices, independent oversight, and immersive workforce training in maintaining the integrity of AI applications.

The narrative further delves into AI governance readiness, illustrating how robust documentation, change review processes, and model risk management practices can fortify AI applications against potential risks. Special attention is given to GenAI, advocating for heightened vigilance and stringent oversight to harness its potential responsibly.

As we journey through this chapter, we will also examine the role of standards and certifications in AI and GenAI, recognizing them as critical markers of an organization's commitment to ethical and high-quality AI practices. By engaging in these areas, organizations demonstrate compliance and contribute to the responsible evolution of AI technologies for societal benefit.

REGULATORY READINESS

As organizations embrace the potential of AI and GenAI, they must contend with a rapidly evolving regulatory landscape. Governments worldwide grapple with AI's potential risks and benefits, and regulatory frameworks are emerging to address these concerns. One of the most significant regulatory developments in recent years is the EU AI Act, which was proposed in 2021.

The EU AI Act seeks to establish a comprehensive framework for developing, deploying, and using AI systems in the EU. The Act covers various topics, including data governance, privacy, algorithmic transparency, and accountability. It also introduces new concepts, such as "high-risk" AI systems, subject to additional requirements and oversight.

One of the critical aspects of the EU AI Act is its focus on ensuring that AI systems are developed and deployed in a way that respects human rights and fundamental freedoms. The Act emphasizes the importance of transparency, explainability, and accountability in AI decision-making processes, and it requires that AI systems be designed with safeguards to prevent potential negative impacts on society.

In addition to the EU AI Act, organizations must consider other regulatory frameworks and guidelines when developing and deploying AI systems. For example, the OECD has developed a set of Principles on Artificial Intelligence, which provide a framework for the responsible development and use of AI. The OECD Principles emphasize the importance of transparency, accountability, and ethical considerations in AI development and deployment.

Similarly, the ISO/IEC has developed a set of standards for AI (see section below), providing guidelines for the ethical design and deployment of AI systems. These standards emphasize the importance of transparency, accountability, and human oversight in AI decision-making processes.

To navigate these regulatory frameworks and guidelines, organizations must establish robust internal infrastructure and processes that ensure compliance with ethical AI practices. This includes developing policies and procedures that address issues such as data governance, algorithmic transparency, and accountability. It also requires establishing roles and responsibilities for ethical AI development and deployment and providing training and resources to ensure employees know the ethical considerations involved in AI development and deployment.

In addition to establishing internal processes and policies, organizations must engage in thoughtful public policy participation. This includes providing input to regulatory agencies on proposed rules and regulations and advocating for policies that support the responsible development and use of AI. It also requires engaging with stakeholders, including civil society organizations, to ensure that AI systems are developed and deployed in a way that respects human rights and fundamental freedoms.

The knowledge base provides various resources and tools to support organizations in navigating the regulatory landscape for ethical AI innovation. This includes regulatory updates and analysis, case studies and best practices, and frameworks and guidelines for ethical AI development and deployment. The knowledge base also provides access to a community of experts and practitioners who can provide guidance and support in addressing the ethical challenges of AI development and deployment.

Regulatory readiness is critical to organizational preparedness for AI and GenAI. Building internal infrastructure, adopting supportive standards, and engaging in thoughtful public policy participation are essential steps toward embracing regulatory compliance. By dedicating resources to understanding and adhering to regulations, organizations demonstrate their commitment to ethical AI practices and contribute to the responsible development and use of AI for the benefit of society.

ETHICAL AI READINESS

As organizations embark on their AI journey, it is crucial to recognize that ethical considerations are just as important as legal compliance. While regulations provide a baseline for legal requirements, ethical principles establish higher aspirational ideals for protecting human rights and welfare. This chapter will explore the importance of ethical readiness in AI development and deployment. We will discuss the core principles that should guide AI development, the role of documented ethical practices, independent oversight bodies, immersive workforce training, participative design, and proactive communication. We will also delve into the additional ethical diligence required for emerging GenAI capabilities and the importance of independent audits and stakeholder participation.

Committing to ethical AI principles requires comprehensive policies, oversight processes, cultural measures, and transparency. Ethical practices codify human-centric design, testing, monitoring, and redress mechanisms tailored to AI risks and use cases. Rigorous testing methodologies evaluate for alignment with principles like fairness and safety before deployment. Ongoing monitoring identifies emerging issues needing mitigation, and feedback channels enable redress for unintended impacts.

Independent oversight bodies of diverse internal and external voices provide multidisciplinary guidance, assess tradeoffs, and uphold principles in practice. Cross-functional teams identify ethical risks and considerations, and external councils spotlight blind spots. Oversight processes steer activities to balance innovation and responsibility.

Immersive workforce training builds skills and enthusiasm for applying ethics through daily choices when developing, testing, and using AI systems. Scenario exercises foster discerning judgments, aligning actions to principles. Education programs cultivate personal responsibility.

Participative design engages affected populations early, often, and iteratively to understand needs holistically and preemptively address concerns. Inclusive involvement empowers improving systems for all, and diverse feedback ensures accessibility.

For emerging GenAI capabilities, additional ethical diligence is warranted, given the more significant risks of uncontrolled or harmful synthesized content. Extensive testing methodologies evaluate for safety, truthfulness, and the absence of unfair biases before integration. Controls like filtering, time limits, and pre-release human reviews help safeguard public systems. Advisory boards guide acceptable use cases based on maturity.

Proactive communication provides visibility into activities, protocols, and controls applied to build understanding and appropriate trust. Transparency demonstrates concrete policies in action across the AI lifecycle. Realistic expectations mitigate hype or fearmongering.

Independent audits verify that intended ethical outcomes are achieved in practice across projects. Assessments highlight priority gaps needing improvement. Benchmarking confirms policies satisfy global standards and best practices.

Genuine, sustained participation enables diverse stakeholders to guide enhancing accessibility and managing risks preemptively. Inclusive involvement empowers steering AI to benefit all equitably. Continued engagement adapts systems to evolving expectations.

With comprehensive policies, oversight processes, cultural adoption, transparency practices, and stakeholder participation deeply embedded into operations, AI merits trust from society to progress in ways that benefit people. However, realizing ethical outcomes depends on a genuine commitment to human principles permeating individual, institutional, and community choices.

Ethical readiness in AI development and deployment is critical to ensure that AI systems are developed and deployed in a way that respects human rights and welfare. By embracing ethical principles, organizations can build trust and demonstrate their commitment to responsible AI development and use. The next chapter will explore the importance of data governance in AI development and deployment.

AI GOVERNANCE READINESS

The realm of AI governance readiness opens a comprehensive narrative, intertwining policies, processes, and controls to align AI development and usage with prevailing regulations, ethical norms, and the overarching organizational strategy. The essence of robust AI governance lies in integrating comprehensive frameworks that guide activities, ensuring compliance is embedded throughout the AI lifecycle. This meticulous approach is pivotal in responsibly managing risks and upholding AI applications' integrity.

Key to this governance structure is the documentation of policies encapsulating the constrained development procedures, which adhere strictly to regulatory requirements and ethical principles. These documented policies become the bedrock upon which fairness testing, thorough documentation, vigilant monitoring, and other mandated practices are enforced before the deployment of AI systems. Additionally, detailed model cards provide a transparent and accountable mechanism to track compliance factors, including data sources, intended use cases, evaluation results, potential biases, and more, for each AI system.

The formalization of change review processes is crucial to the ongoing governance process. These processes ensure that any modifications to models or data strictly adhere to established policies and standards before implementation. Version tracking plays an integral role here, associating each change with accountability. Complementing this, regular automated testing and auditing are essential for verifying sustained alignment with the set requirements and driving continuous improvements in risk management strategies. AI model risk management practices are proactively employed to anticipate and mitigate potential failure points.

GenAI capabilities continue to advance rapidly, and a heightened level of governance vigilance becomes imperative, particularly in managing the risks associated with uncontrolled or harmful synthesized content. Stringent oversight mechanisms, such as output filtering, access limitations, and mandatory human reviews, are crucial for balancing enablement with accountability, especially in open-ended generative models. Additionally, establishing advisory boards focused on safety and ethics is vital for overseeing risks distinct from other types of AI.

To ensure effective governance, immersive workforce training is essential for building the necessary skills to uphold compliance through daily development and usage choices. Scenario exercises are instrumental in fostering discerning judgments that balance the aspiration for innovation with ethical risks. Further, education programs are pivotal in cultivating a culture of personal accountability within the organization.

Proactive communication regarding governance policies and controls is fundamental in providing visibility into activities, fostering public understanding, and building trust in AI systems. Transparency in these processes demonstrates a commitment to managing risks responsibly, and independent audits play a critical role in verifying the intended outcomes.

AI governance readiness is not merely about integrating compliance into frameworks but also building an ethical culture focused on human welfare that permeates the workforce and leadership. Leaders must view governance as a strategic priority that enables innovation rather than a roadblock and promote compliance as a means of competitive differentiation through trust earned from diligent oversight. The combination of governance and culture provides the necessary human oversight, ensuring that policies achieve their intended outcomes in practice despite the inherent subjectivity in interpreting principles.

AI AND GenAI COMPLIANCE

Advancing GenAI demands diligent governance proportionate to emerging abilities and applications. This section outlines a holistic framework guiding responsible innovation through oversight, practices, and stakeholder relationships anchored in shared ethics. Comprehensive policies, controls, transparency, and evaluation underpin safe, purposeful maturation.

A AI/GenAI Governance Board assumes pivotal responsibility through diverse expertise, periodically reviewing development, impacts, and policies. Cross-functional representation fosters balanced consideration across technical, business, and societal spheres aligned with organizational principles.

Regular strategic assessment identifies risks, opportunities, and alignments through multi-perspective stakeholder inquiries. Feedback facilitates continuous improvement by surfacing collaborative solutions' concerns: documentation and versioning archive learning over technological progression.

Established commitment documentation informs you of graduated guidance on approved tools, applications, data sources, and oversight. Scenario analyses foresee effects enabling proactive calibration. Impact assessments inform refinements through open communication, cultivating shared understanding. Evolving standards integration supports proportional progression reflecting collaborative expertise.

Dedicated subject matter advisors contribute ongoing guidance on assurance, investigation, and tailored practice recommendations. Independent review augments stewardship through multidisciplinary perspectives representing diverse interests. Input supports responsive, balanced governance calibrated to developing realities.

Stringent controls establish measured starting points proportionate to formative abilities. Adapted transitioning accommodates maturing as safe operation validates gradually relaxing early strictures, retaining prudent oversight anchored in shared ethics. Ongoing improvement aligns safeguards with advancing competencies and insights.

Early stringent screening, limiting, and flagging proactively identify unacceptable outputs, aims, or behaviors without compromising exploration. Supervision supplements monitoring proportionately. Paused activity preserves safety pending remediation through inclusive dialogue cultivating shared principles.

Controls evolve through human-machine collaboration, systematically reappraising outputs against fairness and safety as abilities progress. Automated validation supplements human discreet monitoring through anomaly detection and alerting of offsetting concerns requiring remediation, enhancing oversight capabilities safely.

Prudent diligence anchors continued risk mitigation proportionate to purposes through documentation, substantiating careful transition guided by collective guardianship. Oversight augments autonomous processes equitably, addressing emerging complexities and respecting human values.

Model documentation substantiates background, limitations, and improvement over technological evolution, cultivating comprehension and responsiveness. Benchmark disclosure gauges progress, bolstering confidence. Clear use case descriptions inform proper applications, maintaining oversight. Interactive exchange fosters shared understanding and collaboratively refined practices.

Metadata records capture development context, facilitating independent impact evaluation and knowledge sharing. Training history archives methodology supporting reproducibility and continual enhancement. Performance substantiates abilities and shortcomings, guiding expectations constructively. Documentation enhances accountability and trust through open practices.

Transparency builds relationships critical for safeguarding benefit realization by disclosing systems, impacts, and oversight. Feedback improves practices anchored collaboratively within shared ethics. Responsible communication nurtures understanding and stewardship of evolving techniques respecting human autonomy.

External assessments supplement internal diligence through subject matter expertise across technical, legal, and human domains. Randomized probing comprehensively evaluates equity, accuracy, and evolving issues. Triggered limits pause concerning activities awaiting remedies guiding improvements. Auditing assesses compliance objectively, bolstering accountability.

Through participatory design, Testing quantifies performance against objectives and diverse, representative conditions. Human-machine collaboration facilitates iterative advancement calibrated within shared security, welfare, and justice principles. Findings enable pre-release improvement and post-deployment remedies respectfully.

Monitoring transparently identifies drift, new concerns, and accomplishments through randomized sampling and collaborative review. Feedback drives rule refinement, balancing opportunities with obligations. Impact documentation archives retrospective analysis cultivating prospective care. Auditing validates conformity objectively on recurring cycles.

Granular records capture model evolution, training practices, reference performance, and appropriate contextualization through clear provenance substantiating responsible application, recall, and evolution and versioning archives technical progression and refinement, impartially bolstering reproducibility, interpretation, and relationships critical for safety.

Technical specifications, constrained training methods, and benchmark disclosure give a line of sight into synthesis history, abilities, and evolving enrichment, transparently addressing foreseeable and unexpected implications constructively through open yet prudent communication. Records retain technical contexts and impact accessibly.

Documentation enhances understanding of applied expertise and collaborative learning through versioning technical development interactively. Accessibility bolsters trust through impartial substantiation of practices, aims, and effects cultivated respectfully within shared commitment. Records substantiate evolution anchored in human priorities through participatory guidance.

Participatory input shapes policies, safeguards, and communication practices through inclusive guidance, representing diverse needs and respecting autonomy. Feedback facilitates continual advancement that is aligned with realities and is collaboratively analyzed through a human-in-the-loop process. Communication nurtures understanding through respectful, proactive information exchange, safely cultivating stewardship of progressing technologies.

Forums invite insights into impacts and appropriate practices improving through shared learning. Transparency substantiates development, respectfully enhancing insight through impartial documentation. Communication invites balanced oversight, sustaining innovation safely through cooperative guardianship.

Multidisciplinary advisory input supports governance through objective subject matter expertise. Participation informs human-centric design facilitated through considerate exchange bolstering mutual understanding. Interactive governance anchors advancement respectfully within shared ethics as experience evolves.

Through diligently expanding safeguards commensurate with maturing abilities validated interactively, organizations can unlock benefits compliantly through prudent yet amenable vigilance anchored in human priorities. An integrated framework cultivates responsible progress equitably guided by collaborative guardianship, proportionately addresses uncertainties, and respects autonomy. Ongoing refinement maintains balance, enhancing confidence through open yet prudent relationships.

AI AND GenAI STANDARDS AND CERTIFICATION

In AI and GenAI, the landscape is ever-evolving, posing unique organizational challenges and opportunities. As we delve into the complexities of compliance readiness, we must acknowledge the pivotal role of standards and certifications. These elements are not mere formalities; they represent a commitment to excellence, a blueprint for responsible innovation, and a guiding light in the labyrinth of digital transformation.

Standards developed by bodies like the ISO/IEC and IEEE offer comprehensive frameworks encompassing transparency, fairness, and security. These frameworks, while voluntary, are instrumental in navigating the intricacies of AI implementation. They are the bedrock upon which organizations can build robust, ethical, and effective AI systems.

Certifications, on the other hand, serve as a testament to an organization's adherence to these high standards. They are not just badges of honor but tangible evidence of an entity's dedication to ethical practices and quality. In a world where trust is paramount, these certifications speak volumes.

Voluntary adoption of standards and pursuit of certifications in AI and GenAI are marks of an organization's commitment to excellence and ethical responsibility. Globally recognized standards such as those from ISO/IEC and IEEE provide critical guidance in transparency, bias mitigation, and security. While not legally binding, these standards shape responsible AI practices.

For instance, the ISO/IEC 23894 (https://www.iso.org/standard/77304.html) outlines reference architectures, metrics, and methodologies for assessing AI across transparency and bias mitigation dimensions. IEEE standards like P7003 (https://standards.ieee.org/ieee/7003/11357/) and P2890 (https://standards.ieee.org/ieee/2890/10318/) set algorithmic bias and transparency benchmarks, offering crucial guidance for organizations navigating these complex territories.

Industry-specific alliances, such as the Financial Services Artificial Intelligence Public-Private Forum (https://www.fca.org.uk/news/news-stories/financial-services-ai-public-private-forum), offer tailored frameworks for sectors like finance, where the risks and rewards of AI are particularly pronounced. These frameworks provide valuable guidance on governance, testing, monitoring, and documentation tailored to the unique challenges of financial services AI.

Certifications play a pivotal role in this ecosystem. They offer independent verification of an organization's commitment to these standards, assuring stakeholders and the public. For instance, certification audits from organizations like Ernst and Young or Deloitte validate an organization's accountability measures in AI against the various approved standards, offering a credible stamp of approval.

Participation in the development of these standards is equally important. Organizations should engage in public comment periods, contributing their experience and insights. This involvement ensures that the standards developed are pragmatic, balancing innovation with appropriate safeguards. For GenAI, which is at the frontier of AI innovation, contributing expertise is crucial. As this technology advances, input on appropriate controls and standards becomes invaluable in managing its novel risks.

A vital part of comprehensive internal governance is adopting standards that provide credible validation and guide innovation toward responsible outcomes. These standards can be used to conduct internal first-party assessments for low-risk use cases, internal or external second-party assessments for medium-risk use cases, and external third-party audits for high-risk use cases. This provides a level of assurance for stakeholders and customers alike.

Embracing AI and GenAI standards and pursuing certifications are not mere compliance exercises but strategic imperatives. They guide organizations in navigating the complex landscape of AI responsibly and effectively. By adopting these standards and seeking certifications, organizations demonstrate a credible commitment to ethical practices and quality in AI.

As leaders in this digital age, our responsibility extends beyond the walls of our organizations. We must actively contribute to shaping the standards that will govern the future of AI and GenAI. Doing so ensures that these technologies advance our business objectives and serve society's greater good.

The journey toward AI compliance readiness is multifaceted. It involves a deep commitment to adopting and shaping global standards, seeking independent certifications, and contributing to developing pragmatic standards. This journey, while challenging, is essential for harnessing the true potential of AI and GenAI in a way that benefits all.

ENVIRONMENTAL IMPACTS OF AI AND GenAI

In AI and GenAI, the conversation is evolving to include technological advancements and their environmental impacts. This aspect, often overshadowed by the remarkable capabilities of these technologies, demands a more profound examination. As we advance in AI, we must also consider the environmental footprint it leaves behind, a footprint characterized by significant energy consumption, water usage, and electronic waste.

Training large-scale AI models like GPT-3/4 is an energy-intensive process, with energy requirements akin to the lifetime emissions of several cars. This considerable demand for energy necessitates a shift in our approach to AI development, prioritizing sustainability and efficiency. Cloud-based AI services also contribute to this carbon footprint while offering scalability and operational efficiency. In response, a shift toward renewable energy sources in cloud services is emerging, reflecting a broader consciousness about the environmental impact of AI.

The environmental footprint of AI also encompasses water usage, especially in the cooling processes of data centers. The substantial water consumption in these facilities poses challenges to local water resources, underlining the need for sustainable water management practices.

Innovations in cooling technologies, such as alternative water sources, are being explored to mitigate this impact.

Furthermore, the rapid pace of hardware advancements in AI contributes to increased electronic waste and resource depletion. In response, sustainable hardware solutions, including modular designs for easy upgrades, are being explored to reduce the ecological impact of AI's hardware requirements.

The development and deployment of AI and GenAI must be approached with environmental sustainability in mind. This entails adopting energy-efficient practices, minimizing water usage, reducing electronic waste, and embedding environmental consciousness into AI development. It also involves creating governance frameworks prioritizing sustainability, fostering collaboration across sectors to promote environmentally responsible AI practices, and ensuring equitable distribution of AI's benefits.

As we embrace AI and GenAI for their transformative potential, we must also be vigilant about their environmental impacts. Addressing these challenges requires a concerted effort across multiple fronts involving governments, industry leaders, researchers, and environmental experts. By prioritizing sustainability in AI development and operation, we can ensure that the benefits of these technologies are harnessed responsibly, paving the way for a sustainable and equitable future.

SOCIAL IMPLICATIONS OF AI

In examining the compliance readiness for AI and GenAI, it's critical to delve deeply into the social implications these technologies bring to the forefront. As a seasoned industry leader, I've observed firsthand the transformative impact of AI on society, stretching far beyond mere operational efficiencies to profoundly affect social dynamics, ethical considerations, and cultural norms.

Data representation in these systems is one of the most significant issues with AI and GenAI. These technologies mirror the data they are trained on, which reflects society – the good, bad, and ugly decisions we have made in the past. This risks amplifying existing societal biases if the data is skewed or incomplete. For instance, facial recognition technologies have faced challenges in accurately identifying individuals from diverse demographic groups due to biases in the training datasets. This issue necessitates a critical reassessment and diversification of these datasets to ensure AI models are fair and representative of the diverse society they serve.

The lack of diversity in AI development teams exacerbates these challenges. The teams' composition significantly influences AI outputs, with a homogenous team often leading to biased AI models. This lack of diversity leads to skewed models and restricts the variety of perspectives and problem-solving approaches. Programs like AI4ALL are making strides in increasing the representation of underrepresented groups in AI, which is crucial for developing unbiased and well-rounded AI systems.

Furthermore, the advancement of AI technologies risks widening the socioeconomic divide. The impact of AI on job markets is not uniform, often disproportionately affecting lower-wage jobs more prone to automation. This issue is not confined to national borders but extends globally, with stark disparities in AI progress and digital access between developed and developing countries. To address these challenges, initiatives like AI for Good leverage AI to promote equitable access to these technologies, aiming to reduce the digital divide and foster global inclusivity.

It becomes increasingly evident that GenAI and AI involve more than technological advancement. It's a path that intersects with ethical, environmental, and social considerations, necessitating a balanced approach to technological progression and ethical responsibility. The future of AI depends not only on its technical prowess but also on its alignment with societal values and ethics. This delicate balance between innovation and responsibility is critical to AI's sustainable and positive societal impact.

In addition to the issues already mentioned, recent studies and experiments have brought to light several other critical considerations in the social implications of AI. For instance, the environmental impact of training large-scale AI models like GPT-3/4 is significant, with substantial energy expenditure comparable to 125 round-trip flights between New York and Beijing. The effects on the environment extend to the use as well. Every 20 prompts made to ChatGPT can consume as much as 500 mL of water. This environmental cost underlines the importance of adopting more sustainable practices in AI development, such as utilizing renewable energy sources and exploring sustainable hardware solutions (https://arxiv.org/pdf/2304.03271.pdf).

Moreover, the rapid pace of hardware advancements in AI contributes to increased electronic waste and resource depletion, further emphasizing the need for sustainable approaches in AI technology. Companies are beginning to explore environmentally friendly hardware options, such as modular designs that allow for easier upgrades without complete hardware replacements. This shift toward a "greener" approach in AI technology is a step toward mitigating the environmental impact of these advancements.

In workforce dynamics, AI's influence extends to diversifying and transforming jobs and industries. The emergence of large language models like ChatGPT has the potential to reshape occupations, requiring new skills and approaches to work. This transformation poses challenges regarding workforce readiness and the need for up-skilling to adapt to the evolving demands of AI-augmented jobs.

Furthermore, integrating AI into various industries raises concerns about the potential displacement of jobs, particularly those more susceptible to automation. This displacement could exacerbate existing socioeconomic disparities, making it imperative for organizations and policymakers to address these challenges proactively. Efforts to leverage AI to enhance human potential and creativity, rather than replacing human labor, are crucial in ensuring a balanced and equitable integration of AI into the workforce.

The social implications of AI and GenAI encompass many issues, from ethical considerations and data representation to environmental impacts and workforce transformation. As we continue to integrate these technologies into our society and industries, we must approach them with a holistic understanding of their multifaceted impacts. By addressing these challenges comprehensively and responsibly, we can harness the full potential of AI and GenAI to benefit society.

EMBRACING HOLISTIC GROWTH

The advancement of AI and GenAI is not just a journey of technological excellence but a quest for harmonizing these innovations with the broader canvas of environmental sustainability and social well-being. As we forge ahead in this era of unprecedented digital transformation, our success will be defined not merely by the sophistication of our algorithms but by how seamlessly they integrate with Environmental, Social, and Governance (ESG) principles. It's about sculpting an AI ecosystem as much about intellectual prowess as ethical consciousness and humanitarian concern.

The integration of ESG considerations into every facet of AI development and deployment marks a significant shift in the trajectory of technological progress. It demands a new ethos in the evolution of AI – an ethos where environmental conservation and social responsibility are integral to AI's DNA. This paradigm shift calls for a proactive approach, ensuring that AI's path forward is paved with advanced capabilities and a deep-seated commitment to sustainable and ethical practices.

This new era of AI evolution beckons us to a future where technological advancement aligns harmoniously with our planet's health and societal equity. As AI technologies evolve rapidly, creating many possibilities, we are tasked with a dual responsibility: to embrace and foster these innovations while remaining vigilant and responsive to their environmental and social impacts. This constant vigilance and adaptability are crucial in steering AI toward a future that is intelligent, efficient, wise, and considerate in interacting with our world and its diverse inhabitants.

In encapsulating the journey of AI and GenAI, it's evident that we are charting a course where technological prowess and ethical stewardship are intertwined. This journey is about pioneering a future where AI transcends computational excellence to become a beacon of positive transformation, aligning with the greater good and ensuring a symbiotic relationship with our environmental and societal framework. As we navigate this path, our collective wisdom, creativity, and ethical commitment will be the guiding lights, shaping a future where AI catalyzes holistic growth and harmonious coexistence.

FINAL THOUGHTS

As we transition from Chapter 10, focus on navigating the intricate landscape of AI and GenAI compliance. We now embark on Chapter 11, which emphasizes the crucial role of comprehensive AI readiness assessments in enabling organizations to integrate various elements into cohesive and strategic AI solutions effectively.

Chapter 11 underscores the importance of regular evaluations to diagnose the maturity of an organization across critical dimensions such as culture, skills, data, infrastructure, systems, and compliance. These assessments are vital for illuminating priority areas needing improvement, allowing organizations to shape pragmatic roadmaps that align with their specific needs and objectives.

Chapter 11 outlines the value of these assessments, comparing them to a chef routinely tasting a dish during preparation. Regular comprehensive evaluations are crucial for gaining visibility into the current state of AI readiness and assessing progress on goals, mindset, values, and accountability. This process includes evaluating culture, ethics, strategy, and technical capabilities through questionnaires, interviews, audits, and benchmarks.

The methodology for these assessments is structured to guide organizations across interdependent dimensions of AI readiness. This includes evaluating foundational organizational readiness, performing in-depth technical readiness reviews, verifying the integration of readiness ingredients, and analyzing the outputs to shape pragmatic roadmaps.

Chapter 11 also highlights the importance of ongoing assessment cycles to reflect organizational and external changes. As the AI field matures, new priority focus areas emerge, necessitating continual assessment updates and adaptations.

The realization of value from these assessments is emphasized as crucial for developing integrated AI solutions that deliver tangible business results. Chapter 11 advocates combining insights from assessments into actionable plans focusing on culture, skills, data, systems, governance, and ethics.

Operationalizing these assessments requires embedding them into the organization's operational framework. This includes prioritizing assessments at the leadership level, integrating findings into governance policies, and cultivating a culture that views assessments as a regular and constructive practice.

Chapter 11 presents a comprehensive guide for organizations to assess and enhance their AI readiness effectively. The chapter emphasizes that regular and comprehensive AI readiness assessments are not just about identifying gaps or compliance issues but are integral to understanding and leveraging the organization's unique AI journey. This proactive approach enables organizations to successfully navigate the complex landscape of AI implementation, aligning with strategic goals and ensuring ethical and sustainable AI practices. Chapter 11 underscores the need for organizations to continuously assess and adapt their AI strategies, ensuring they deliver value for the business, stakeholders, and society at large.

KEY TAKEAWAYS AND ACTIONS

REGULATORY READINESS

- **Actionable Steps:** Stay informed and comply with emerging AI regulations like the EU AI Act.
- **Implementation:** Develop internal processes to ensure compliance with legal requirements on data governance, privacy, and algorithmic accountability.

ETHICAL AI READINESS

- **Actionable Steps:** Embed ethical principles in AI development and deployment.
- **Implementation:** Create ethical AI guidelines, establish oversight bodies, and conduct immersive training for the workforce to maintain AI integrity.

AI GOVERNANCE READINESS

- **Actionable Steps:** Implement robust AI governance frameworks.
- **Implementation:** Document AI policies, conduct change reviews, manage model risks, and ensure governance over GenAI for responsible usage.

STANDARDS AND CERTIFICATION IN AI AND GenAI

- **Actionable Steps:** Adopt and contribute to AI standards like ISO/IEC and IEEE.
- **Implementation:** Pursue certifications that validate compliance with ethical and quality standards in AI development.

ENVIRONMENTAL IMPACTS OF AI AND GenAI

- **Actionable Steps:** Address the environmental footprint of AI technologies.
- **Implementation:** Opt for renewable energy-powered cloud services, innovate in sustainable hardware design, and consider water usage in AI operations.

SOCIAL IMPLICATIONS OF AI

- **Actionable Steps:** Ensure fair and diverse representation in AI data and workforce.
- **Implementation:** Diversify training datasets, enhance workforce diversity, and address the socioeconomic and global digital divide in AI advancements.

Assessing Your Readiness

INTRODUCTION

This chapter critically explores the comprehensive AI readiness assessments that provide continuous insights, enabling organizations to integrate key ingredients into cohesive solutions that meet strategic needs. This chapter is dedicated to guiding leaders through the complexities of conducting regular evaluations to diagnose and enhance their organization's AI capabilities.

In this chapter, we delve into the multifaceted process of AI readiness assessment. We explore the value of these assessments in providing visibility into an organization's current state across various critical dimensions, including culture, skills, data, infrastructure, systems, and compliance. This is akin to a chef constantly tasting and adjusting a dish during its preparation. Through ongoing evaluations, organizations can identify priority areas needing improvement, crafting pragmatic roadmaps that accelerate their AI capabilities.

The assessment methodology is dissected, highlighting the importance of evaluating foundational organizational readiness, including culture, skills, and strategy. We also look into in-depth technical readiness reviews, focusing on infrastructure, data, and platform assessments. This structured approach ensures a thorough understanding of the organization's actions regarding AI readiness and what areas require immediate attention and investment.

As we progress, this chapter emphasizes the importance of ongoing assessment cycles. These regular updates are crucial as they reflect changes in organizational activities and the external AI landscape. They

 DOI: 10.1201/9781003486725-12

help sustain an updated understanding of AI readiness, ensuring that the organization remains agile and responsive to new developments and challenges in AI.

In the pursuit of realizing the value of these assessments, this chapter discusses how to combine insights from evaluations into actionable plans judiciously. This is crucial for avoiding stalled or ineffective AI initiatives that arise from unidentified gaps. This chapter argues for the need for governance processes and a culture that adopts insights from these assessments to strengthen and scale AI solutions effectively.

Operationalizing these assessments is vital; This chapter guides how to embed them into the organization's DNA. This includes prioritizing assessments at the leadership level, integrating findings into governance policies, and fostering a culture that views regular assessments as beneficial practices rather than burdensome audits.

This chapter asserts that comprehensive AI readiness assessments are indispensable for organizations aiming to harness AI effectively. These evaluations illuminate the path forward, while governance and cultural adoption of insights power the journey to achieving significant business impact.

THE VALUE OF ASSESSMENTS

Regular comprehensive assessments are crucial to illuminate priority areas needing improvement in an organization's AI readiness. Ongoing evaluations diagnose progress and gaps to shape pragmatic roadmaps accelerating capabilities. Assessments provide much-needed visibility into the current state of AI readiness across critical dimensions. Evaluating culture, ethics, and strategy readiness via questionnaires, interviews, and audits assesses progress on goals, mindset, values, and accountability. Culture drives priorities, so understanding motivations and perceptions is crucial. Ethics audits verify policies translate into ethical practices. Strategy alignment confirms activities map to business objectives.

Reviewing technical capabilities through infrastructure audits and benchmarks quantifies the maturity of data, platforms, tools, and systems. Data assessments reveal coverage, quality, labeling, biases, and accessibility. Compute infrastructure audits to uncover bottlenecks. Platform evaluations highlight integration gaps between data lakes, feature stores, model management systems, and deployment tools.

Analyzing skills and proficiency through assessments highlights role-based development needs for disciplines like data scientists, machine learning (ML) engineers, and product managers. Skill gaps impact delivery capacity.

Ongoing assessments also track readiness over time through pulse checks, updated audits, and benchmarking. Pulse checks like questionnaires or interviews spot shifting mindsets and new gaps or blockers needing resolution. Progress benchmarking confirms foundational practices are maturing. Updating audits highlights new weaknesses or strengths.

Comparing assessment results against peers, industry benchmarks, and AI best practices spotlights improvement opportunities. New priorities emerge as innovations, regulations, and public expectations advance.

The insights from regular assessments crucially inform data enhancement initiatives, infrastructure upgrades, capability development, project prioritization, policy improvements, training investments, and evolving AI capability roadmaps.

Root cause analysis on process breakdowns or project failures highlights specific weaknesses needing remediation. Project post-mortem extracts critical lessons learned for strengthening development and operational methodologies. Documenting success highlights achievements and best practices to celebrate, reinforce, and replicate.

Assessment findings feed pragmatic action plans to incrementally tackle priority gaps identified across culture, skills, data, systems, and policy compliance. Just as chefs adjust recipes based on taste, organizations refine AI practices based on assessments.

The path forward entails tightly integrating continuous readiness evaluations into operations to consistently benchmark against AI leaders, rapidly rectify breakdowns, and showcase achievements. Assessments signal where organizations need assistance progressing their AI journey amidst complex, ever-evolving environments. However, realizing results requires acting upon the insights through governance and culture.

Comprehensive readiness assessments provide crucial visibility to evaluate culture, skills, data, infrastructure, systems, and compliance. They uncover priority gaps needing improvement and track progression over time versus milestones. Assessments compare against peers to reveal opportunities, analyze failures to strengthen methodologies, and highlight successes to reinforce best practices. The findings directly inform pragmatic action plans and roadmaps.

With readiness continuously diagnosed across ingredients, organizations can judiciously combine culture, skills, data, systems, governance, and ethics into integrated AI solutions that fulfill business needs. Regular checkups empower data-driven planning. However, realizing value requires governance and culture adopting insights to accelerate capabilities. Ongoing assessments illuminate the path forward.

ASSESSMENT METHODOLOGY

The path to effectively harnessing AI extends far beyond adopting new technologies. It demands a comprehensive and strategic assessment of an organization's readiness, encompassing a spectrum of critical factors that range from internal culture and data management to technological infrastructure, regulatory compliance, and ethical considerations.

AI readiness is not a linear path but a multifaceted endeavor that requires a nuanced understanding of various organizational dimensions. This includes an in-depth evaluation of organizational readiness, which delves into the internal preparedness of an organization, assessing aspects such as culture, structure, capacity, and strategic alignment with AI objectives. It's about ensuring that the leadership's vision and innovation strategies are not only ambitious but also pragmatically aligned with the practicalities and nuances of AI integration.

Architectural Readiness, another crucial dimension, focuses on the technical backbone of AI implementation. This involves critically assessing the existing infrastructure's capability to adapt to and integrate emerging AI technologies. It's about creating a robust and agile architecture that can respond to the evolving AI landscape, ensuring that the organization remains adaptable and poised for future advancements.

Data Readiness is equally vital, scrutinizing the organization's capability to manage, process, and effectively utilize data for AI applications. This dimension covers data quality, governance, architecture, and infrastructure, ensuring the data ecosystem is primed for AI deployment. High-quality data, governed effectively and supported by modern architecture, lays the foundation for reliable and impactful AI applications.

Specifically addressing AI and generative AI (GenAI), the AI Readiness and GenAI Readiness assessments delve into the organization's capabilities regarding team skills, future-proofing strategies, quality assurance, and governance. These assessments are critical in evaluating the organization's approach to expanding AI use cases, developing AI team skills, and integrating new data types to enhance AI model quality.

Lastly, Compliance Readiness is essential in assessing an organization's ability to meet regulatory, ethical, and accountability standards in AI deployment. This dimension provides insights into the organization's capacity to manage risks, adhere to regulations, uphold ethical practices, and consider environmental, social, and governance (ESG) impacts.

In essence, a comprehensive AI readiness assessment is a strategic imperative for organizations seeking to navigate the complexities of digital transformation successfully. It ensures that organizations are technically prepared and culturally, structurally, and ethically aligned to leverage AI technologies effectively. The assessment should be able to understand and evaluate the maturity of an organization on several key topics that may have varying levels of importance. This thorough readiness assessment is a testament to an organization's commitment to innovation, competitive advantage, and long-term success in an AI-driven future.

ORGANIZATIONAL READINESS

In today's rapidly evolving digital era, integrating AI into business operations is not just a trend but a critical pivot toward future growth and sustainability. As organizations navigate this transformation, assessing Organizational Readiness becomes paramount. This assessment transcends traditional technological evaluations, delving into the very fabric of the organization's structure, culture, and strategic vision. It's a comprehensive process that examines an organization's readiness to adopt AI and embed it effectively into its core operations and strategies. This readiness encompasses various facets, from future-proofing the organization's approach to AI, nurturing a culture conducive to innovation, structuring the organization for agility, and ensuring robust governance and accountability in AI deployment. Let's explore these critical sub-dimensions that define an organization's preparedness to embrace and excel in the AI-driven future.

Organizational Future-Proofing

In the realm of AI, the future-proofing of an organization is not a mere buzzword but a strategic imperative. It starts at the top, with leadership crafting a vision that anticipates the evolving landscape of data and AI and aligns seamlessly with the organization's long-term business goals. This vision is the compass that navigates the organization through the complexities of AI integration. An effective innovation strategy is paramount here, balancing risks and returns and shaping informed decisions about AI investments. Technology roadmaps are not just plans but blueprints for capability development, ensuring a systematic approach to acquiring and integrating AI technologies.

The cornerstone of AI readiness is building a talent pool equipped for the future. This involves up-skilling the current workforce and strategically attracting new talent versed in AI. Ecosystem partnerships are invaluable in this regard, opening doors to new capabilities and insights, thus propelling AI adoption and innovation within the organization.

Adapting the business architecture and processes is critical for effectively embedding AI into organizational operations. This adaptation is more than a technical overhaul; it's about fostering a culture that embraces AI, facilitated by change management practices that address resistance and encourage acceptance.

Scenario planning and trend monitoring are indispensable tools for strategic planning. They ensure the organization remains agile and responsive, ready to pivot in the face of the ever-changing AI landscape. Aligning the portfolio strategy with future AI opportunities is about positioning the organization to capitalize on emerging AI trends and innovations.

Organizational Culture

An organization's culture is the fertile ground where AI adoption flourishes or withers. A culture that champions innovation and creativity sets the stage for successful AI implementation. New ideas are welcomed and nurtured in such environments, and creative thinking is the norm. Openness to experimenting with new technologies, a tolerance for ambiguity and reasonable risk, and collaboration across various disciplines enhance the organization's capacity to leverage AI effectively.

A continuous learning and growth culture is non-negotiable in the AI domain, where technologies and best practices are in constant flux. Customer-centricity and a focus on generating business value are the lenses through which AI initiatives must be viewed, ensuring alignment with customer needs and business objectives. Data-driven decision-making and a commitment to transparency and diversity lay the foundation for an ethical and inclusive AI adoption process.

Organizational Structure

The structure of an organization can significantly influence its AI readiness. Cross-functional and interdisciplinary teams are the lifeblood of AI projects, fostering collaboration and bringing together complementary skills. Internal mobility, leadership development, and recruiting top-tier talent are essential in building a workforce adept at driving AI initiatives.

The organizational design must facilitate the free flow of information, with roles such as the Chief Data Officer symbolizing a commitment to data and AI. Teams that balance optimization with exploration, distributed authority to circumvent bottlenecks, and transparent decision rights are the hallmarks of an organization primed for sustained innovation.

Organizational Capacity and Strategy

For AI to be effective, it must be in lockstep with the business strategy. This involves dedicated teams and resources focused on strategy execution, underpinned by well-defined business metrics and key performance indicators (KPIs). Robust data and analytics capabilities are not just support systems but the backbone of AI projects. Tools that enable self-service access, a value-based prioritization framework, and an effective pipeline for identifying and scaling high-impact initiatives are critical components of AI readiness.

Organizational Accountability

In the world of AI, responsibility extends beyond functionality. Embedding responsible AI principles throughout lifecycles, establishing ethics oversight for high-risk cases, and executive commitment to ethics and compliance are non-negotiable. The demand for explainability and auditability, training on ethics, and incentives aligned with responsible innovation are pillars of ethical AI use.

In essence, assessing organizational readiness for AI is a comprehensive process scrutinizing various organizational dimensions. It evaluates how well the organization's leadership, culture, structure, capacity, strategy, and accountability align with AI technologies' multifaceted demands and opportunities. This assessment is not just a procedural step but a strategic endeavor crucial for organizations seeking to integrate AI into their operations successfully. It's about ensuring that organizations are technically, structurally, and ethically equipped to leverage AI for innovation, competitive advantage, and long-term success.

ARCHITECTURAL READINESS

The readiness of an organization's architecture to support and enhance AI initiatives is a critical factor in determining its success in this domain. Architectural Readiness for AI is not just about having the latest technology. It ensures that the entire architectural framework of the organization is robust, agile, and adaptable enough to integrate new data sources and emerging capabilities seamlessly. This readiness encompasses a comprehensive evaluation of various architectural components, including future-proofing strategies, data architecture, AI architecture, GenAI architecture, and integrating these architectures. Let's delve into these critical areas to understand how they collectively form the backbone of an organization's AI strategy and contribute to its ability to leverage AI technologies effectively.

Architectural Future Proofing

In the context of AI, the architectural future-proofing of an organization is a strategic endeavor that goes beyond mere technical upgrades. It's about ensuring the overall architecture is robust and agile enough to seamlessly integrate new data sources and emerging capabilities. This level of flexibility is critical for handling diverse data types, such as images and videos, and for incorporating new delivery channels. A future-proof architecture distinguishes itself by its ability to harness capabilities from various cloud platforms, fostering an environment conducive to rapid experimentation with emerging technologies.

The essence of a future-proof architecture lies in its modularity, allowing for minimal impact when swapping components. This modularity is critical to maintaining agility and responsiveness in a fast-paced digital landscape. Employing open standards is a strategic move to avoid vendor lock-in, keeping the organization's options open and adaptable. Incorporating event-driven capabilities for real-time processing, underpinned by a foundation of microservices and Application Programming Interface (APIs) is instrumental in facilitating agile development and swift adaptation to evolving technological needs.

Data Architecture

A modern data architecture is at the foundation of AI readiness, crucial for powering downstream analytics and AI applications. This architecture requires a well-organized inventory of data sources, each with clearly defined access requirements and usage protocols. Efficient and reliable data pipelines are the lifelines that move and transform data from its sources to its destinations. A comprehensive data catalog enhances visibility into the available data assets, while data lakes provide a flexible repository for storing raw data assets.

Data warehouses, data lakes, and data lake houses are pivotal in optimizing data for business analytics and reporting. Master data management (MDM) is a strategic move to ensure data consistency and minimize duplications. Monitoring data quality across various sources and usage points is vital for preserving the integrity of AI applications. Metadata management adds another layer of value, offering context and meaning to data assets, while robust data governance enforces necessary security, access, and lifecycle management policies.

AI Architecture

A robust AI architecture is characterized by an mature machine learning operations (MLOps) pipeline designed to develop, deploy, and monitor ML models efficiently. The practice of versioning models and meticulously tracking metadata from development through production is essential for maintaining control and traceability. Centralized feature storage is critical, enabling access and monitoring across various models. The ability to compare experiments and transition the best-performing models to production is a testament to an effective AI architecture.

Adherence to trusted AI principles, including fairness, explainability, and robustness, is non-negotiable in ensuring ethical AI use. Continuous monitoring of models in production and re-training to counteract data or concept drift are integral practices. The democratization of AI through AutoML/AI empowers a broader range of users, while collaborative tools like notebooks and shared workspaces are instrumental in fostering teamwork during model development.

GenAI Architecture

Developing generative models is a nuanced process that significantly benefits from iterative feedback at each stage, ensuring the generated content is appropriate and contextualized. Curating data to minimize bias and safety issues, coupled with consistent human oversight, is crucial in this process. Transparency in source data, training methods, and limitations is provided to maintain clarity and trust.

Integration of Architectures

The integration of various architectures is a critical component of AI readiness. This integration is facilitated through APIs and events, ensuring seamless connections between different systems and platforms. Identity and access management are pivotal in integrating authorization across these architectures. Monitoring and observability extend across data, ML, and GenAI architectures, providing a comprehensive view of the system's health and performance. CI/CD pipelines, covering code, configurations, and assets, along with shared source repositories, are essential for maintaining consistency and efficiency across environments.

In essence, assessing architectural readiness for AI is a comprehensive process that scrutinizes an organization's infrastructure across multiple dimensions. It evaluates the organization's capacity to adapt to new technologies, manage data effectively, develop and deploy AI models, and integrate various architectural components. This assessment is crucial for organizations aiming to leverage AI technologies successfully, as it ensures that the underlying architecture not only supports but also enhances AI initiatives, contributing significantly to the organization's overall AI strategy and objectives.

DATA READINESS

The readiness of an organization's data infrastructure plays a pivotal role in AI reshaping business paradigms. Data Readiness for AI is not just about having vast amounts of data; it's about ensuring it is primed and aligned with the organization's AI objectives. This readiness thoroughly evaluates the organization's data capabilities, including future-proofing strategies, data quality, governance, architecture, and infrastructure. Let's delve into these crucial aspects to understand how they underpin the organization's ability to harness AI technologies effectively, contributing significantly to its overall AI strategy and success.

Data Future Proofing

The future-proofing of an organization's data capabilities for AI is a strategic endeavor that extends beyond current needs. It involves forward-thinking plans to expand analytics into new realms and proactively identify new data types. This approach is pivotal in adapting data governance policies to the ever-changing landscape of regulations and in evolving the data infrastructure to capitalize on emerging capabilities. Skills development is critical to this puzzle, equipping staff to use new technologies adeptly. Balancing innovation with prudence in technology standards is a tightrope walk that organizations must master.

Modularity and abstraction are not mere buzzwords but essential attributes that facilitate flexibility and scalability. Integrating external data opens doors to new insights, necessitating adjustments in data quality processes to accommodate new data types. Change enablement is critical in helping users adapt to and adopt new capabilities, while cloud services offer the required flexibility for burgeoning initiatives. Data governance policies must underscore ethical data use, and a commitment to automation is vital to enhancing data quality over time. Cultivating a culture that prioritizes data-driven decision-making and democratizes data access is fundamental in future-proofing data capabilities.

Data Quality

In AI, high data quality is not a luxury but a necessity. Data must be complete, current, and possess the granularity needed for specific use cases. Uniform formatting, adherence to regulatory requirements, and identifying and documenting biases in data are imperative. Accuracy is non-negotiable, and comprehensive metadata descriptors and data dictionaries are essential. Robust data integrity validation processes and sourcing data from authoritative sources are foundational to maintaining data integrity. The documentation of data lineage, structuring data for analytics use cases, and the vigilant monitoring of data quality KPIs are critical practices. Addressing issues in data quality assessments promptly and ensuring that data quality processes are both sustainable and repeatable is crucial to maintaining the integrity of AI applications.

Data Governance

Effective data governance is the backbone of AI-related data management. Clearly defined responsibilities, well-documented policies and procedures, and the assignment of data stewards to manage critical data assets form the framework of robust data governance. An operating model that supports data governance activities, balanced policies that cater to business needs while respecting constraints, and a workforce aware of their data governance responsibilities are essential. Executive sponsorship plays a pivotal role in the success of data governance activities, necessitating regular reviews and updates. Comprehensive data governance must encompass structured, unstructured, and external data backed by established regulatory compliance processes.

Data Architecture

A modern data architecture that supports analytics and AI use cases is critical to data readiness. It should facilitate the rapid integration of new data and automate data movement between systems. Data lineage mapping, normalization for downstream uses, and the application of master data management principles are strategic elements of a modern data architecture. Maximizing the separation of storage and compute, supporting real-time and batch data processing, and scalable data storage with disaster recovery protections are non-negotiable requirements. The architecture must also facilitate enterprise data integration, enable the reuse of data objects, and support role-based data access control.

Data Infrastructure

An organization's data infrastructure must be robust enough to provide adequate storage and compute capacity, catering to concurrent users and supporting in-memory processing. It should deliver the necessary network throughput and support hybrid and multi-cloud environments. Sufficient ETL processing power, high availability levels, and the protection of sensitive data are crucial. Cost optimization, adherence to defined architectures, support for disaster recovery processes, and efficient monitoring for usage and performance are vital. Efficient change management, proactive capacity planning for future needs, and secure access methods are integral components of a robust data infrastructure.

In essence, assessing data readiness for AI is a comprehensive process that evaluates an organization's infrastructure across multiple dimensions, including data quality, governance, architecture, and infrastructure. This assessment is vital for organizations aiming to leverage AI technologies successfully, ensuring that the underlying data capabilities not only support but also enhance AI initiatives, thereby contributing significantly to the organization's overall AI strategy and objectives.

AI READINESS

In an era where AI is becoming a cornerstone of competitive advantage, assessing AI Readiness within an organization is a critical and comprehensive task. It goes beyond the mere possession of advanced tools and technologies; it's about ensuring that the entire organizational ecosystem is aligned and prepared for the effective adoption and utilization of AI. This assessment, rooted in detailed and strategic questions, probes deep into the organization's capabilities across various domains, such as team skills, future-proofing strategies, quality assurance, governance, architecture, and infrastructure. Let's explore these key areas to understand how they collectively determine an organization's readiness to implement AI and do so in a way that aligns with its broader strategic objectives and ethical standards.

AI Future Proofing

The future-proofing of an organization's AI capabilities is a strategic process that requires foresight and adaptability. It involves crafting a roadmap to expand AI into new use cases, continuously evaluating and developing the AI team's skills, and adapting AI governance to align with evolving regulations and public expectations. Identifying new data types to enhance AI model accuracy and growing the AI infrastructure to capitalize on emerging capabilities are critical steps in this journey. Balancing innovation with prudence in AI technology standards is essential, as is ensuring that AI systems are designed with modularity and abstraction for maximum flexibility.

Integrating external data sources is critical to unlocking new AI capabilities, necessitating adjustments in AI quality processes to accommodate new data and model types. The AI infrastructure must be equipped with technologies capable of supporting growth, and change enablement processes are vital to facilitate the adoption of new AI capabilities. Cloud services offer the needed flexibility for new AI initiatives, while AI governance policies must emphasize the ethical and fair use of AI. Cultivating a culture that embraces AI-driven decision-making and democratizing access to AI are fundamental aspects of future-proofing an organization's AI capabilities.

AI Quality

Systems must adhere to stringent performance thresholds for accuracy and undergo rigorous testing for biases and unfair outcomes. The explainability of AI model decisions to stakeholders is a non-negotiable aspect, ensuring transparency and trust. AI models must be reproducible from their project artifacts, and continuous monitoring is necessary to detect and address accuracy drift over time. Incorporating human oversight into AI systems is crucial to address potential weaknesses, and compliance with regulatory requirements specific to the domain is mandatory.

AI Governance

Effective governance in AI is about establishing clear responsibilities and ethical frameworks. Policies must mandate AI systems' safe and ethical development, supported by well-documented processes. An operating model that underpins AI governance activities is essential, as is the awareness and involvement of employees in these governance responsibilities. AI projects require executive oversight, and governance policies should encompass the protection of personal information and cover the entire model lifecycle.

AI Architecture

A modern software architecture is the backbone of rapid AI development, supporting automated ML pipeline orchestration. This architecture should facilitate the labeling, pre-processing, and versioning of data and enable the integration of new data sources. It must support various development stages – from development to staging and production – and promote the sharing and discoverability of models. Scalable infrastructure to accommodate increasing model complexity and support for both real-time and batch model deployment are critical components.

AI Infrastructure

The infrastructure for AI must provide adequate storage capacity for models and data, with the capability for linear scaling as needed. It should deliver the necessary operational Infrastructure Operations (IOps) performance for model development and support multiple concurrent model-building jobs. Adequate compute capacity for training and deployment, in-memory processing for low latency predictions, and sufficient network throughput are essential. The infrastructure must also support hybrid on-premises and multi-cloud deployments and provide the necessary data processing power.

In essence, assessing AI Readiness is evaluating an organization's preparedness across multiple dimensions, ensuring that the underlying capabilities support and enhance AI initiatives. This assessment is crucial for organizations aiming to successfully leverage AI technologies, as it contributes significantly to the organization's overall AI strategy and objectives. It's a strategic endeavor beyond technical readiness, encompassing cultural, structural, and ethical alignment with AI technologies.

GenAI READINESS

The specific focus on GenAI readiness within an organization marks a significant stride beyond traditional AI preparedness. Assessing GenAI Readiness is a nuanced and comprehensive process that critically examines an organization's ability to adopt and effectively utilize GenAI technologies. This assessment, grounded in detailed questions, delves into the organization's capabilities, specifically targeting areas such as future-proofing strategies, quality assurance, governance, architecture, and infrastructure, all tailored for GenAI. Let's explore these key areas to understand how they collectively shape an organization's ability to implement GenAI and do so in a manner that aligns with its broader strategic goals and ethical considerations.

GenAI Future Proofing

Future-proofing for GenAI is a strategic process that demands foresight and adaptability. It involves crafting a roadmap to expand GenAI into new and diverse use cases over time. This roadmap necessitates the regular evaluation and development of the GenAI team's skills, alongside adapting GenAI governance to align with the dynamic landscape of regulations and public expectations. Identifying new data types to enhance generative model quality and evolving the infrastructure to capitalize on emerging GenAI capabilities are pivotal steps in this journey. Balancing innovation with prudence in GenAI technology standards is essential, as is ensuring that GenAI systems are designed with modularity and abstraction for maximum flexibility.

Integrating external data sources is vital to unlocking new GenAI capabilities, necessitating process adjustments to accommodate new data types and generative model paradigms. The GenAI infrastructure must be equipped with technologies capable of supporting growth, and change enablement processes are vital to facilitate the adoption of new generative capabilities. Cloud services offer the needed flexibility for new GenAI initiatives, while governance policies must emphasize the ethical and safe use of GenAI. Cultivating a culture that embraces GenAI-driven creation and democratizing access to GenAI are fundamental aspects of future-proofing an organization's GenAI capabilities.

GenAI Quality

GenAI systems must adhere to stringent performance thresholds, producing high-quality artifacts and content. Testing must validate outputs' coherence, accuracy, and uniqueness, and generative outputs should be scrutinized for harmful, toxic, or biased content. Testing data should cover a wide array of use cases and creative scenarios. Generative systems must be reproducible from their project artifacts, and continuous monitoring is necessary to detect and address drift in output quality. Incorporating human oversight into GenAI systems is crucial to address potential weaknesses, and compliance with regulatory requirements specific to content generation is mandatory.

GenAI Governance

Effective governance in GenAI requires establishing clear responsibilities and ethical frameworks. Policies must mandate generative systems' safe and ethical development, supported by well-documented processes. An operating model that underpins GenAI governance activities is essential, as is the awareness and involvement of employees in these governance responsibilities. GenAI projects require executive oversight, and governance policies should encompass the protection of personal information and cover the entire generative model lifecycle.

GenAI Architecture

A modern software architecture is the backbone of rapid GenAI development, supporting automated orchestration of generative pipelines. This architecture should facilitate the processing and versioning of training data and enable the integration of new data sources. It must support various development stages – from development to staging and production – and promote the sharing and discoverability of generative models. Scalable infrastructure to accommodate increasing model complexity and support for both real-time and batch model deployment are critical components.

GenAI Infrastructure

The infrastructure for GenAI must provide adequate storage capacity for models and data, with the capability for linear scaling as needed. It should deliver the necessary IOPS performance for model development and support multiple concurrent model-building jobs. Adequate compute capacity for training and deployment, in-memory processing for low latency predictions, and sufficient network throughput are essential. The infrastructure must also support hybrid on-premises and multi-cloud deployments and provide the necessary data processing power.

In essence, assessing GenAI Readiness evaluates an organization's preparedness across multiple dimensions, ensuring that the underlying capabilities support and enhance GenAI initiatives. This assessment is crucial for organizations that leverage GenAI technologies, as it contributes significantly to their overall AI strategy and objectives. It's a strategic endeavor beyond technical readiness, encompassing cultural, structural, and ethical alignment with GenAI technologies.

COMPLIANCE READINESS

Assessing Compliance Readiness for AI and GenAI deployment within an organization is a critical and comprehensive endeavor. This process goes far beyond mere adherence to regulatory norms; it's an in-depth evaluation of an organization's readiness to meet regulatory, ethical, and accountability standards in deploying AI and GenAI technologies. This assessment, meticulously based on a detailed set of questions, provides essential insights into the organization's ability to manage risks, adhere to regulations, uphold ethical practices, ensure accountability, and consider ESG impacts. Let's delve into these critical areas to understand how they collectively form an integral part of an organization's strategy to deploy AI responsibly and sustainably, ensuring it meets compliance standards while upholding its ethical and social responsibilities.

Compliance Future Proofing

Future-proofing for compliance in AI and GenAI is a strategic endeavor that extends beyond current operational needs. It involves a proactive approach to expanding AI and GenAI use cases while adeptly managing associated risks. This necessitates the development of skills that enable prudent innovation and the adaptation of policies to keep pace with evolving regulations. Designing systems that facilitate responsible controls and aiming to exceed compliance standards are fundamental. Incorporating external perspectives is vital to mitigate blind spots, and fostering a culture of critical introspection and continuous learning is vital to staying ahead in compliance. Infrastructure supporting real-world testing and evaluating new techniques for their risks and benefits are integral to this strategy. Embedding ethics into AI and GenAI processes through democratization initiatives and ensuring stakeholder inclusion in oversight activities are essential for robust compliance future-proofing.

Regulation

Regulatory readiness is a proactive stance involving continuously monitoring regulatory requirements and ensuring that systems undergo necessary certification for compliance. Legal counsel plays a crucial role in reviewing initiatives and contracts, and mandatory assessments are imperative before deploying systems. Transparent management of relationships with regulators and adherence to regional rules and restrictions are essential. Internal audits that verify ongoing compliant practices and policies that mandate documentation for traceability are foundational. Protecting confidential information appropriately and designing systems that can be turned off to comply with lawful orders are critical aspects of regulatory readiness.

Ethics

Ethical practices in AI and GenAI are not optional but a core requirement. Policies must mandate ethical practices throughout AI and GenAI lifecycles, and risk assessments should carefully weigh benefits against potential harms. Executive commitment to responsible AI and GenAI is a non-negotiable aspect, and ethical practices should be integral to organizational evaluations. Involving diverse voices in ethical considerations and seeking guidance from ethics advisory panels are vital practices. Transparency in public communications about AI and GenAI limitations, rigorous testing to avoid biases, and strict adherence to privacy and consent are essential to upholding ethical standards in AI and GenAI.

Accountability

Accountability in AI and GenAI clearly defines responsibilities and fosters a culture where risk and compliance processes support this accountability. Documentation that traces decisions for traceability and controls that enable monitoring of AI and GenAI systems in production is crucial. Errors and issues must trigger comprehensive assessments, and regular audits should evaluate practices against established policies. Transparency reporting to disclose progress and limitations and empowering employees to question practices are vital. Leadership must demonstrate unwavering commitment to responsible AI and GenAI.

ESG Impact

ESG impact considerations are increasingly becoming a cornerstone of AI and GenAI readiness. This includes assessing the environmental sustainability of AI and GenAI initiatives, their impact on climate change, and optimizing energy efficiency in infrastructure. Sustainable sourcing policies for hardware, minimizing waste and water use, and selecting providers with robust ESG practices are critical. Additionally, considering workforce welfare, community impacts, corporate citizenship, ethical supply chain policies, data stewardship, and responsible marketing practices are integral to a comprehensive ESG strategy.

In essence, assessing Compliance Readiness for AI and GenAI is a multifaceted process that evaluates an organization's readiness across various dimensions. It's a crucial step for organizations aiming to leverage AI and GenAI technologies responsibly and sustainably, ensuring compliance with standards while upholding ethical and social responsibilities. This assessment is a procedural necessity and a strategic imperative, integral to the organization's commitment to responsible AI deployment.

The essence of this methodology lies in its ability to provide a multidimensional view of readiness, encompassing Organizational, Architectural, Data, AI, GenAI, and Compliance Readiness. Each dimension is meticulously evaluated, revealing insights into the organization's capabilities, potential gaps, and areas for improvement. This process is not just about ticking boxes; it's about understanding the depth and breadth of an organization's readiness to embrace AI. From ensuring that the leadership's vision aligns with AI objectives to evaluating the robustness of data governance and the agility of technological infrastructure, this assessment methodology is a comprehensive guide for organizations navigating the complexities of AI integration.

Concluding this assessment, it's evident that readiness for AI and GenAI is a nuanced and dynamic process requiring continuous evaluation and adaptation. Organizations must be technically prepared and culturally and structurally attuned to the demands of an AI and GenAI-driven future. This readiness is a testament to an organization's commitment to innovation, competitive advantage, and long-term success in an increasingly digital world. As AI and GenAI continues to evolve and reshape industries, this assessment methodology is crucial for organizations to chart their course in the AI and GenAI landscape, ensuring they are not just participants but leaders in this transformative era.

ONGOING ASSESSMENT CYCLES

In an era where technology, particularly AI and GenAI, is advancing at an unprecedented pace, ongoing assessment cycles become relevant and essential for organizations aiming to stay at the forefront of innovation. This continuous evaluation is a strategic imperative in an organization's AI readiness and adaptability journey. As an industry leader with extensive experience, I have observed how the rapid advancement of AI and GenAI technologies can swiftly turn today's breakthroughs into tomorrow's outdated methods. In such a fast-paced environment, ongoing assessment cycles are beneficial and crucial for ensuring that an organization's AI strategies and implementations remain cutting-edge, effective, and in sync with the latest technological advancements.

The essence of continuous evaluation in AI and GenAI readiness lies in its proactive and dynamic nature. AI and GenAI are fields characterized by rapid changes and advancements. Technologies that were groundbreaking a few months ago may soon become obsolete. This rapid evolution extends beyond technology to regulatory landscapes, ethical considerations, and market expectations. Regular reassessment, therefore, is a critical exercise, enabling organizations to identify and address gaps in their AI and GenAI capabilities, realign AI and GenAI strategies with the latest trends, and anticipate and prepare for future developments.

Moreover, the unprecedented pace of AI and GenAI advancement means that regular updates are not just a matter of staying current but are essential for maintaining a competitive edge. AI and GenAI's influence permeates various business operations, impacting everything from customer interactions to product development, supply chain management, and strategic decision-making. The interconnected nature of AI and GenAI with these business aspects means that changes in AI and GenAI can have significant and far-reaching implications. Ongoing assessment cycles ensure that organizations are aware of these implications and strategically positioned to respond effectively. They allow for the recalibration of AI and GenAI strategies in line with broader business objectives, ensuring that AI initiatives drive meaningful value and contribute to sustainable growth.

AI and GenAI's complexity and multifaceted nature further underscore the need for continuous reassessment. AI and GenAI encompass diverse technologies and applications, each presenting unique challenges and opportunities. Ongoing evaluation enables organizations to develop a deep and nuanced understanding of these various aspects, allowing them to tailor their AI and GenAI initiatives to specific needs and contexts. It promotes a culture of learning and adaptation, where insights from ongoing assessments inform and refine AI and GenAI strategies, ensuring they are robust, relevant, and effective.

Ongoing assessment cycles are indispensable for AI and GenAI readiness and adaptation. They represent a proactive approach to navigating the rapidly evolving AI and GenAI landscape, ensuring that organizations remain agile, informed, and strategically aligned with the latest developments in A and GenAI I. As leaders in this digital age, we must recognize the critical importance of these continuous evaluations and integrate them into our organizational strategies. Doing so protects our current AI investments and lays a solid foundation for future innovations and success in this transformative era.

KEY COMPONENTS OF ONGOING ASSESSMENT CYCLES IN THE CONTEXT OF AI READINESS

In the rapidly evolving landscape of AI and GenAI, where technological advancements occur at an unprecedented pace, AI and GenAI readiness transcends a one-time evaluation. It necessitates a continuous assessment cycle characterized by regular monitoring, updating, and dynamic adaptation. These components are not just operational necessities but strategic imperatives that ensure an organization's AI and GenAI initiatives remain aligned with the latest technological advancements and business objectives.

Regular Monitoring and Updating

The first critical component of ongoing assessment cycles is Regular Monitoring and Updating. In the realm of AI and GenAI, where new developments and breakthroughs are a constant, an organization's readiness today might not suffice tomorrow. Regular monitoring involves a comprehensive review of the organization's AI and GenAI strategies, technologies, and methodologies in light of the latest advancements and industry standards. This process is akin to recalibrating instruments in a rapidly changing environment, ensuring the organization's AI and GenAI roadmap remains relevant and practical.

Updating assessments is crucial to reflect these new developments. It involves revisiting and revising the AI and GenAI readiness framework to incorporate new technologies, methodologies, and industry benchmarks. This continuous updating process ensures that the organization's AI and GenAI initiatives are built on current best practices and emerging trends rather than becoming obsolete relics of past understanding.

Dynamic Adaptation

The second component, Dynamic Adaptation, is about the organization's ability to pivot and adjust its AI and GenAI strategies based on insights gained from ongoing assessments. This component is where the true agility of an organization is tested. Dynamic adaptation involves reshaping AI and GenAI strategies and operations in response to emerging challenges and opportunities identified through regular monitoring.

This adaptability is crucial in a landscape where AI and GenAI's potential and implications constantly expand. It ensures that AI and GenAI initiatives are not static but evolve in alignment with the organization's changing needs and the external environment. Dynamic adaptation allows organizations to make informed decisions, whether it's about adopting a new AI and GenAI technology, altering a development approach, or realigning AI and GenAI objectives with broader business goals.

The critical components of ongoing assessment cycles in AI and GenAI readiness – Regular Monitoring and Updating and Dynamic Adaptation – are vital in ensuring that an organization's AI and GenAI initiatives are effective today and poised for future success. These components enable organizations to stay ahead of the curve, respond effectively to new developments, and fully harness the transformative power of AI and GenAI. As leaders guiding digital transformations, we are responsible for embedding these components into our organizational strategies, ensuring our AI and GenAI initiatives are robust, relevant, and resilient in rapid technological change.

STRATEGIES FOR IMPLEMENTING ONGOING ASSESSMENT CYCLES IN AI READINESS

Implementing ongoing assessment cycles is crucial for maintaining an organization's competitive edge and alignment with technological advancements. These cycles ensure that AI and GenAI strategies and operations are continuously optimized. Let's explore practical strategies for implementing these cycles, focusing on Scheduled Re-Evaluations, Real-Time Monitoring Tools, and Feedback Mechanisms.

Scheduled Re-Evaluations

Scheduled Re-Evaluations are essential in the ongoing assessment process. These structured intervals, whether quarterly or bi-annually, provide opportunities for organizations to review and update their AI and GenAI readiness systematically. This approach ensures that AI and GenAI strategies remain relevant and practical despite rapid technological changes and evolving business goals.

During these re-evaluations, organizations should assess various aspects of AI and GenAI readiness, such as data infrastructure, governance, compliance, and workforce skills. It's a time to reflect on progress, identify improvement areas, and adjust strategies accordingly. The key is to find a balance in scheduling these evaluations – frequent enough to stay current, yet spaced adequately to allow for the implementation of significant changes.

Feedback Mechanisms

Incorporating Feedback Mechanisms into the assessment cycle is crucial for a holistic understanding of AI and GenAI readiness. Feedback from employees, customers, and stakeholders offers invaluable insights into AI and GenAI initiatives' practical impact and effectiveness.

Employee feedback can shed light on operational challenges, training needs, and the practical utility of AI and GenAI tools. Customer feedback is essential for gauging user experience and satisfaction with AI and GenAI-driven products and services. Stakeholder feedback from industry partners provides an external perspective on the organization's AI and GenAI strategy and its alignment with industry trends.

Establishing structured channels for collecting and analyzing this feedback ensures that AI and GenAI strategies are grounded in real-world experiences and needs. This approach helps organizations develop AI and GenAI solutions that are technologically sound and resonate with and bring value to their intended users.

The successful implementation of ongoing assessment cycles in AI and GenAI readiness requires a combination of regular re-evaluations, real-time monitoring, and active feedback collection. This comprehensive approach ensures that an organization's AI and GenAI initiatives are continually refined and aligned with the latest technological developments, operational requirements, and strategic goals. As leaders in AI and GenAI, we are responsible for integrating these strategies into our organizational practices, ensuring a proactive and informed approach to AI adoption and utilization.

HARMONIZING ASSESSMENTS WITH ORGANIZATIONAL DYNAMICS

Integrating assessment processes with an organization's core functions and ethos is paramount. This integration ensures that AI and GenAI initiatives are not isolated endeavors but are deeply rooted in the organization's strategic and cultural fabric. Let's explore how this can be achieved through alignment with business objectives and incorporation into corporate culture.

Alignment with Business Objectives

The key to successful AI and GenAI integration is ensuring that ongoing assessments harmonize with the organization's broader business strategy and objectives. This alignment means that AI and GenAI initiatives should directly contribute to the organization's overarching goals, whether enhancing operational efficiency, improving customer experience, or driving innovation.

To achieve this, AI and GenAI assessments should be designed to evaluate the technical capabilities and how these capabilities translate into tangible business outcomes. Regular reviews should be conducted to ensure that AI and GenAI strategies are contributing to key performance indicators and strategic milestones. This approach ensures that AI and GenAI initiatives are always relevant and add value to the organization.

Incorporation into Corporate Culture

Embedding the assessment process into the organizational culture is crucial for its acceptance and effectiveness. This integration means moving beyond seeing assessments as mere formalities or compliance activities. Instead, they should be considered integral components of the organizational ethos, driving continuous improvement and innovation.

Fostering a culture that values data-driven decision-making, continuous learning, and adaptability is essential to embed these processes. Encouraging open communication about AI and GenAI initiatives and their impact, recognizing and rewarding teams for AI and GenAI-driven achievements, and providing ongoing training and development opportunities are ways to achieve this. By making AI and GenAI assessments a part of the daily conversation, organizations can ensure that their AI strategies are technically sound and culturally ingrained.

The effective integration of AI and GenAI assessments within an organization demands that they are aligned with business objectives and woven into the corporate culture. This approach ensures that AI and GenAI initiatives are strategically relevant and culturally embraced, leading to a more holistic and impactful adoption of AI and GenAI technologies. As leaders in digital transformation, our role is to guide this integration, ensuring that AI is not just a tool but a fundamental aspect of how the organization operates and evolves.

NAVIGATING CHALLENGES IN SUSTAINED ASSESSMENT PRACTICES

Organizations inevitably encounter various challenges in the journey of continuous AI and GenAI readiness assessment. Two primary hurdles are managing change fatigue and ensuring assessment methodologies' ongoing relevance and accuracy. Addressing these challenges effectively is crucial for maintaining the momentum and integrity of AI and GenAI integration efforts.

Managing Change Fatigue

Change fatigue, a common byproduct of constant evolution and reassessment, can lead to team resistance or apathy. To mitigate this, adopting strategies that foster resilience and adaptability is essential. One practical approach is communicating the purpose and benefits of ongoing assessments and aligning them with individual and organizational goals. This alignment helps in cultivating a sense of ownership and understanding among employees.

Another strategy is to pace the changes and assessments in a manageable way for the organization. This pacing can be achieved by prioritizing areas of evaluation based on urgency and impact, thus avoiding overwhelming employees with too many changes at once. Additionally, providing adequate support and resources, such as training and counseling, can help employees adapt to and embrace change more readily.

Ensuring Relevance and Accuracy

Maintaining assessment tools' and methodologies' relevance and accuracy is critical, especially as AI technology and business landscapes evolve rapidly. Regular updates and revisions of assessment tools and criteria are necessary to ensure that assessment practices remain effective. This process involves staying abreast of the latest developments in AI and GenAI and related fields and incorporating these insights into the assessment framework.

Involving a diverse group of stakeholders in the review and update process can also enhance the relevance and accuracy of assessments. This diversity brings various perspectives, ensuring the assessments cover all critical AI and GenAI readiness aspects. Furthermore, leveraging data analytics and feedback mechanisms can provide insights into the effectiveness of current assessment practices, guiding necessary adjustments.

Addressing the challenges of managing change fatigue and ensuring the relevance and accuracy of ongoing assessments is crucial for the success of AI and GenAI readiness initiatives. Organizations can navigate these challenges effectively by adopting thoughtful strategies and staying vigilant to the changing technology and business dynamics. This vigilance ensures that their AI readiness assessments remain a robust and responsive tool in their journey toward digital transformation and AI and GenAI excellence.

The implementation of ongoing assessment cycles stands as a cornerstone for organizations striving to harness the full potential of AI and GenAI technologies. These cycles are not mere procedural steps but strategic imperatives that ensure organizations remain agile, informed, and ahead in the race for technological advancements. As a leader in this field, I recognize the critical importance of embedding these continuous evaluations into our organizational strategies, ensuring our AI and GenAI initiatives are robust, relevant, and resilient.

AI and GenAI readiness is continuous and ever-evolving. It demands a proactive approach, where organizations are not just reacting to changes but anticipating and preparing for them. Through regular monitoring and updating, dynamic adaptation, and the integration of assessments into organizational processes, we ensure that our AI and GenAI strategies and operations are continuously optimized. This optimization is not limited to technical aspects but extends to aligning AI and GenAI initiatives with broader business objectives and embedding them into the corporate culture.

However, this has its challenges. Managing change fatigue and ensuring assessment methodologies' ongoing relevance and accuracy are critical hurdles organizations must navigate. Addressing these challenges effectively is crucial for maintaining the momentum and integrity of AI and GenAI integration efforts. By fostering resilience, adaptability, and a culture of continuous learning, we can mitigate the impact of change fatigue. Simultaneously, staying vigilant to the changing dynamics of technology and business ensures that our assessment methodologies remain relevant and accurate.

The path is a nuanced and dynamic process requiring continuous evaluation and adaptation. It's about ensuring that organizations are technically prepared and culturally and structurally attuned to the demands of an AI and GenAI -driven future. This readiness is a testament to an organization's commitment to innovation, competitive advantage, and long-term success in an increasingly digital world. As AI and GenAI continues to evolve and reshape industries, our commitment to ongoing assessment cycles will be crucial in charting our course in the AI and GenAI landscape, ensuring we are not just participants but leaders in this transformative era.

REALIZING THE VALUE

With comprehensive maturity diagnosed across essential ingredients, pragmatic roadmaps can develop integrated AI and GenAI solutions fulfilling strategic business needs. Regular assessments empower data-driven planning and implementation, avoiding stalled or failed initiatives resulting from unidentified gaps.

Assessments provide visibility into how to judiciously combine culture, skills, data, systems, governance, and ethics into an enterprise AI and

GenAI practices greater than isolated parts. They highlight which specific recipe ingredients require attention and investment to achieve objectives.

This understanding accelerates adoption and business value delivery by informing training priorities, funding allocation, project scoping, and capability development based on quantified diagnostics. Assessments spotlight adoption blockers needing timely resolution. They provide metrics demonstrating progression versus milestones to celebrate incremental successes.

However, realizing impactful results requires governance processes and cultural readiness to adopt assessment insights across initiatives. Leadership must visibly sponsor and participate in evaluations to demonstrate commitment. Assessment findings need integration into strategy planning and investment roadmaps. The workforce mindset needs to embrace frequent checkups as constructive opportunities rather than passing audits.

With maturity continuously diagnosed across all AI and GenAI readiness dimensions, organizations can confidently scale AI and GenAI solutions that responsibly deliver tangible business results. Assessments provide data-driven insights illuminating the path forward. Integrated governance practices and culture then accelerate the journey through guided enhancements.

Regular AI and GenAI readiness assessments empower data-driven planning and implementation to realize value at scale. They highlight recipe ingredients needing attention, avoiding stalled initiatives from gaps. Assessments inform investments, projects, capabilities, and more to accelerate adoption. However, governance and culture must adopt insights to strengthen solutions holistically. Assessments illuminate the path, while governance and culture fuel the engine of business impact.

OPERATIONALIZING ASSESSMENTS

Leadership must champion assessments as a strategic priority, participating personally in evaluations, acting upon insights, and investing in capabilities. Governance policies must mandate regular checkups organization-wide and integrate findings into planning processes and funding roadmaps. At the cultural level, assessments should become accepted routine wellness practices versus feared audits.

With maturity benchmarks woven into operations, readiness gaps and achievements readily gain visibility to guide enhancement efforts. Assessment metrics are tracked over time alongside product KPIs to show progress. Findings directly inform project planning, team building, and resources to ensure initiatives are able to stay within unidentified weak points.

Education builds workforce skills in conducting assessments while fostering enthusiasm for regular checkups as constructive ways to accelerate collective capabilities versus passing audits. Starting with small, low-risk assessments demonstrates value through early wins, earning buy-in for further adoption. As organizational muscle memory develops, periodic assessments become habitual components of project initiation and completion.

Immersive training empowers teams to self-diagnose readiness as part of development routines. Standard tools and templates aid consistency across groups. Peers assist via assessment reviews to spread skills. With assessments demystified through learning and practice, capabilities grow collaboratively.

Over time, comprehensive assessments can be embraced, like routine health checkups sustaining long-term well-being, rather than undergoing invasive surgery only when problems are acute. Preventative insights avert painful failures down the line. Continued gains build confidence and appetite for achieving higher maturity levels through pragmatic enhancement efforts informed by insights.

Operationalizing assessments requires leadership prioritization, governance integration, and cultural adoption. With benchmarks woven into operations, insights guide efforts. Education and small wins build enthusiasm and skills. Regular wellness checkups have become accepted best practices for sustaining collective capabilities over the long term.

Comprehensive AI and GenAI readiness assessments provide invaluable continuous insights, enabling organizations to combine ingredients into integrated solutions fulfilling strategic needs.

Regular evaluations thoroughly diagnose maturity across critical cultural, skills, data, systems, governance, and ethics dimensions. They illuminate priority gaps and progression over time versus milestones. Comparing against peers reveals opportunities, while analyzing failures and successes informs strengthening practices. The quantified findings shape pragmatic enhancement plans and roadmaps tailored to the organization's needs and objectives.

But simply conducting assessments alone is insufficient. Realizing results requires governance processes to adopt insights and invest in identified capabilities. An ethical culture focused on responsible AI and GenAI needs to embrace regular checkups as constructive opportunities rather than audits. Assessments provide data-driven visibility into the current state. Integrated governance practices fuel the journey forward through prioritization, training, and solution strengthening guided by the insights. With readiness continuously diagnosed across ingredients, organizations can confidently combine elements into AI and GenAI solutions, delivering business impact more significantly than the sum of isolated parts. Regular assessments illuminate needs, while governance and culture power the acceleration.

FINAL THOUGHTS

Assessing your organization's readiness to embrace AI and GenAI technologies is pivotal. This chapter is a comprehensive guide for leaders navigating the complexities of AI integration, offering insights into the multifaceted aspects of readiness spanning culture, skills, data, infrastructure, systems, and compliance. The ultimate goal is to ensure that your organization is equipped and culturally and strategically aligned for AI adoption.

AI readiness is not static; it's a dynamic process necessitating regular and thorough assessments. These evaluations are essential in understanding your organization's AI and GenAI journey and where it needs to go. It is a periodic health check, essential for diagnosing current conditions and proactive planning and improvement. This chapter outlines a detailed methodology for conducting these assessments, addressing critical areas, including organizational and architectural readiness and data, AI, GenAI, and compliance.

Organizational readiness is a cornerstone of your AI and GenAI journey. It involves examining your organization's culture, structure, strategy, and capacity for AI adoption. This is where leadership's vision and strategy for AI and GenAI must align with practical implementation capabilities. On the other hand, architectural readiness focuses on the technical framework supporting AI initiatives. This includes your data architecture, your infrastructure's robustness, and your systems' adaptability to emerging AI and GenAI technologies.

Data readiness is pivotal in the AI and GenAI readiness spectrum. High-quality data, effectively managed and governed, lays the foundation for successful AI and GenAI applications. The readiness of your AI and GenAI capabilities is also critical. This involves assessing the technical aspects and ensuring that ethical and governance frameworks are in place. Compliance readiness completes the picture, encompassing regulatory, ethical, and accountability standards crucial in the AI and GenAI landscape.

The process of ongoing assessment cycles is integral to maintaining AI and GenAI readiness. These cycles, encompassing regular monitoring, updating, and dynamic adaptation, ensure your AI strategies and operations remain cutting-edge and in sync with the latest technological advancements. These assessments are not merely procedural but strategic imperatives that guide your organization in navigating the rapidly evolving AI and GenAI landscape.

Operationalizing these assessments is vital. This involves integrating them into your organization's core functions, aligning them with business objectives, and embedding them into the corporate culture. Leadership is critical here, championing assessments as strategic priorities and acting upon their insights. Moreover, navigating the challenges in sustained assessment practices, such as managing change fatigue and ensuring ongoing relevance and accuracy, is crucial for the success of your AI and GenAI initiatives.

In essence, comprehensive AI and GenAI readiness assessments are indispensable tools for organizations looking to harness the full potential of AI and GenAI. They provide a detailed view of your current state, highlight improvement areas, and offer a roadmap for future development. But remember, the value of these assessments lies not only in their execution but also in how their insights are operationalized through governance and cultural adoption. As you embark on this journey, let these assessments guide you, illuminating the path forward and helping your organization embrace AI and GenAI holistically for long-term success.

KEY TAKEAWAYS AND ACTIONS

COMPREHENSIVE AI READINESS ASSESSMENTS ARE ESSENTIAL ACROSS VARIOUS ORGANIZATIONAL DIMENSIONS

- **Actionable Step:** Regularly evaluate culture, skills, data, infrastructure, systems, and compliance.
- **Implementation:** Schedule periodic assessments, use standardized tools for evaluation, and involve cross-functional teams for a holistic view.

METHODOLOGY OF AI AND GenAI READINESS ASSESSMENT INVOLVES BOTH FOUNDATIONAL AND TECHNICAL ASPECTS

- **Actionable Step:** Evaluate organizational readiness (culture, skills, strategy) and technical readiness (infrastructure, data, platforms).
- **Implementation:** Develop a checklist for each assessment area, gather data through surveys and interviews, and analyze results to identify gaps.

IMPORTANCE OF ONGOING ASSESSMENT CYCLES TO KEEP PACE WITH CHANGES IN TECHNOLOGY AND ORGANIZATIONAL NEEDS

- **Actionable Step:** Implement regular updates and reassessments of AI readiness.
- **Implementation:** Establish a recurring assessment schedule, update assessment criteria based on the latest AI advancements, and document changes in organizational needs.

COMBINING INSIGHTS INTO ACTIONABLE PLANS TO AVOID STALLED AI AND GenAI INITIATIVES

- **Actionable Step:** Create and update AI implementation plans using assessment insights.
- **Implementation:** Translate assessment findings into strategic priorities, develop action plans, and allocate resources for implementation.

OPERATIONALIZING ASSESSMENTS TO MAKE THEM AN INTEGRAL PART OF ORGANIZATIONAL STRATEGY

- **Actionable Step:** Embed assessment processes into the organization's operational framework.
- **Implementation:** Incorporate assessment results into regular business reviews, ensure leadership endorsement, and integrate findings into strategic decision-making.

REGULAR COMPREHENSIVE ASSESSMENTS ARE VITAL FOR DIAGNOSING PROGRESS AND GAPS IN AI READINESS

- **Actionable Step:** Conduct assessments to shape AI strategies and roadmaps.
- **Implementation:** Use results to prioritize AI projects, align with business objectives, and adjust strategies as needed.

ANALYZING SKILLS AND PROFICIENCY THROUGH ASSESSMENTS HIGHLIGHTS DEVELOPMENT NEEDS

- **Actionable Step:** Assess role-based AI skills and organizational proficiency.
- **Implementation:** Identify skill gaps, develop targeted training programs, and encourage a continuous learning culture.

CHAPTER 12

The Chief AI Officer, One Leader for AI

INTRODUCTION

In AI's dynamic and transformative realm, the Chief AI Officer (CAIO) emerges as pivotal in guiding organizations through the intricate maze of technological evolution and strategic implementation.

Chapter 1 laid the foundation, highlighting the critical shift from traditional AI, rooted in data science and machine learning, to the generative AI (GenAI) field. This evolution underscore the importance of aligning AI strategy with core business objectives. The CAIO, in this context, became the architect of this alignment, ensuring that AI initiatives are not merely technological endeavors but strategic assets driving tangible business outcomes. The CAIO sets the stage for AI's successful integration into business strategies by learning from past AI applications and focusing on building organizational and technical capacity.

Chapter 2, confronted the uncomfortable truth of AI's overhyped promises versus its actual delivery. Chapter 2 criticized the superficial adoption of AI, terming it a "scam" in the context of its underutilization and misapplication. Here, the CAIO's role transcended mere implementation; it involves a holistic reevaluation of AI strategies, focusing on practical, human-centric approaches and ensuring that AI initiatives are deeply integrated into business operations, driving real value.

Chapter 3 further emphasized the connection of AI with tangible business value. It advocated for a strategic synthesis of AI capabilities with

DOI: 10.1201/9781003486725-13

business goals, requiring an organizational cultural shift. The CAIO emerged as a critical driver of this shift, promoting a culture that embraced AI, ensuring ethical AI practices, and aligning AI initiatives with business objectives for substantial impact.

In Chapter 4, the narrative delved into cultivating an AI-ready culture, a task that fell squarely on the shoulders of the CAIO. This involved fostering innovation, embedding ethical AI practices, igniting enthusiasm for AI across the organization, and ensuring leadership commitment. Breaking down silos and advocating externally for the organization's AI initiatives are also crucial aspects of the CAIO's role.

The succeeding chapters – "Organizational Structure," "Infrastructure Readiness," "Data Readiness," "AI Readiness," "GenAI Readiness," and "Compliance Readiness" – comprehensively covered the various facets an organization must consider to be genuinely AI-ready. These chapters highlighted the importance of a well-structured approach, robust infrastructure, quality data, ethical considerations, and compliance with regulations for effective AI implementation. In these chapters, the CAIO is portrayed as the linchpin in orchestrating these elements, ensuring the organization's structure, culture, strategy, and operations are optimally aligned for AI success.

Finally, Chapter 11 on "Assessing Your Readiness" provided the tools and frameworks for organizations to evaluate and measure their AI maturity and preparedness. These assessments are crucial for the CAIO to understand where the organization stands in its AI journey, enabling it to make informed decisions, strategize effectively, and drive it toward AI excellence.

The CAIO, as depicted, is not just a technological leader but a strategic visionary, a cultural catalyst, an ethical guide, and a business strategist. Their role is integral in navigating the complex landscape of AI, transforming it from a misunderstood and underutilized technology into a powerful driver of innovation, efficiency, and growth. The CAIO's leadership is essential in ensuring that AI is leveraged not just as a tool but as a transformative force, aligned with the organization's core objectives and ethical standards, and capable of propelling the organization to new heights in the digital era.

INTRODUCING THE ROLE OF CHIEF AI OFFICER

In the transformative landscape of today's business world, marked by rapid advancements in AI, the emergence of the CAIO is a testament to the critical importance of AI in shaping organizational strategies and operations. This role, evolving beyond the traditional confines of technological expertise, signifies a shift toward a more integrated, strategic approach to AI in business.

The CAIO stands at the intersection of strategy, technology, and organizational culture, championing the integration of AI in a way that aligns with and amplifies the company's core objectives. This vital role involves implementing AI for innovation's sake and integration as a critical driver of the company's strategic ambitions.

The multifaceted responsibilities of the CAIO underscore the breadth and depth of this role in an organization. A CAIO navigates the complex terrain of aligning AI initiatives with overarching business goals, ensuring that AI investments contribute meaningfully to the company's success. This alignment is crucial for several reasons: it guarantees that AI projects support and enhance the broader strategic objectives of the company and ensures that resources dedicated to AI are utilized in the most impactful manner.

Developing a comprehensive, adaptable AI strategy is a cornerstone of the CAIO's role. Under the CAIO's stewardship, this strategy requires a holistic view of the organization's capabilities and needs, both present and future. It encompasses evaluating the current technological infrastructure, identifying skill gaps within the workforce, and understanding the company's readiness to harness the power of data. This strategic component is not static; it evolves in response to technological advancements and market shifts, requiring the CAIO to maintain agility and foresight.

Regarding technology, the CAIO's purview includes overseeing the organization's development and implementation of AI systems. This responsibility entails staying abreast of the latest AI and data science developments and understanding their potential applications within the company. The CAIO ensures that the AI technologies adopted align with the specific needs and goals of the company and are integrated seamlessly into existing systems and workflows.

Culturally, the CAIO plays a pivotal role in reshaping the organization's approach to AI. This involves fostering a culture of innovation where AI is embraced across various departments, encouraging teams to leverage AI in their work. This cultural shift, often challenging due to entrenched practices and mindsets, is critical as the success of AI initiatives frequently hinges on the organization's willingness to embrace new technologies.

Ethical AI governance constitutes another crucial aspect of the CAIO's role. Establishing robust governance frameworks is essential in an era where AI's potential risks, such as bias and privacy concerns, are increasingly scrutinized. These frameworks guide the responsible and ethical development and use of AI, encompassing policies on data usage, model transparency, and algorithmic accountability. The CAIO ensures these policies are adhered to, safeguarding the company, and building stakeholder trust.

Furthermore, the CAIO is instrumental in building the organization's AI talent pool. This involves attracting top AI and data science talent and fostering the existing workforce's skills and capabilities. The CAIO collaborates with HR and learning and development teams to create comprehensive training programs that enhance AI literacy across the organization, ensuring the company possesses the internal capabilities to develop, implement, and manage AI systems effectively.

A fundamental responsibility of the CAIO is fostering enterprise AI strategy alignment. This alignment ensures that AI initiatives are synchronized across various departments, forming a company-wide strategy. This unifying role demands strong leadership skills and the ability to foster collaboration across diverse groups such as IT, data science, marketing, and operations. Effective communication and stakeholder engagement is vital, as the CAIO articulates the value of AI initiatives in terms that resonate across the organization.

The CAIO plays a pivotal role in resource allocation for AI initiatives. By aligning AI projects with business objectives, the CAIO justifies investments in technology, talent, and infrastructure, demonstrating their potential ROI. This approach ensures efficient and effective resource allocation, prioritizing AI projects based on their strategic importance and potential impact.

The CAIO also continually monitors the progress of AI initiatives, assessing their impact on business objectives. Establishing key performance indicators (KPIs) and metrics to measure success allows the CAIO to refine and adjust AI strategies, ensuring they remain aligned with evolving business goals and market dynamics.

Effective change management is critical in accelerating AI adoption, a vital responsibility of the CAIO. This involves navigating the skill gap within the organization, securing necessary budgets, and managing resistance to change. Creating a conducive environment for AI integration involves more than just managing the technical transition; it requires transforming the organization's culture and mindset. The CAIO drives this cultural shift, championing the benefits of AI and embedding it into the organizational fabric.

Championing ethical and responsible AI practices is integral to the CAIO's role. Establishing fairness, accountability, and transparency standards in AI systems is crucial. Regular audits of AI systems, training on ethical AI practices, and fostering a culture where ethical considerations are at the forefront of AI development and deployment are key responsibilities. The CAIO also engages with industry groups, policymakers, and the public to shape the broader conversation around ethical AI.

Driving business value through AI initiatives involves adopting an iterative delivery model. This model focuses on incremental development, targeted solutions, and quick wins, ensuring AI initiatives align with business objectives and yield measurable benefits. The iterative model allows for continuous feedback and improvement, keeping the organization's AI strategy at the forefront of innovation.

Addressing the talent gap in AI and data science is a significant challenge the CAIO addresses. Developing comprehensive training programs, recruiting strategies, and fostering a diverse AI and data science workforce are critical components of this effort.

Instituting integrated AI governance is a crucial responsibility of the CAIO. This involves overseeing privacy and data security, performance monitoring of AI systems, and ethical considerations. Establishing a governance framework that integrates these various aspects is vital for the responsible and sustainable utilization of AI technologies.

Quantifying the business impact of AI initiatives is critical to the CAIO's role. Defining measurable objectives, establishing metrics, and calculating ROI are essential steps. Communicating the business impact of AI to stakeholders and using insights from current AI projects to inform future strategies are also critical aspects of the CAIO's role.

Elevating AI leadership to the executive level through the CAIO role marks a significant shift in organizational strategy. This elevation underscores the strategic importance of AI in business and ensures that AI initiatives are led with the necessary vision and oversight. The CAIO's role is pivotal in guiding organizations through the transformative journey of AI integration, balancing innovation with ethical responsibility and strategic alignment.

The CAIO is central to an organization's successful navigation of the AI-driven business environment. Key responsibilities include aligning AI initiatives with business goals, facilitating cultural and organizational adaptation to AI, enforcing ethical AI practices, driving business value through AI, and addressing the talent gap in AI and data science. The CAIO's role reflects the critical importance of AI in business strategy, ensuring that AI initiatives are led with the necessary vision and oversight.

This role is pivotal in guiding organizations through the transformative journey of AI integration, balancing innovation with ethical responsibility and strategic alignment.

STRATEGIC LEADERSHIP AND AI INITIATIVE ALIGNMENT

The CAIO is the strategic linchpin in aligning AI initiatives with an organization's overarching business goals and objectives. This alignment is crucial, as it bridges the gap between the potential of AI and the practical needs of the business, ensuring that AI initiatives propel the organization toward its strategic targets.

The CAIO's role transcends mere technological oversight; it involves a nuanced understanding of how AI can be harnessed to meet specific business objectives. This requires deep diving into the company's strategic goals and identifying areas where AI can provide the most significant leverage. The CAIO must have dual lenses: one keenly focused on the advancements and possibilities within the AI landscape and another that maintains a clear view of the company's strategic roadmap.

At the core of this responsibility is the ability to translate complex AI capabilities into tangible business outcomes. The CAIO must discern which AI technologies and applications align best with the company's strategic goals: enhancing customer experience, streamlining operations, or driving innovation. This involves carefully analyzing the company's current position, market trends, and competitive landscape.

A critical aspect of the CAIO's role is ensuring that AI initiatives are not isolated endeavors but are integrated components of the broader business strategy. This integration necessitates a cohesive approach where AI initiatives complement and enhance other strategic projects within the organization.

The CAIO achieves this by working closely with various business units, understanding their unique challenges and objectives, and identifying how AI can catalyze achieving these goals. This collaborative approach ensures that AI initiatives are grounded in real business needs and are designed to deliver measurable impact.

Developing a strategic AI roadmap is a primary responsibility of the CAIO. This roadmap outlines how AI will be deployed across the organization, detailing timelines, key milestones, and expected outcomes. The CAIO must ensure that this roadmap is flexible yet robust and can adapt to rapid technological changes while staying aligned with the company's long-term strategic vision.

During this planning phase, the CAIO identifies key investment areas in AI, technology, talent, or infrastructure. Prioritizing these investments based on their potential to drive strategic objectives is a balancing act that the CAIO must master. This involves understanding AI projects' technical feasibility, scalability, integration with existing systems, and the overall return on investment (ROI).

Effective communication is paramount in the CAIO's role. They must articulate the strategic value of AI initiatives to stakeholders at all levels, from C-Suite executives to operational teams. This communication is about conveying the technical details of AI projects and, more importantly, linking them to key business outcomes and demonstrating their value in achieving strategic objectives.

The CAIO must also manage expectations, ensuring that stakeholders have a realistic understanding of what AI can and cannot do. This involves dispelling myths about AI, setting achievable goals, and aligning AI initiatives with the organization's capacity for change and adaptation.

Finally, the CAIO must ensure that AI initiatives align with the organization's evolving business goals and strategies. This requires a continuous loop of feedback, evaluation, and adaptation. By regularly assessing the impact of AI initiatives against strategic objectives, the CAIO can make necessary adjustments, whether in redirecting resources, scaling efforts, or shifting focus to new AI opportunities.

The CAIO's role in strategic leadership and AI initiative alignment is pivotal in transforming AI from a conceptual technology into a strategic business driver. By meticulously aligning AI initiatives with the organization's goals, the CAIO ensures that AI becomes an integral, value-adding component of the business strategy, driving the organization toward its future vision in an increasingly AI-driven world.

DEVELOPING AND IMPLEMENTING AI STRATEGY

In AI, the CAIO is pivotal in sculpting a comprehensive and adaptable AI strategy. This strategy, tailored to the unique contours of the organization, involves a thorough assessment of current capabilities, identification of skill gaps, and an in-depth understanding of the company's data readiness.

Developing an AI strategy under the guidance of the CAIO is akin to constructing a bridge between the present state of the organization and its envisioned future. This strategy is not a static blueprint but a dynamic plan responsive to the rapid advancements in AI technology and shifting market demands. The CAIO, leveraging their deep understanding of AI's potential, crafts a strategy that aligns with and amplifies the company's strategic goals.

A crucial element of this strategy is its comprehensive nature. It encompasses various dimensions of the organization, from operational workflows and customer interactions to product development and market positioning. The CAIO ensures that the AI strategy touches every facet of the business where AI can bring transformative value.

An honest and thorough assessment of the organization's current capabilities forms the foundation of an effective AI strategy. The CAIO evaluates the existing technological infrastructure, software systems, data management practices, and analytical tools. This evaluation is about taking stock of the hardware and software and understanding how these technologies are integrated into the business processes and where AI can enhance their efficacy.

In tandem with assessing technological capabilities, the CAIO identifies skill gaps within the organization that could impede the successful implementation of AI. This involves analyzing the current workforce's proficiency in AI-related skills and understanding the gaps in knowledge and expertise. The CAIO collaborates with human resources and department heads to map out a detailed skill landscape, pinpointing areas where up-skilling or re-skilling is required.

Developing a talent strategy is critical to the CAIO's responsibilities. This strategy may include internal training programs to enhance AI literacy among existing employees, recruitment drives to bring in new talent with specialized AI skills, and partnerships with academic institutions to tap into cutting-edge research and emerging talent pools.

A cornerstone of any AI initiative is the availability and quality of data. The CAIO assesses the company's data readiness, which involves evaluating the quality, quantity, diversity, and accessibility of data. They examine data collection methods, storage infrastructure, data governance policies, and compliance with data protection regulations.

Understanding data readiness also means evaluating the organization's ability to utilize data for AI applications effectively. This includes assessing data integration across various systems and platforms, the scalability of data infrastructure to handle AI-driven analytics, and the existence of data silos that may hinder comprehensive data analysis.

Developing an AI strategy is not a one-time endeavor but an ongoing process. The CAIO ensures that the strategy remains adaptable and responsive to new developments in AI technology and shifts in business strategy. They establish mechanisms for regular review and refinement of the AI strategy, incorporating feedback from implementation experiences, changes in business priorities, and emerging AI trends.

The CAIO also plays a crucial role in advocating for and securing the necessary resources to implement the AI strategy effectively. This involves securing financial investments and ensuring organizational buy-in and support for AI initiatives.

The role of the CAIO in developing and implementing an AI strategy is central to the organization's journey toward leveraging AI for strategic advantage. By crafting a comprehensive, adaptable approach that considers current capabilities, skill gaps, and data readiness, the CAIO positions the organization to harness the full potential of AI. This strategy is the roadmap that guides the organization through the complexities of AI adoption, ensuring that AI initiatives are aligned with business objectives and are poised to deliver transformative impact.

The CAIO oversees an organization's development and implementation of AI technologies. This responsibility involves ensuring that these technologies embody the state-of-the-art in AI advancements and align intricately with the company's specific needs and overarching goals.

The CAIO's role in overseeing AI technology development is multifaceted. It involves staying attuned to the latest advancements in AI and evaluating how these innovations can be strategically applied within the organization. This evaluation is not just about the allure of new technology; it's about discerning which AI tools and systems will drive real value for the company.

A significant part of this oversight is the strategic selection of AI projects. The CAIO must identify which AI initiatives are most likely to impact the company's strategic objectives. This involves carefully exploring innovative AI solutions and focusing on technologies that address specific business challenges. The CAIO leads this charge, ensuring that AI development is not a pursuit of technology for technology's sake but a strategic endeavor aimed at specific business outcomes.

One of the primary responsibilities of the CAIO is to ensure that the AI technologies developed to align with the company's needs and goals. This alignment requires a deep understanding of the business's processes, challenges, market position, and strategic objectives.

The CAIO works closely with various business units to understand their unique needs and challenges. This collaboration is critical to developing AI solutions tailored to specific business contexts and can provide practical and impactful solutions.

Ensuring this alignment involves the CAIO in the architectural decisions of AI systems. The CAIO guides the technical teams in designing AI systems that are scalable, integrable with existing IT infrastructure, and capable of evolving with the company's growth and changing market dynamics.

Beyond the development of AI technologies, the CAIO oversees their implementation and integration into the company's existing systems and processes. This involves managing the complexities of integrating new AI technologies into existing IT infrastructure, which often requires navigating compatibility challenges and ensuring that AI systems enhance rather than disrupt existing workflows.

The CAIO also plays a crucial role in managing the change associated with implementing AI systems. This includes preparing the workforce for new AI-enabled processes, ensuring minimal disruption to business operations, and fostering a receptive culture to AI-driven changes.

Post-implementation, the CAIO's role shifts to monitoring and evaluating the performance of AI systems. This involves setting up metrics and KPIs to measure the effectiveness of AI solutions in achieving intended business outcomes. Continuous monitoring identifies areas where AI systems can be improved, ensuring they align with business needs and objectives.

The CAIO also ensures that AI systems are maintained and updated in line with technological advancements and changing business requirements. This ongoing maintenance is crucial to keep AI systems relevant and effective over time.

The CAIO's role in technology oversight and AI systems implementation is central to ensuring that AI initiatives within an organization are successful and aligned with business goals. This role encompasses a strategic evaluation of AI technologies, close collaboration with business units, careful oversight of AI development and implementation, and ongoing monitoring and maintenance of AI systems. Through effective oversight and implementation, the CAIO ensures that AI technologies are advanced, innovative, and pragmatically aligned with the company's strategic needs, driving tangible business value.

CULTURAL TRANSFORMATION AND AI ADOPTION

The CAIO is pivotal in steering an organization's cultural transformation toward embracing AI. This transformative process is essential for the effective adoption of AI technologies and for fostering an environment where innovation and data-driven decision-making become integral to the company's ethos.

The journey to AI adoption begins with cultivating a culture of innovation within the organization. The CAIO leads this cultural shift, advocating for an environment where exploration, experimentation, and embracing new technologies are valued and encouraged. This culture of innovation is crucial in preparing the ground for AI integration, as it involves breaking away from traditional ways of working and being open to new, AI-driven approaches.

The CAIO's role in fostering this culture goes beyond mere advocacy; it involves engaging with various departments to inspire and motivate teams to think innovatively. This includes organizing workshops, training sessions, and collaborative projects highlighting AI's potential and applications in improving business processes and outcomes.

In an AI-empowered organization, decision-making increasingly relies on data and analytics. The CAIO plays a crucial role in promoting a data-driven culture, where decisions are made based on insights derived from data analysis rather than solely on intuition or traditional methods.

This shift to data-driven decision-making requires not just the availability of data but also the tools and skills to analyze it effectively. The CAIO ensures teams can access the necessary data, tools, and training to make informed decisions. This involves investment in data infrastructure, analytics tools, and employee up-skilling programs.

One of the significant challenges in cultural transformation is overcoming resistance to change. Introducing AI into business processes can be met with apprehension, as it often involves changes in job roles, workflows, and the need for new skills. The CAIO must address these concerns proactively, engaging with employees at all levels to communicate the benefits of AI, addressing fears, and clarifying misconceptions.

This change management process involves transparent communication about the AI initiatives, their objectives, and the anticipated impact on the organization and its employees. The CAIO facilitates forums for discussion, feedback, and collaboration, ensuring that employees feel heard and involved in the AI transformation journey.

For AI adoption to succeed, it must be embedded into the organization's DNA. This means integrating AI into everyday workflows and processes, making it a natural part of the organization's operations. The CAIO leads this integration, working closely with department heads and team leaders to identify opportunities for AI implementation and ensuring that AI tools are accessible and user-friendly.

The CAIO also plays a crucial role in setting up governance structures for AI usage, ensuring that AI is used ethically and responsibly within the organization. This includes establishing AI usage and privacy protocol guidelines and ensuring compliance with relevant regulations.

In summary, the CAIO's role in cultural transformation and AI adoption is multifaceted and crucial for successfully integrating AI within an organization. By fostering a culture of innovation, advocating for data-driven decision-making, addressing resistance to change, and embedding AI into the organizational DNA, the CAIO paves the way for a transformative AI journey. This journey prepares the organization to harness the full potential of AI but also shapes a future-ready workforce that thrives in an AI-augmented environment.

ETHICAL AI GOVERNANCE AND POLICY DEVELOPMENT

In the rapidly evolving landscape of AI, the CAIO assumes a critical responsibility for establishing and enforcing ethical AI practices within an organization. This role involves developing comprehensive policies that address key concerns such as data usage, model transparency, and algorithmic accountability, ensuring that AI is used practically, ethically, and responsibly.

The CAIO's first task is establishing what constitutes ethical AI within the organization's context. This involves defining clear principles that guide the development and use of AI. These principles typically revolve around fairness, non-discrimination, privacy, security, and transparency. The CAIO collaborates with various stakeholders, including legal, IT, and data science teams, to articulate these ethical guidelines clearly and comprehensively.

One of the fundamental aspects of ethical AI governance is ensuring the responsible usage of data. The CAIO plays a crucial role in developing policies that govern how data is collected, stored, processed, and shared. These policies must comply with relevant data protection and privacy laws, such as GDPR in Europe, and ensure that data is used to respect user privacy and consent.

In addition to compliance, the CAIO's policies on data usage also focus on the integrity and quality of data. This includes measures to prevent data collection and processing biases, which can lead to biased AI outcomes. The CAIO ensures that data handling practices are transparent and clarifies how and why data is used in AI systems.

Model transparency is another crucial aspect of ethical AI. The CAIO ensures that AI models developed and used by the organization are transparent and their workings understandable, not only to the data scientists who create them but also to the end-users. This transparency is essential for building trust in AI systems among users and stakeholders.

The CAIO also advocates for the development of explainable AI models. Explainable AI involves creating AI systems whose actions and decisions can be easily understood by humans. This is particularly important in sectors where AI decisions have significant impacts, such as healthcare, finance, and law enforcement.

Algorithmic accountability is a cornerstone of ethical AI governance. The CAIO ensures mechanisms are in place to hold the AI systems accountable for their decisions and actions. This involves setting up processes for regular audits of AI algorithms and assessing their fairness, accuracy, and impact.

The CAIO also establishes channels for addressing and rectifying any issues or biases that arise from AI algorithms. This includes setting up response teams to handle incidents related to AI systems and ensuring accountability and responsiveness in case of AI-related errors or failures.

Given the dynamic nature of AI and its regulatory environment, the CAIO ensures that AI governance policies are not static. They establish a framework for the continuous review and adaptation of these policies. This includes staying abreast of the latest AI ethics and regulation developments and incorporating new learnings and guidelines into the organization's AI governance framework.

The CAIO's role in ethical AI governance and policy development ensures that organizations use AI technologies responsibly. The CAIO fosters an ethical AI environment by establishing clear guidelines on data usage, providing model transparency, enforcing algorithmic accountability, and adapting policies in line with evolving standards and regulations. This mitigates risks and builds trust and credibility, ensuring the organization uses ethically sound and socially responsible AI.

TALENT DEVELOPMENT AND AI SKILLS CULTIVATION

In the dynamic field of AI, the role of the CAIO extends significantly into talent development and AI skills cultivation. The CAIO undertakes a comprehensive approach to building the organization's AI talent pool, recognizing that a skilled and knowledgeable workforce is the bedrock of any successful AI initiative. This approach is characterized by a blend of internal training and development and strategic external recruitment, all aimed at fostering a workforce proficient in AI and data science.

Central to the CAIO's strategy is developing internal training programs to uplift the existing employees' AI and data science capabilities. These programs are tailored to cater to various levels of AI proficiency across the organization. For the broader workforce, the focus is on imparting a foundational understanding of AI principles and applications, ensuring a basic level of AI literacy throughout the organization. This foundational training is crucial for nurturing an organizational culture that is receptive and appreciative of AI's potential. The CAIO implements more advanced training for technical teams directly engaged in AI projects, such as IT and data analytics departments, delving into specialized AI technologies and methodologies directly relevant to the organization's specific AI endeavors.

Furthermore, understanding the importance of informed decision-making in AI investments and strategies, the CAIO also focuses on equipping the leadership and managerial staff with knowledge that spans the business aspects of AI. This includes insights into the ROI of AI projects, strategic alignment, and ethical considerations of AI deployment. Recognizing the rapidly evolving nature of AI, the CAIO fosters an environment of continuous learning and development through regular workshops, seminars, and access to online courses, ensuring that the workforce stays abreast of the latest developments and skills in the AI field.

The CAIO employs strategic external recruitment to attract top-tier AI talent to complement the internal up-skilling initiatives. Identifying skill gaps that cannot be adequately filled internally is a critical first step. The CAIO, in response, initiates targeted recruitment drives to attract AI specialists, such as machine learning engineers, AI researchers, and data scientists with niche expertise. In addition, the CAIO establishes partnerships with universities and academic institutions to ensure a steady influx of new talent. These collaborations, from joint research initiatives to internship and recruitment programs, open doors to fresh talent well-versed in the latest AI technologies and research paradigms. A crucial aspect of these recruitment efforts is building an attractive employer brand. The organization's commitment to cutting-edge AI work and innovative culture is highlighted in a highly competitive AI talent market, creating an employer brand that resonates with top AI professionals seeking impactful and stimulating work environments.

An integral part of the CAIO's talent development strategy is fostering diversity within the AI team. Diversity in AI talent is not just a matter of social responsibility but a strategic imperative. A diverse team brings a range of perspectives and experiences that are critical in mitigating biases in AI development and enhancing the creativity and innovation of AI solutions. To this end, the CAIO ensures that recruitment practices are inclusive and aims to build a team that reflects a rich tapestry of backgrounds, experiences, and perspectives. Training programs are designed to be accessible and inclusive, catering to various learning styles and backgrounds and ensuring equitable opportunities for all employees to advance their AI skills.

The CAIO's comprehensive strategy for talent development and AI skills cultivation underscores the significance of human capital in an organization's AI journey. By harmoniously blending internal training with external recruitment and emphasizing the importance of diversity, the CAIO forges a robust AI talent pool and creates an ecosystem where AI can thrive. This strategic emphasis on talent ensures that the organization is well-prepared to leverage AI for groundbreaking innovation and maintain a competitive edge in the ever-evolving landscape of AI.

FOSTERING ENTERPRISE AI STRATEGY ALIGNMENT

The CAIO is pivotal in aligning AI initiatives across an organization's various departments, ensuring that these initiatives harmonize with the company's strategic direction. This alignment is vital for the cohesive and effective integration of AI technologies into the broader business framework, facilitating a unified approach toward achieving the company's goals.

In undertaking this responsibility, the CAIO embarks on a journey of collaboration and synchronization. Their approach involves profoundly understanding each department's unique functions and objectives and identifying how AI can augment these areas to align with the enterprise's strategic vision. This understanding allows the CAIO to tailor AI initiatives to suit the specific needs of different departments while ensuring that these initiatives collectively drive the organization toward its central goals.

The CAIO's task involves more than just the technical implementation of AI; it is about weaving AI into the fabric of the organization's operations. They work closely with department heads and teams, fostering a culture of open communication and collaboration. This collaborative environment is crucial for the seamless integration of AI, as it enables the sharing of insights, challenges, and successes across different business areas.

A significant part of the CAIO's strategy ensures that AI initiatives are not perceived as isolated technological projects but as integral components contributing to the organization's strategic narrative. To achieve this, the CAIO articulates how each AI initiative aligns with and supports the broader business objectives. This articulation is not limited to showcasing the technical prowess of AI solutions. Still, it extends to demonstrating their practical impact on enhancing business processes, improving customer experience, driving innovation, and ultimately contributing to the company's growth and success.

The CAIO also strongly emphasizes measuring the impact of AI initiatives. They establish KPIs and metrics that reflect the effectiveness of AI solutions in achieving defined business objectives. Regularly reviewing these metrics allows the CAIO to adjust and fine-tune AI initiatives, ensuring their continued alignment with the evolving business strategies and market conditions.

Furthermore, the CAIO navigates the challenges of integrating AI into existing systems and workflows. They address potential obstacles such as compatibility issues, data integration complexities, and the need for upskilling employees to work effectively with new AI tools. This involves technical acumen and change management skills, ensuring that the transition to AI-enhanced processes is smooth and well-received across the organization.

The CAIO's role in fostering enterprise AI strategy alignment is a testament to their strategic vision and leadership in AI. By synchronizing AI initiatives across departments and ensuring their cohesive integration with the company's strategic direction, the CAIO plays an instrumental role in transforming AI from isolated projects into a core driver of the organization's success. Their approach not only maximizes the impact of AI initiatives but also positions the organization to leverage AI as a strategic asset, poised to meet the challenges and opportunities of the digital era.

CHANGE MANAGEMENT AND AI ADOPTION ACCELERATION

In adopting AI, the CAIO is crucial in managing the sweeping organizational changes accompanying this technological shift. The CAIO's responsibilities in this arena are comprehensive, addressing various facets of the organization – from skill gaps and budgeting to overcoming resistance to change – to ensure a smooth and effective transition into AI-enhanced operations.

One of the key challenges in AI adoption that the CAIO confronts is the skill gap within the organization. As AI technologies evolve and become more integrated into business processes, a workforce proficient in these new technologies becomes essential. The CAIO, therefore, focuses on identifying areas where the existing workforce lacks the necessary AI skills and knowledge. This identification is followed by targeted training and development programs to up-skill employees and equip them with the competencies to work with AI effectively. This proactive approach to talent development is pivotal in ensuring that the organization does not just adopt AI technology but is adept at leveraging it to its full potential.

Budgeting for AI initiatives is another critical aspect of the CAIO's role in change management. AI adoption can be a significant financial investment, involving costs associated with technology acquisition, system integration, and workforce training. The CAIO strategically advocates for and secures the necessary budget allocations. This consists of presenting a compelling business case for AI investments and ensuring the budget is used efficiently and effectively. The CAIO is tasked with demonstrating how AI initiatives align with and support the broader business objectives, justifying their financial implications.

However, perhaps the most nuanced challenge in this transition is managing resistance to change within the organization. Introducing AI into business operations often disrupts established workflows and processes, which can lead to apprehension and resistance among employees. The CAIO's role extends beyond the realm of technology implementation into the domain of organizational psychology. They must engage with employees at all levels, communicating the benefits of AI, addressing concerns, and dispelling fears. This engagement is crucial for fostering an organizational culture that is receptive to AI and sees it as a valuable tool for innovation and growth.

The CAIO implements strategies to facilitate a smooth transition to AI-enhanced processes. This involves designing AI implementation plans that minimize disruption to ongoing operations and ensuring that employees are supported throughout the change process. The CAIO employs regular communication and transparent discussions about AI's impact and provides platforms for feedback and concerns to ease the transition.

Moreover, the CAIO also plays a vital role in embedding a sense of ownership and participation among the workforce. By involving employees in the AI implementation process and decision-making, the CAIO fosters a sense of empowerment and collective responsibility. This approach alleviates resistance to change. It encourages innovation and creative thinking among employees.

The CAIO's role in managing organizational change in the context of AI adoption is multifaceted and integral to successfully integrating AI into the business fabric. By addressing skill gaps, managing budgetary aspects, and skillfully navigating resistance to change, the CAIO ensures that the transition to AI is both technologically successful and organizationally harmonious. Their strategic approach to change management facilitates the acceleration of AI adoption, positioning the organization to fully capitalize on the opportunities presented by AI while simultaneously preparing it to meet future technological advancements with agility and confidence.

DRIVING BUSINESS VALUE THROUGH ITERATIVE AI DELIVERY

The CAIO drives business value through an iterative delivery model. This approach, centered on agility and continuous improvement, ensures that AI initiatives align with the organization's strategic goals and deliver tangible, measurable outcomes.

The CAIO's leadership in this domain is characterized by a focus on delivering quick wins, implementing targeted solutions, and fostering a culture of continuous improvement. Unlike traditional project methodologies that often pursue large-scale, comprehensive AI implementations, the iterative delivery model advocates for breaking AI projects into smaller, manageable segments. This breakdown allows for rapid development, testing, and deployment, allowing the organization to adapt swiftly to changing requirements and market conditions.

A vital aspect of the iterative approach championed by the CAIO is the emphasis on achieving quick wins. These early successes play a crucial role in demonstrating the value of AI initiatives to stakeholders across the organization. Quick wins serve as tangible proof points of the effectiveness of AI, bolstering confidence in AI investments and fostering a broader organizational buy-in. By showcasing the immediate benefits of AI, the CAIO not only builds momentum for ongoing AI projects but also paves the way for more ambitious AI endeavors.

The CAIO also ensures that AI initiatives under the iterative model are highly targeted. This focus on addressing specific business challenges or opportunities ensures that AI solutions are directly tied to critical operational or strategic objectives. By concentrating efforts on areas where AI can have a marked impact, the CAIO ensures that technological and Human Resources are utilized effectively, enhancing AI projects' overall efficacy and effect.

Central to the iterative AI delivery model is the principle of continuous improvement. Under the CAIO's guidance, each iteration of AI deployment is followed by a phase of evaluation and refinement. This process involves gathering feedback, analyzing performance data, and incorporating insights into subsequent iterations. The CAIO establishes mechanisms to measure the performance of AI solutions continuously, using metrics and KPIs that align with the organization's strategic objectives. This ongoing development cycle, assessment, and enhancement ensures that AI initiatives remain relevant, effective, and aligned with the organization's evolving needs.

Moreover, the CAIO fosters a culture where learning from each phase of AI implementation is valued. Lessons learned from early iterations are applied to future projects, gradually increasing the sophistication and impact of AI solutions. This culture of learning and adaptation is vital to keeping the organization's AI strategy agile and responsive to new developments in AI.

The CAIO's implementation of an iterative delivery model for AI initiatives represents a strategic approach to maximizing the business value of AI. The CAIO ensures that AI projects are technically successful and closely aligned with the organization's strategic goals by focusing on quick wins, targeted solutions, and continuous improvement. This approach accelerates the delivery of AI-driven business outcomes and establishes a foundation for sustainable AI growth and innovation within the organization. Through this iterative model, the CAIO navigates the complexities of AI implementation, driving tangible business value and positioning the organization to leverage AI as a critical driver of competitive advantage.

In the dynamic landscape of modern business, where AI plays an increasingly pivotal role, the CAIO is responsible for quantifying AI's business impact. This task is not just about measuring outcomes but articulating the value that AI brings to an organization in a tangible, understandable manner. It involves a meticulous process of defining objectives, establishing metrics, and calculating the ROI, which collectively paint a clear picture of AI's contribution to the organization's success.

The CAIO starts by defining specific, measurable objectives for each AI initiative. These objectives are closely aligned with the organization's broader strategic goals. Whether it's about enhancing operational efficiency, improving customer engagement, driving revenue growth, or fostering innovation, these objectives are benchmarks against which AI initiatives' success is measured. The CAIO's expertise lies in identifying areas where AI can significantly impact, ensuring that each AI project undertaken is purpose-driven and strategically relevant.

Establishing metrics is the next critical step. The CAIO develops a framework of KPIs tailored to assess the effectiveness of each AI initiative. These metrics offer insights into how well AI applications meet set objectives, providing a quantitative basis for evaluating AI's performance. For example, in an AI-driven marketing campaign, metrics might include customer conversion rates, engagement levels, and the cost-effectiveness of the campaign. Such measurements enable the CAIO to present a clear and factual account of how AI initiatives contribute to the organization's goals.

Calculating the ROI of AI projects is paramount in quantifying AI's business impact. This calculation is multifaceted, encompassing the total costs associated with AI initiatives – from development and deployment to maintenance and ongoing operation. Simultaneously, the CAIO assesses AI's direct and indirect benefits. Direct benefits might include immediate cost savings and increased revenues, while indirect benefits could cover aspects like enhanced customer satisfaction and brand reputation. The CAIO skillfully navigates this complex landscape, offering a comprehensive view of the financial impact of AI on the organization.

Communicating the business impact of AI to stakeholders forms an integral part of the CAIO's role. This involves presenting the data and metrics and crafting a narrative that underscores the strategic value of AI investments. The CAIO articulates how AI initiatives contribute to the organization's competitive advantage, operational efficiency, and long-term strategic goals. This communication is vital for securing ongoing support for AI projects and aligning the organization's leadership and workforce with the AI strategy.

Moreover, the CAIO employs a forward-looking approach, leveraging insights from current AI initiatives to inform future AI strategies and investments. This proactive stance involves identifying emerging AI trends and technologies, assessing their potential impact on the business, and aligning future AI initiatives with the organization's strategic direction.

In summary, the CAIO's role in quantifying AI's business impact is comprehensive and multifaceted. By effectively defining objectives, establishing metrics, calculating ROI, and communicating the value of AI, the CAIO validates the organization's investment in AI and guides strategic decision-making regarding future AI endeavors. This approach ensures that AI initiatives are aligned with the organization's goals and contribute meaningfully to its growth and success.

QUANTIFYING AI'S BUSINESS IMPACT

The elevation of AI leadership to the executive level, epitomized by the role of the CAIO, marks a significant evolution in the strategic landscape of modern businesses. This shift underscores the recognition of AI as a technological tool and a fundamental pillar of business strategy that demands high-level oversight and integration at the core of organizational decision-making.

Positioning the CAIO at the executive level is a clear testament to the strategic importance of AI in today's business environment. AI's potential to transform business models, redefine customer experiences, optimize operations, and create new market opportunities necessitates a leadership perspective that transcends traditional IT or data science roles. As an executive leader, the CAIO ensures that AI is not merely an operational tool but a strategic asset, integrated across various facets of the organization and aligned with overarching business objectives.

The CAIO's role at this level involves a holistic approach to AI strategy and its implementation. By being part of the executive team, the CAIO is uniquely positioned to collaborate effectively with other C-level leaders, such as the Chief Information Officer (CIO), Chief Technology Officer (CTO), Chief Financial Officer (CFO), and Chief Marketing Officer (CMO). This cross-functional collaboration is crucial for developing and implementing AI strategies coherent with the organization's overall goals, ensuring that AI initiatives deliver value across all business units.

In addition to strategic alignment, the CAIO's presence at the executive level enables effective advocacy for the necessary resources and support for AI initiatives. This includes securing funding, attracting top talent, and investing in cutting-edge technology. The CAIO's role in communicating the value and potential of AI to the board and other stakeholders is instrumental in garnering organizational buy-in and facilitating the strategic allocation of resources toward AI projects.

Navigating the complex ethical, legal, and regulatory challenges associated with AI is another critical aspect of the CAIO's executive role. In an era where AI's impact extends far beyond business operations, encompassing societal, ethical, and regulatory dimensions, the CAIO ensures that AI applications adhere to ethical standards and comply with relevant laws and regulations. This responsibility is critical to maintaining the organization's reputation and stakeholder trust.

Furthermore, the CAIO leads the cultural transformation required for AI adoption at an organizational level. AI implementation is not merely a technological upgrade but a corporate culture and mindset shift. The CAIO drives this change, fostering a culture of innovation, data-driven decision-making, and continuous learning. This cultural shift is essential for successfully integrating AI into business processes and realizing its full potential.

Finally, having AI leadership at the executive level sends a strong signal to the market, customers, and competitors about the organization's commitment to and focus on AI as a critical driver of innovation and growth. It positions the company as a forward-thinking entity, keen on harnessing the latest technological advancements for strategic advantage, and attracts top talent, partners, and investors eager to be associated with a leader in AI application.

Elevating the CAIO to the executive level is not just a structural change but a strategic imperative. It reflects the critical importance of AI in shaping business strategies and the need for a dedicated, high-level leadership role focused on the strategic integration and oversight of AI technologies. The CAIO's role at this level is pivotal in guiding organizations through the transformative journey of AI integration, ensuring that AI initiatives are innovative, ethically responsible, and strategically aligned with the business's long-term objectives.

FINAL THOUGHTS

As we conclude this chapter, it's evident that the emergence and evolution of the CAIO role marks a pivotal shift in the strategic landscape of modern businesses. This chapter points out the multifaceted responsibilities of the CAIO, emphasizing the role's critical importance in integrating AI into the organizational fabric and ensuring that AI initiatives are not only innovative but strategically aligned and ethically grounded.

The CAIO emerges as a strategic visionary, bridging the gap between AI's potential and business needs. By aligning AI initiatives with the organization's overarching goals, the CAIO ensures that AI is not an isolated technological endeavor but a fundamental component driving tangible business outcomes. The development and implementation of a comprehensive, adaptable AI strategy under the stewardship of the CAIO are paramount in navigating the complexities of AI adoption.

The CAIO's role in overseeing AI technology development and fostering a culture of innovation is crucial. The CAIO positions AI as a critical driver of innovation and efficiency by staying abreast of AI advancements and ensuring that AI technologies are aligned with the company's needs. Cultivating a culture that embraces AI across departments is instrumental in successfully integrating AI into business processes.

Establishing ethical AI governance and policy development is another cornerstone of the CAIO's mandate. In an era where AI's impact transcends business operations, encompassing societal, ethical, and regulatory dimensions, the CAIO ensures AI applications adhere to ethical standards and comply with relevant laws and regulations.

Talent development and AI skills cultivation are central to the CAIO's strategy. Building and enhancing the organization's AI talent pool is vital to forging a robust AI ecosystem. Through internal training and strategic recruitment, the CAIO ensures a workforce proficient in AI and data science, fostering diversity and inclusivity within the AI team.

The CAIO is pivotal in fostering enterprise AI strategy alignment. Ensuring synchronization of AI initiatives with the organization's strategic direction is vital for a cohesive and effective integration of AI technologies. This alignment facilitates a unified approach toward achieving the company's goals.

The CAIO's most nuanced challenges are change management and AI adoption acceleration. Navigating organizational changes for effective AI integration requires addressing skill gaps, securing budgets, and managing resistance to change. In driving business value through iterative AI delivery, the CAIO adopts a model focused on agility and continuous improvement. This approach maximizes the impact of AI initiatives and establishes a foundation for sustainable AI growth and innovation. Quantifying AI's business impact is a crucial responsibility of the CAIO. By effectively measuring the impact of AI on business objectives, the CAIO validates the organization's investment in AI and guides strategic decision-making regarding future AI endeavors.

The elevation of AI leadership to the executive level through the CAIO role underscores AI's strategic importance in business. This elevation ensures that AI initiatives are led with the necessary vision, oversight, and integration at the core of organizational decision-making. Suppose you are not implementing a CAIO role. In that case, you're not taking the complexities of AI and GenAI implementation seriously and are unlikely to successfully gain value from your investments in AI and GenAI. Without the role of CAIO, AI and GenAI will continue to be scams for you.

KEY TAKEAWAYS AND ACTIONS

BRIDGING AI POTENTIAL AND BUSINESS NEEDS

- **Actionable Steps:** Align AI initiatives with the organization's strategic goals.
- **Implementation:** The CAIO must work closely with various departments to understand their unique needs and align AI strategies accordingly, ensuring AI initiatives complement the broader business strategy.

CRAFTING A COMPREHENSIVE AI STRATEGY

- **Actionable Steps:** Develop a dynamic, comprehensive AI strategy encompassing current capabilities and future needs.
- **Implementation:** The CAIO should assess the existing infrastructure, identify skill gaps, and ensure data readiness, adapting the strategy in response to technological and market changes.

OVERSEEING AI TECHNOLOGY DEVELOPMENT

- **Actionable Steps:** Guide the strategic selection and implementation of AI technologies.
- **Implementation:** The CAIO must stay abreast of AI advancements, ensuring that AI technologies align with the company's specific goals and integrate into existing systems.

FOSTERING A CULTURE OF INNOVATION

- **Actionable Steps:** Cultivate a culture that embraces AI across all departments.
- **Implementation:** The CAIO should lead cultural transformation initiatives, promoting AI literacy and fostering an environment conducive to AI adoption and innovation.

ESTABLISHING ETHICAL AI PRACTICES

- **Actionable Steps:** Develop and enforce ethical AI governance policies.
- **Implementation:** The CAIO must define ethical guidelines for AI usage, ensuring transparency, fairness, and accountability in AI systems.

TALENT DEVELOPMENT AND AI SKILLS CULTIVATION

- **Actionable Steps:** Build and enhance the organization's AI talent pool.
- **Implementation:** The CAIO should focus on internal training programs for up-skilling employees and strategic recruitment to attract specialized AI talent.

FOSTERING ENTERPRISE AI STRATEGY ALIGNMENT

- **Actionable Steps:** Ensure synchronization of AI initiatives with the enterprise's strategic direction.
- **Implementation:** The CAIO must facilitate cross-departmental collaboration, align AI projects with organizational goals, and measure their impact using KPIs.

CHANGE MANAGEMENT AND AI ADOPTION ACCELERATION

- **Actionable Steps:** Navigate organizational changes for effective AI integration.
- **Implementation:** The CAIO should address skill gaps, secure budgets, and manage resistance to change, ensuring a smooth transition to AI-enhanced processes.

DRIVING BUSINESS VALUE THROUGH ITERATIVE AI DELIVERY

- **Actionable Steps:** Implement an iterative AI delivery model to drive business value.
- **Implementation:** Focus on achieving quick wins and continuous improvement in AI projects, aligning them closely with business objectives.

QUANTIFYING AI'S BUSINESS IMPACT

- **Actionable Steps:** Measure and communicate the impact of AI on business.
- **Implementation:** The CAIO must define clear objectives for AI, establish metrics to measure success, and calculate ROI, effectively communicating these to stakeholders.

ELEVATING AI LEADERSHIP TO EXECUTIVE LEVEL

- **Actionable Steps:** Position the CAIO role at the executive level to emphasize AI's strategic importance.
- **Implementation:** The CAIO should collaborate with C-level executives, lead ethical AI practices, and drive the cultural transformation required for AI adoption.

CHAPTER 13

Pulling it All Together to Build Your AI iQ

REFLECTING ON THE AI JOURNEY

As we embark on this retrospective voyage through the annals of artificial intelligence (AI), it's pivotal to acknowledge the monumental shifts that have defined this journey. From its nascent stages to the groundbreaking advent of Generative AI (GenAI), AI's evolution has been a technological feat and a transformative saga reshaping the digital and business landscapes.

The early days of AI were marked by a focus on data science and machine learning, which primarily leveraged data for insights and decision-making. The essence of this period was rooted in harnessing vast volumes of data – a digital goldmine, if you will – and applying statistical models to glean insights. These were the days when data science was the vanguard of AI, a discipline that combined statistical prowess with computing power to solve complex problems. Machine learning, a subset of AI, revolutionized how we processed and interpreted data, moving beyond static algorithms to systems that could learn from data and improve over time.

Yet, as revolutionary as these technologies were, they represented just the tip of the iceberg. The true paradigm shift occurred with the advent of GenAI. This wasn't merely an incremental step in the AI journey; it was a quantum leap, a foray into uncharted territories where AI was no longer just analyzing data but creating it. GenAI, epitomized by technologies like OpenAI's Generative Pre-trained Transformer (GPT) models, has brought about a tectonic shift from traditional data analysis to creativity and innovation.

DOI: 10.1201/9781003486725-14

This transition from the old-school AI of data science and machine learning to the new school of GenAI represents a profound transformation in our understanding and application of AI. Whereas traditional AI is about understanding and predicting the world based on existing data, GenAI is about creating new realities, content, and possibilities. It's a shift from reactive to proactive, from understanding to creating.

GenAI models, using advanced algorithms, are now capable of synthesizing text, generating realistic images, and even composing music, tasks that were once deemed exclusively human. This leap is not just technological but philosophical, forcing us to rethink the boundaries of machine capabilities and the nature of creativity itself.

However, with great power comes great responsibility. The rise of GenAI has opened up a Pandora's box of ethical and practical challenges. The capacity to generate realistic content has profound implications for everything from media integrity to personal privacy. As industry leaders, we are now tasked with navigating these uncharted waters, ensuring that the power of GenAI is harnessed responsibly, ethically, and in ways that augment human potential rather than undermine it.

This journey from the early stages of AI to the advent of GenAI is more than a technological evolution; it's a narrative of transformation, innovation, and responsibility. It's about how we, as leaders and innovators, adapt to and harness these changes, integrating them into our business strategies and operations. It's a journey that demands technological acumen, strategic foresight, ethical consideration, and a commitment to sustainable, inclusive growth.

As we look back on this journey, it's clear that AI has changed how we do business and redefined the fabric of innovation and creativity. The future beckons with limitless possibilities, and it is incumbent upon us to steer this ship with a steady hand, ensuring that the power of AI is used to illuminate and uplift rather than to obscure and divide. The journey of AI, from its humble beginnings to the dizzying heights of GenAI, is a testament to human ingenuity and a clarion call for responsible stewardship in the age of digital transformation.

FROM SCAM TO STRATEGIC IMPERATIVE

The narrative surrounding AI in business has dramatically transformed, evolving from initial skepticism to becoming a strategic imperative for organizations worldwide. This evolution is not just a story of technological advancement but a saga of changing perceptions, understanding, and strategic realignment in the context of AI.

In the early stages of its corporate journey, AI, particularly in its nascent forms of data science and machine learning, was often met with a blend of intrigue and skepticism. The potential was immense, yet so were the pitfalls. Many organizations leaped onto the AI bandwagon, expecting miraculous transformations and unprecedented efficiency gains. However, the reality was frequently a stark contrast. Projects floundered, investments turned sour, and AI, in some circles, was hastily labeled a "scam." This label stemmed from a fundamental misalignment – a disconnect between the technological capabilities of AI and the strategic objectives it was expected to achieve. The problem was not with AI but with how it was perceived, implemented, and integrated into business models.

However, this period of disillusionment was a necessary phase in the maturation of AI in the business context. It sparked a vital dialogue about the realistic capabilities of AI and the need for strategic alignment. The narrative shifted from AI as a standalone solution to a tool that, when strategically integrated, could offer significant competitive advantages. The conversation moved from unrealistic expectations to pragmatic implementations, focusing on how AI could enhance, rather than replace, human capabilities and business processes.

The turning point in this journey was the understanding that AI is not a plug-and-play solution but a sophisticated tool requiring strategic thought, careful planning, and alignment with business objectives. This realization paved the way for AI's transition from a perceived "scam" to a strategic imperative. Organizations began to recognize the value of data as a strategic asset and the importance of aligning AI initiatives with broader business goals. AI strategies were increasingly tied to practical business outcomes, such as enhancing customer experience, optimizing operations, and driving innovation.

Furthermore, the advent of GenAI marked a new era in the AI journey. It expanded the horizons of what AI could achieve, adding creative capabilities to its repertoire. This advancement bolstered the strategic importance of AI, presenting new opportunities for businesses to innovate and differentiate themselves in the market. GenAI has provided new tools for content creation and data analysis and opened avenues for unprecedented personalization and customer engagement.

Today, AI has become an integral part of the strategic toolkit for businesses. It is no longer a question of whether AI should be implemented but how it can strategically align with business goals to maximize its potential. This journey from skepticism to strategic implementation has been a path of learning and adaptation. It underscores the importance of understanding the capabilities and limitations of AI and integrating it into the business fabric in a way that complements and enhances human skills and organizational goals.

In conclusion, the evolution of AI in the business context is a narrative of transformation and strategic realignment. From being viewed with skepticism to being embraced as a strategic imperative, AI's journey reflects the evolving understanding of its potential and the strategic acumen required to harness it effectively. As business leaders, our task is to continue this journey, leveraging AI as a technological tool and a strategic asset that can drive innovation, efficiency, and sustainable growth in the digital age.

AI STRATEGY AND BUSINESS INTEGRATION

In the modern business landscape, integrating AI into strategic planning is not just an advantage but a necessity. The significance of aligning AI with business strategies cannot be overstated. It marks the shift from viewing AI as a mere technological tool to recognizing it as a strategic asset capable of reshaping business models and driving substantial value.

Harmonizing AI with business strategies requires a deep understanding of both AI's capabilities and the specific objectives and challenges of the business. It's about marrying the potential of AI with each organization's unique context, creating a synergy that propels companies forward. This integration demands a meticulous approach, where AI initiatives are not isolated projects but integral components of broader business strategies.

The role of AI as a strategic asset is multifaceted. First and foremost, AI acts as a catalyst for innovation. By harnessing AI, businesses can unlock new possibilities in product development, service delivery, or operational efficiency. AI's ability to analyze vast datasets can uncover hidden patterns and insights, leading to more informed decision-making and a deeper understanding of customers and markets.

Moreover, AI is reshaping business models. In sectors ranging from healthcare to finance, AI is enabling new service offerings and business models that were previously unimaginable. For instance, AI-driven personalized recommendations are transforming the retail and entertainment industries, while AI enables more accurate diagnoses and customized treatment plans in healthcare.

However, integrating AI into business strategies is not without its challenges. It requires a thoughtful approach to data governance, ethical considerations, and organizational change management. Businesses must navigate these challenges carefully, ensuring that AI initiatives are ethical, transparent, and aligned with the company's values and objectives.

To effectively integrate AI into business strategies, organizations must foster a culture that supports innovation and continuous learning. This involves not only investing in technology but also in people. Up-skilling the workforce to understand and work alongside AI technologies is crucial. Additionally, collaboration across departments and teams is essential to ensure that AI initiatives are aligned with business goals and that insights gained from AI are effectively applied across the organization.

Moreover, leadership is critical in successfully integrating AI into business strategies. Leaders must champion AI initiatives, providing the vision and support necessary to drive them forward. They must also ensure that AI initiatives are technically sound, strategically aligned with the organization's goals, and responsive to the needs of customers and stakeholders.

In summary, the integration of AI into business strategies is a journey that requires careful planning, strategic alignment, and a commitment to continuous learning and adaptation. AI, as a strategic asset, has the potential to reshape business models, drive innovation, and create significant value. However, realizing this potential requires a synergistic approach where AI is seamlessly integrated into business strategies, guided by thoughtful leadership and a culture that embraces change and innovation. As we continue to navigate the ever-evolving landscape of AI, the businesses that succeed will be those that not only harness the technological power of AI but also strategically integrate it into their core business strategies.

BUILDING AN AI-READY ORGANIZATION

The journey toward becoming an AI-ready organization transcends mere technological adoption; it necessitates a profound cultural transformation. This transformation is pivotal in ensuring that AI is not just integrated but ingrained into the very fabric of an organization. It involves rethinking traditional processes, fostering a mindset of innovation, and embedding ethics and enthusiasm at the core of AI adoption.

To begin with, cultural readiness for AI requires fostering an environment of innovation. This means nurturing a workplace where experimentation is encouraged and failure is not seen as a setback but as a stepping stone to innovation. Employees across all levels should be motivated to think outside the box, challenge the status quo, and explore new possibilities AI can offer. Innovation in AI requires a blend of creativity and technical acumen, where imaginative ideas meet data-driven decision-making.

However, innovation alone is not enough. As we embrace AI, ethical considerations must take center stage. Integrating AI into business processes brings about a host of ethical dilemmas and responsibilities. From data privacy concerns to the potential biases in AI algorithms, organizations must be equipped to handle these challenges. Building an AI-ready culture means instilling a strong sense of ethical responsibility, where every AI initiative is scrutinized for its impact on stakeholders and society. It involves establishing clear ethical guidelines and ensuring that all AI projects adhere to these principles.

Another critical element in building an AI-ready is fostering enthusiasm for AI across the company. This requires demystifying AI, making it accessible and understandable to all employees, not just those in technical roles. Enthusiasm for AI can be kindled through continuous education and engagement. This might involve regular workshops, seminars, and hands-on sessions that allow employees to see AI in action and understand its practical applications.

Building this culture also means addressing any apprehension or misconceptions about AI. It's about communicating the benefits of AI clearly and transparently, showing how AI can augment human capabilities rather than replace them. Leaders play a crucial role in this regard. They must act as champions of AI, driving its adoption with a clear vision and communicating its benefits and implications to their teams.

Moreover, to truly embed AI into the organizational culture, it is essential to integrate AI literacy into the professional development paths of employees. Training programs should focus on building technical competencies and developing an understanding of how AI can be leveraged in various roles across the organization. This approach ensures that AI is not seen as a tool limited to IT departments but as a cross-functional asset that can drive value in various facets of the business.

In summary, building an AI-ready organization requires a holistic cultural shift. This shift involves fostering a culture of innovation, embedding solid ethical foundations, and generating enthusiasm for AI across the organization. It's a journey that requires commitment and leadership at all levels, continuous learning and adaptation, and a clear vision of how AI can be leveraged to enhance, not replace, human capabilities. As we move forward in the age of AI, the success of organizations will depend not just on their technical prowess but on their ability to adapt and embrace the transformative power of AI culturally.

STRUCTURING FOR AI

Organizational design and talent acquisition play crucial roles. For AI to deliver its promise, organizations must strategically align their structures and people. This alignment is critical in fostering an environment where AI can thrive, driving innovation and yielding sustainable business value.

Optimizing organizational structures for AI involves more than just creating new roles or departments; it requires a fundamental rethinking of how teams are organized, how they collaborate, and how decisions are made. A structure conducive to AI promotes agility and flexibility, allowing quick adaptation as AI technologies and applications evolve. This might involve flattening hierarchies to facilitate faster decision-making or forming cross-functional teams that combine diverse skill sets to drive AI initiatives.

Such teams should include data scientists, AI specialists, domain experts, operational staff, and business strategists. This diversity ensures that AI solutions are not developed in a vacuum but are deeply integrated with business processes and goals. It's about creating a symbiotic relationship between AI and various business functions, ensuring that AI initiatives are aligned with and directly contribute to strategic business objectives.

The role of diverse and inclusive teams is central to the successful structuring of AI. Diversity in AI teams goes beyond just gender or ethnic diversity; it encompasses a diversity of thought, experience, and expertise. Diverse teams are better equipped to identify and mitigate biases in AI algorithms, leading to more equitable and effective AI solutions. They bring various perspectives that can lead to more innovative and creative AI applications, ensuring that these solutions are robust, fair, and resonate with a broad user base.

The importance of inclusive teams in AI also extends to the representation of various stakeholders who will be affected by AI technologies. Inclusion in this context means involving individuals who can represent the interests and concerns of different user groups, ensuring that AI solutions are developed with empathy and an understanding of the diverse needs of end-users.

Moreover, acquiring talent in the AI space must be strategic and forward-thinking. The rapid evolution of AI technologies means that the skills needed today might be different tomorrow. Therefore, organizations must focus on hiring the best talent and nurturing a culture of continuous learning and development. This involves investing in training programs to up-skill existing employees, enabling them to stay abreast of the latest AI developments and trends.

Additionally, organizations should look beyond traditional talent pools when recruiting for AI roles. This might involve partnerships with academic institutions, involvement in AI communities, and tapping into non-traditional sources of talent who may bring fresh perspectives to AI initiatives.

In conclusion, structuring AI and fostering diverse and inclusive teams are indispensable in realizing the full potential of AI in business. This involves creating organizational structures that are agile and conducive to AI integration, building diverse and inclusive teams, and strategically acquiring and developing talent. By doing so, organizations can ensure that their AI initiatives are technically sound, aligned with their business goals, and capable of driving innovation and value in an increasingly competitive and fast-paced business environment.

INFRASTRUCTURE AS THE BEDROCK OF AI

Implementing AI in any organization fundamentally depends on the robustness of its underlying infrastructure. This infrastructure acts as the bedrock, enabling AI technologies to function optimally and efficiently. The significance of a well-designed and resilient infrastructure cannot be overstated in the current landscape, where AI is increasingly becoming a cornerstone for strategic decision-making and operations.

Firstly, specialized computing resources are essential for AI. Unlike traditional computing tasks, AI algorithms require significant computational power, especially those involving deep learning. This demand is due to the nature of these algorithms, which include processing vast amounts of data and performing complex calculations. To meet these requirements, organizations must invest in hardware specifically designed for AI workloads. This includes, but is not limited to, high-performance graphics processing units (GPUs) and Tensor Processing Units (TPUs). These specialized processors can handle the parallel processing tasks characteristic of machine learning and deep learning algorithms much more efficiently than conventional CPUs.

Furthermore, scalable data platforms form another critical component of AI infrastructure. AI systems learn and derive insights from data, making the management, storage, and accessibility of data crucial. A scalable data platform ensures that as the organization grows and the volume of data increases, the system can scale accordingly without compromising performance or security. This scalability is vital in handling the current data load and future-proofing the organization against rapidly increasing data volumes and complexities.

Unified analytics is another crucial aspect of AI infrastructure. AI initiatives often involve diverse data sources, including real-time and historical data and structured and unstructured data. Managing these disparate data sources can be a significant challenge. Unified analytics platforms address this challenge by providing a cohesive environment where data from various sources can be collected, processed, analyzed, and visualized harmonized. These platforms streamline the data analytics process, making it more efficient and effective. They enable data scientists and analysts to focus on extracting insights rather than spending time on data management and integration.

Integrating specialized computing, scalable data platforms, and unified analytics into an organization's infrastructure lays a strong foundation for AI initiatives. It enables organizations to rapidly develop, deploy, and scale AI solutions, ensuring they are reliable, efficient, and capable of delivering meaningful insights.

In conclusion, the importance of robust infrastructure in supporting AI initiatives cannot be understated. As we venture further into the age of digital transformation, organizations must prioritize developing an infrastructure capable of supporting the demanding requirements of AI. This involves investing in specialized computing resources, scalable data platforms, and unified analytics solutions. Such an investment supports current AI initiatives and allows the organization to embrace future AI technology advancements seamlessly. Robust infrastructure is not just required for effective AI implementation; it is a strategic asset that can provide a competitive edge in the rapidly evolving business landscape.

CULTIVATING DATA READINESS

In the AI era, data is not just an asset; it is the lifeblood that fuels AI systems. The effectiveness of AI initiatives is intrinsically tied to the quality, governance, and accessibility of data. Cultivating data readiness is paramount for any organization aspiring to harness the full potential of AI. It's about creating a robust data culture that transcends mere collection and storage, focusing instead on the strategic use of data for insightful, AI-driven decision-making.

A robust data culture is foundational for effective AI initiatives. It involves a shift in mindset where data is viewed as a strategic asset central to all business operations. In this culture, data is not an afterthought but a key consideration in every business decision. This shift requires the right technology and processes and a change in organizational behavior where every employee understands the value of data and is empowered to use it in their respective roles.

Data quality is a critical element in the data readiness spectrum. High-quality data is accurate, complete, and timely, making it a reliable foundation for AI algorithms. Poor quality data, on the other hand, can lead to erroneous AI insights, potentially causing significant business harm. Therefore, organizations must establish stringent data quality protocols, including regular audits, validation processes, and cleansing routines. Ensuring data quality is not a one-time activity but an ongoing process that needs to be ingrained in the data management lifecycle.

Data governance is another crucial component. It encompasses the policies, standards, and procedures that ensure data is managed appropriately and ethically throughout the organization. Effective data governance provides a framework for data usage, security, privacy, and compliance. It ensures that data is used effectively and responsibly, addressing concerns such as data privacy and ethical AI use. In an age where data breaches and privacy concerns are rampant, robust data governance is not just a best practice; it's a necessity.

Accessibility of data is equally important in building data readiness. Accessibility refers to the ease with which authorized personnel can access and use data. This requires a delicate balance between making data readily available to those who need it for decision-making and ensuring it is protected against unauthorized access. Organizations must invest in technologies and processes that facilitate secure, easy access to data. This includes adopting modern data platforms supporting data democratization and allowing non-technical users to access and analyze data without compromising security or compliance.

Cultivating data readiness is fundamental for any organization looking to succeed in AI. It requires building a robust data culture, ensuring data quality, implementing effective data governance, and enhancing data accessibility. These elements are not standalone but interdependent facets of a comprehensive data strategy that underpins successful AI initiatives. As businesses continue to navigate the complexities of the digital landscape, the ones that thrive will be those that recognize the centrality of data and make concerted efforts to cultivate a culture of data readiness. This readiness prepares organizations for the present and prepares them for future success in an increasingly data-driven world.

PREPARING FOR THE AI-DRIVEN FUTURE

As businesses venture into the AI-driven future, AI readiness becomes a critical determinant of success. AI readiness is not just about having the right technology; it encompasses a holistic approach that includes quality, governance, accessibility, and culture. This readiness is a strategic blueprint for pragmatic and sustainable AI adoption, ensuring that organizations can effectively and ethically leverage AI.

The first pillar of AI readiness is quality. Quality in AI refers to AI algorithms' precision, reliability, relevance, and the data they process. High-quality AI systems are developed with rigorous testing, validation, and continuous improvement processes. These systems are designed to deliver accurate and reliable results, minimizing risks of errors or unintended consequences. Quality also extends to the data used by these systems. As AI models are only as good as the data they analyze, ensuring high-quality, unbiased, and representative data is crucial.

Governance is the second pillar and is arguably as critical as the technological aspects of AI. AI governance involves establishing a framework that defines how AI is used within the organization. This framework covers ethical considerations, compliance with regulations, and alignment with organizational values and objectives. Effective governance ensures that AI initiatives are transparent and accountable and do not infringe on privacy or other ethical standards. It also involves setting up oversight, audit, and control mechanisms to manage the risks associated with AI deployments.

Accessibility, the third pillar, pertains to the availability and usability of AI tools and systems across the organization. AI should not be confined to silos or limited to certain elite groups within the organization. Instead, it should be accessible to various departments and skill levels, enabling diverse teams to leverage AI for multiple applications. This requires providing various stakeholders with the necessary tools, platforms, and training, ensuring that AI can be used effectively to support decision-making and innovation across the organization.

The final pillar, culture, is the most challenging yet vital aspect of AI readiness. Cultivating a culture that embraces AI involves fostering an environment where innovation is encouraged and AI is seen as a tool to augment human capabilities. It requires a shift in mindset from fearing AI as a threat to jobs to understanding it as a partner in enhancing efficiency and creativity. This cultural shift also involves educating the workforce about AI, demystifying its capabilities, and promoting an understanding of how AI can benefit various roles and functions.

In conclusion, preparing for the AI-driven future requires a comprehensive approach encompassing quality, governance, accessibility, and culture. Organizations must develop strategic blueprints that guide AI's pragmatic and sustainable adoption. These blueprints should be dynamic, allowing for adaptation as AI technologies and applications evolve. By focusing on these four pillars, organizations can ensure that they are not only ready for the AI present but are also well-prepared to embrace the AI future, leveraging its potential to drive innovation, efficiency, and competitive advantage.

NAVIGATING GenAI

GenAI represents a frontier in the AI landscape, offering unprecedented creative potential and unique challenges. As we navigate this realm, understanding and strategically integrating GenAI becomes essential for organizations aiming to harness its capabilities responsibly and creatively.

GenAI, characterized by its ability to generate new content and ideas, is shifting from AI systems that interpret to those that create. This leap forward unlocks immense potential across various sectors, from designing innovative products and personalizing customer experiences to creating new forms of entertainment and art. However, the very power that makes GenAI so compelling also introduces complex challenges. These challenges revolve around ensuring ethical usage, maintaining authenticity and trust, and handling the unpredictable nature of generated content.

A crucial aspect of responsibly navigating GenAI is addressing the ethical implications. As GenAI systems can create indistinguishable content from human-generated content, issues around authenticity and intellectual property rights emerge. There's a fine line between use and misuse; establishing ethical guidelines is imperative. Organizations must develop policies that define acceptable uses of GenAI, ensuring that its applications do not deceive or manipulate users and that they respect intellectual property and individual rights.

Another challenge is managing the unpredictability and quality of GenAI outputs. While GenAI can produce highly innovative and valuable outputs, it can generate irrelevant or inappropriate content. Establishing mechanisms to monitor and filter these outputs is vital to maintaining the quality and relevance of the content. This requires a combination of automated checks and human oversight to ensure that the outputs align with the organization's standards and objectives.

Integrating GenAI creatively into business strategies also demands a nuanced approach. Organizations should look beyond conventional applications, exploring how GenAI can add value uniquely and innovatively. This might involve using GenAI to enhance creative processes, improve customer engagement, or generate novel solutions to complex problems. It requires a mindset that views GenAI as a tool for efficiency and as a partner in creativity.

To harness the full potential of GenAI, organizations must also invest in talent and skills development. This involves training AI specialists and equipping creative professionals with the understanding and tools to collaborate with GenAI systems. Fostering a culture where technology and creativity intersect is vital to realizing GenAI's innovative potential.

In conclusion, navigating the future of creative technology with GenAI demands a balanced approach that addresses ethical challenges, manages the quality and unpredictability of outputs, and integrates GenAI into business strategies creatively. Organizations that succeed in this endeavor will view GenAI as an opportunity to enhance their creative capabilities, engage with customers in novel ways, and drive innovation. As we step into this new era of AI, the focus should be on harnessing the creative potential of GenAI responsibly, ethically, and innovatively.

NAVIGATING THE COMPLIANCE LANDSCAPE IN AI AND GenAI

In the evolving world of AI and GenAI, navigating the compliance landscape is a complex but essential task. The rapid advancement in AI technologies necessitates heightened vigilance in AI regulations, ethics, and governance. Understanding and adhering to regulatory frameworks and cultivating a readiness for ethical AI is crucial to ensure responsible and sustainable AI development and deployment.

The first step in navigating this landscape is understanding the existing and emerging regulations that govern AI and GenAI. These regulations vary by region and are often in response to the unique challenges posed by AI technologies, including privacy concerns, data security, and ethical implications. For instance, the European Union's General Data Protection Regulation (GDPR) has set precedents in data privacy, impacting AI strategies globally. Similarly, other regulatory frameworks are being developed to address the specific challenges of AI, such as bias, transparency, and accountability. Organizations must stay informed about these regulations and ensure their AI systems comply.

Beyond legal compliance, there is a pressing need for ethical AI readiness. This involves developing AI solutions that are not only technically sound but also ethically responsible. Ethical AI readiness requires a thorough understanding of the ethical implications of AI technologies and implementing practices that mitigate potential risks. This includes ensuring fairness, avoiding bias in AI algorithms, protecting user privacy, and being transparent about AI decision-making processes.

Ethical AI readiness also involves establishing robust governance structures. These structures should oversee the development and deployment of AI systems, ensuring they adhere to ethical guidelines and regulatory requirements. This governance should include diverse stakeholders, including ethicists, data scientists, legal experts, and end-users, to ensure a comprehensive approach to ethical AI.

Moreover, organizations must foster a culture of ethical awareness and responsibility. This culture should permeate all levels of the organization, from top leadership to operational teams. Training and continuous education about the ethical implications of AI are vital in cultivating this culture. Employees should be encouraged to consider the ethical dimensions of their work with AI, and mechanisms should be in place for reporting and addressing ethical concerns.

In conclusion, navigating the compliance landscape in AI and GenAI is a multifaceted endeavor that requires vigilance, foresight, and a commitment to ethical principles. Organizations must keep abreast of evolving AI regulations and integrate ethical AI readiness into their strategies and operations. By doing so, they can ensure that their use of AI and GenAI drives innovation and competitive advantage and aligns with societal values and ethical standards. As AI continues to reshape industries and societies, the role of regulatory frameworks and ethical AI readiness will become ever more critical in guiding its responsible and beneficial use.

ASSESSING YOUR AI iQ

In the rapidly evolving landscape of AI, assessing an organization's AI readiness is beneficial and essential for long-term success. AI readiness assessments provide a comprehensive overview of an organization's preparedness for integrating AI into its operations and strategy. These assessments are pivotal in identifying strengths, uncovering gaps, and developing effective AI strategies.

The methodology of AI readiness assessments is multifaceted, encompassing a range of factors from technological infrastructure and data management capabilities to cultural readiness and ethical considerations. The first step in these assessments often involves evaluating the existing technical infrastructure. This evaluation examines whether the current IT landscape can support advanced AI applications, including computational power, data storage capacity, and network reliability.

Another critical area of assessment is data readiness. This involves examining the quality, accessibility, and governance of the organization's data. High-quality, well-governed data is the fuel for effective AI systems, and its readiness is a strong indicator of AI success. Additionally, assessing the skills and knowledge of the workforce concerning AI is crucial. This includes the technical competencies of IT personnel and the broader AI literacy across the organization.

Beyond these tangible factors, AI readiness assessments also delve into more subjective areas such as organizational culture and mindset. This involves evaluating whether the organization's culture supports innovation, risk-taking, and continuous learning – all critical for successful AI adoption. Furthermore, ethical readiness must be assessed, ensuring that the organization is prepared to responsibly handle the ethical implications of AI technologies.

Once the assessment is conducted, the results must be translated into actionable strategies. This involves addressing identified gaps, leveraging strengths, and setting realistic goals for AI integration. Regular evaluations are essential in this process. AI continuously advances, and regular assessments ensure an organization's AI strategies and capabilities evolve accordingly. These evaluations allow organizations to stay ahead of technological trends, adapt to new market demands, and continually refine their AI initiatives.

In conclusion, conducting comprehensive AI readiness assessments is a crucial step for any organization aiming to harness the power of AI. These assessments provide valuable insights into the organization's current state, guiding the development of strategic roadmaps for AI integration. Regular evaluations in this process cannot be overstated – they are essential for keeping AI strategies relevant and effective in the fast-paced world of AI development. By embracing this comprehensive and iterative approach to AI readiness, organizations can position themselves to adopt AI successfully and lead in the AI-driven future.

THE PIVOTAL ROLE OF THE CHIEF AI OFFICER

In the dynamic and increasingly complex world of AI, the role of a Chief AI Officer (CAIO) has become pivotal for businesses. The CAIO is at the forefront of AI integration, acting as a strategic leader who bridges the gap between advanced AI technologies and business goals. This role is not just about overseeing the technical aspects of AI but also about driving the strategic direction of AI initiatives within the organization.

The strategic role of the CAIO involves ensuring that AI is integrated into the company's broader business strategy. This means aligning AI projects with the organization's objectives and ensuring these initiatives drive tangible business value. The CAIO is responsible for developing a comprehensive AI vision and strategy that is both innovative and practical, aligning AI investments with business outcomes.

One of the primary responsibilities of the CAIO is to advocate for and manage the AI transformation across all levels of the organization. This involves not only the deployment of AI technologies but also the fostering of an AI-centric culture. The CAIO must champion the adoption of AI, communicating its benefits and potential to enhance efficiency, drive innovation, and create new business opportunities. They must also address any resistance to AI adoption, helping to alleviate fears and misconceptions about AI among employees.

Another critical responsibility is overseeing the ethical implementation of AI. This includes ensuring that AI systems are developed and used in a way that is ethical, transparent, and compliant with existing laws and regulations. The CAIO must navigate the complex ethical landscape of AI, setting standards and practices that safeguard against biases, protect data privacy, and ensure the responsible use of AI.

Furthermore, the CAIO faces the challenge of building and maintaining a skilled AI team. This involves hiring the right talent and fostering an environment of continuous learning and development. The CAIO must update the team with AI advancements and methodologies, ensuring the organization remains at the cutting edge of AI technology.

In conclusion, the CAIO plays a critical and multifaceted role in successfully integrating AI within an organization. From aligning AI strategies with business objectives and advocating for AI adoption to ensuring ethical AI practices and building a skilled AI team, the responsibilities of a CAIO are extensive and vital. As AI continues to transform the business landscape, the role of the CAIO will be crucial in harnessing the potential of AI to drive innovation, operational efficiency, and competitive advantage in the marketplace.

IMPLEMENTING AI SUCCESSFULLY

As we gaze into the future of AI and GenAI, it becomes increasingly evident that their evolution is set to usher in a new era of groundbreaking developments, reshaping how businesses operate and interact with customers and the environment. The integration of AI in business processes is expected to deepen beyond routine tasks to encompass complex decision-making processes, fundamentally altering the core of business operations. Natural Language Processing (NLP) will significantly advance, leading to more sophisticated human-AI interactions. This evolution will be further enhanced by the emergence of multimodal AI models capable of interpreting a blend of text, images, and voice inputs, thereby creating more intuitive and versatile AI applications.

The realm of personalized customer experiences is poised for a revolution driven by AI and GenAI's ability to predict individual preferences and behaviors with remarkable accuracy. This shift will transform marketing strategies and revolutionize customer service and product customization. In healthcare, AI's expansion will be particularly noteworthy, encompassing advanced diagnostics, personalized treatment plans, and accelerated drug discovery, leading to more effective and tailored healthcare solutions.

Ethical considerations in AI will gain unprecedented focus. Organizations are expected to develop comprehensive frameworks to ensure responsible AI usage, address biases, ensure transparency, and maintain accountability in AI systems. Alongside ethical AI, the security of these systems will become a top priority, with enhanced measures to protect against cyber threats and ensure the integrity and reliability of AI applications.

AI's role in sustainability and environmental efforts will also expand, playing a crucial role in energy optimization, resource management, and environmental protection. This aligns with the global push toward more sustainable business practices. In content creation, the capabilities of GenAI will broaden, encompassing areas like video, audio, and design, opening new avenues in media, entertainment, and advertising.

The transformation of business models driven by AI and GenAI will be particularly evident in finance, retail, and manufacturing industries, leading to more innovative and efficient ways of delivering products and services. This transformation will also necessitate a shift in workforce dynamics, with an increasing need for AI literacy across all employment levels. Organizations will invest in training and development to equip their employees with the necessary skills to work effectively alongside AI.

In navigating these future trends, organizations must adhere to core principles of agility and adaptability, ethical considerations and social responsibility, and strategic alignment with organizational goals. The ability to quickly adapt to new AI advancements and market changes will be crucial, involving a culture of innovation and flexibility in strategy and operations. Prioritizing ethical considerations and social responsibility will be paramount as AI systems grow in capability and influence, ensuring fairness, privacy, and transparency. Additionally, AI initiatives must align with and support the overall objectives and values of the organization, ensuring that AI contributes positively to the organization's mission and adapts to new developments in the field.

The future of AI and GenAI presents a dynamic and transformative landscape where organizations that prioritize agility, ethical considerations, and strategic alignment will be best positioned to harness the benefits of AI and navigate its challenges effectively. This future is not just about technological advancements; it's about responsibly integrating them into society and business, fostering an innovative, inclusive, and sustainable world.

Index

Printed in the United States
by Baker & Taylor Publisher Services